TRANSMEN AND FTMs

Transmen and FTMs

*Identities, Bodies,
Genders, and Sexualities*

Jason Cromwell

University of Illinois Press
Urbana and Chicago

Library of Congress Cataloging-in-Publication Data
Cromwell, Jason, 1952–
Transmen and FTMs : identities, bodies, genders, and sexualities
/ Jason Cromwell.
p.   cm.
Includes bibliographical references and index.
ISBN 0-252-02439-7 (cloth : acid-free paper)
ISBN 0-252-06825-4 (pbk. : acid-free paper)
1. Transsexuals. 2. Sex change—Psychological aspects.
3. Gender identity. I. Title.
HQ77.9.C76   1999
305.9'066—ddc21   99-6186
CIP

1 2 3 4 5 C P 5 4 3 2

To Bonnie for being my rock yet never clipping my wings,
and to our son, Spencer, for teaching me the meaning
of unconditional love and still considering me a hero,
and
in memory of Louis G. Sullivan (1941–91),
who was a guiding light for so many.

Truths and Lies

I have been told
that I am a figment
of my own imagination,
that what I am cannot be,
that my truths are lies
and their lies are truths.
But I know that I am
and that my truths are not lies
and their lies are not truths.
They may keep me
outside the boundaries
of their imaginations,
but I refuse to be invisible.

— Jason Cromwell

Contents

Acknowledgments

I am indebted to Sue-Ellen Jacobs for pushing and prodding me to finish my dissertation, which eventually became this book. Without her encouragement it might not have come to pass. My appreciation to Ann Bolin, Evelyn Blackwood, Mildred Dickemann, and Sue-Ellen Jacobs for numerous discussions of some of this material. A special thanks to those who read the various manifestations of the manuscript—Mike Hernandez, Spencer Bergstedt, Kelly, Daniel C., C. Jacob Hale, and an anonymous reviewer— and especially Evelyn Blackwood for her many suggestions and comments. I am particularly grateful to Rena Davis Phoenix and Jackal for graciously reading the manuscript and making editorial comments and for engaging in stimulating conversation during the last phases of writing. I greatly appreciate the confidence of Liz Dulany, the enthusiasm of David Perkins, and the deft copyediting of Mary Giles of the University of Illinois Press. My gratitude goes also to Dallas Denny, who maintains the Transgender Archives of the American Education Gender Information Service in Atlanta, for locating some difficult-to-find materials and mailing copies to me at her personal expense. A special thanks to the partners of FTMs/ transmen who agreed to my last-minute requests for interviews and for permission to quote them: Amy H., Kristen K., Bonnie C., Eric K., Allie H., and Gabriel M.

Finally, without the transmen and FTMs who participated in my research it would have been impossible to write this book. My deepest appreciation to Dennis, Timothy Joshua, Taylor P., Marcelle, Audrey, Jamie W., Andy, David S., Geoff, Randall, Vern, Michael Hernandez, Jay P., Maxwell Anderson, Stephen Whittle, Michael M., David Hughes, Aaron, Taylor M., Miles, Kai, Kory Martin Damon, Jerry S., Dean D., James E., Billy Lane, Jack Hyde, Spencer Bergstedt, C. Jacob Hale, Carlos, Spencer, Alex W., Daniel C., Toné, Frances, Sky Renfro, Jamison Green, Dave, Charles, Les, Paul T., Danny B., Rafe, Justin, Dan M., Gauge McLeod, Jackal, Aidan Key, Skye Walker, P.B.,

Jeremiah, Kitt Kling, Sean, Mark Craig, Rich, Gary Bowen, Arthur Freeheart, Mitch G., Justin M., Del La Grace Volcano, Chris K., Joshua Goldberg, J. Kelly M., Starr, Mikhail McM., Rob, Jack Watson, Ilya Pearlman, Lou Sullivan, and to those who wish to remain anonymous. The interpretations, and final rendering, of their voices remain my responsibility.

TRANSMEN AND FTMs

Prologue

Naming and then owning is the essence of integration.
—Husain 1996:xviii

San Francisco: December 1992

Silence engulfed the room as though an unspeakable dread had descended. Except for the anxiety on our faces, we appeared to be a relatively typical group of men. We might have been part of a mythopoetic men's group, or an AA meeting, or even an ad hoc committee for some social or political cause. We numbered thirteen and ranged in age from the mid-twenties to the mid-forties. Most of us were white, but there were also three African Americans—two of whom also held claim to being partly Native American—two Latinos, a Native American, an East European Jew, and an Italian.

We were gathered in a loosely formed circle, sitting on chairs, a sofa, and the floor in the living room of a nice suburban home. I'd asked a simple question but one I knew would make everyone uncomfortable. I'd always experienced discomfort whenever someone asked it of me. Many of the men began to fidget, and the glances of some flitted from person to person. No one spoke, and the tension began to build.

I felt responsible for causing everyone's unease, not only because of the question but also because these men had gathered to meet me. It was only a few moments before I broke the strained silence, but as is often the case it seemed a small eternity. "Okay, I'll go first. My name was Jeannie Babbette."

Immediately the tension began to ease. Shoulders and hands relaxed, and the furtive glances and fidgeting ceased. A few laughed quietly. A couple of them who'd known me for awhile guffawed loudly. Then someone else said, "Okay, I'll tell. My parents named me . . ."

Eventually all thirteen of us said what our given names had been—some more reluctantly than others. The majority had been bestowed with very feminine names: Cynthia, Susan, Bernadette, Beatrice, Tamara, Pamela, and Penelope as well as Christine, Elizabeth, Martha, Margaret, and Jeannie. There was one, Terry, who had chosen a less androgynous name.

After we'd all said what our names had been I commented, "I noticed that we all seemed so vulnerable when we were sharing our given names." "Yeah," someone replied, "no one looked into anyone's eyes." Someone else volunteered, "I feel so relieved. That's felt like such a dark secret." Several men nodded in agreement.

We then launched into a discussion of why the question had caused so much tension and anxiety. We described how we had coped with our given names, tried to shorten them to make them androgynous or even masculine, and avoided the issue by using initials or nicknames. We also discussed the childhood and teenaged associations centered around our names, how they had affected our relationships with others, and even how funny and inappropriate they seemed, considering what we looked like now.

Names have not only the power to help identify us but also to shape how others perceive us. For the men in the room, our given names had painful associations with how others had conceived of us as female and the behaviors that society expected of girls and women. But each of us, in spite of our female bodies and those around us (family, friends, teachers, ministers, store clerks, in short, everyone), had grown up seeing and believing ourselves to be boys who would someday grow up to men.

For some, the vision and belief became lost as we matured and went through puberty. A few had laid down visions and set aside beliefs before going into the world determined to make sense of things that in some ways made little sense. A few had become mothers, and almost all had become lovers to men or to women (or both). Some became or tried to become lesbians. Only one had begun to live as a man (i.e., to be perceived as such by others) before the age of twenty. The rest would wait until their early or mid-twenties, or even their late thirties and early forties. Nonetheless, all of us remained to varying degrees masculine, and we deeply wished to be true to our visions.

Excerpts from a Journey

Gender changes have their own agenda.
—Harrison 1997:129

It should be obvious from the prologue that I am a transman. I could have concealed this. For I can "pass" as "normal." But I would be hiding behind the mask of the academician. It would be a lie by omission not to come out as a transman. Writing this book has been part of my own journey.

My first knowledge of transsexuals came when I was seventeen.[1] While waiting for a doctor's appointment I came across an article on transsexuals, one of whom was female-to-male.[2] Although our circumstances were different, there was an instant recognition of what I had felt and struggled with my entire life. For the first time I had a word that described how I felt and thought about myself. Before reading the article I had already decided that once I was free of family constraints I was going to begin living my life as a man.

Being a lesbian did not fit. I had heard about lesbians and read about them, and even though I did not meet an "out" lesbian until I was twenty-one, I knew I was not one. Lesbians loved women, and although I was attracted to women I was also attracted to men. At the time it also seemed clear that lesbians identified as women. I did not. I do not believe that I ever did so despite some brief efforts to please my parents and to follow the requirement to wear "female attire" until my senior year in high school. If I could have gotten away with it—and if my family would have allowed me to do so—I would have gone to school as a boy. But I lived in small communities where everyone knew I had a female body; my family would not have permitted me to wear boys' clothes to school.

What the article offered, or so I thought, was help in facilitating living as a man via hormones and surgery. I knew that to talk with anyone about how I felt was somehow taboo. I secretly did library research and found as much information as I could. (I lied when my mother discovered the information and told her that it was for a school project.) The research was to point out my error regarding the possibility of getting hormones and having surgery unless I was willing to admit to a diseased mind (psychosis, neurosis, schizophrenia, and delusions as well as perversion, bouts of depression, and paranoia) and submit to surgical mutilation. I did not believe I was insane or in need of psychiatric help (although I had experienced bouts of depression and moments of paranoia and recognized the possibility of being perverted because of having sexual desires for both men and women). Nor did I desire mutilation.

Although there was little literature specific to female-to-males, what there was insisted that I must be obsessed with having a penis and also be a heterosexual attracted only to very feminine women who had low self-esteem or had been sexually abused and felt safe with a "penis-less" man. In the literature that critiqued transsexualism, if and when it mentioned female-to-males, I again learned that my sanity was questioned and my self-image perverted. Criticism also asserted that I was seeking male privilege, or that I must have felt too ugly to be a woman, or that I was a lesbian in denial or a woman who had false consciousness, or some combination of all of these.

All my young life I knew I was a boy. For years I thought I was a boy just like my brothers. But I was wrong—my penis never did grow. Contrary to what I read, I did not find being without a penis much of a problem. I knew I was supposed to think it was a problem, but it was not. No one ever asked me to prove that I had one. Growing up, the problems I incurred concerned others' perceptions of my gender more than my body. I learned to see it as a housing for my spirit and intellect. I believe that a lot of battered and otherwise abused children learn to regard their bodies in a similar manner. Of course, I had read that my background had "caused" my transsexualism. I could not help wondering why more people were not transsexual if that were really the cause. Then I remembered that gays and lesbians are "perverts" also. In fact, I learned we were all lumped together as people in need of psychiatric help.

The language I read in the medico-psychological discourse shamed me into hating myself, as it does many other transpeople. (That feeling of shame began to disappear after I met others like myself.) The literature also taught me that I should hate my body and feel shame because I was "trapped in the wrong body." I did hate my breasts and their seeming permanency, and I hated menstruating. Both marked me as female. Nonetheless, I liked the rest of my body, and it did not feel wrong to me.

Within a year of beginning to live as a man (initially on a part-time basis), I located a support group for transsexuals. Group members were not supportive and in fact reinforced messages that I was both less than a "real" man and not "really" a transsexual. I was "less than a man" because I did not strive for a "manly" occupation, ironically because I wanted to be a writer. I was once again not really a transsexual because I was not obsessed with having genital surgery, which, more than anything else, based on what I had seen, would only result in mutilation.

The leaders of the group were a psychologist and one or two of his students. Within weeks of joining I was coerced into taking a battery of tests supposed to determine whether I was really a transsexual. It was concluded that I was not a "good candidate." I had been uncooperative (either refusing to answer many of their questions or doing so in an unexpected manner) and was obstinate in my objections to being tested and too feminine as well (my career choices were especially damning but so were my sexual desires). Thus they deemed that I would be unsuccessful as a man.

Based on everything I read and my experiences in the so-called support group, I concluded that I was and was not a transsexual. Nonetheless, I still believed that I was a man and went about living my life as such. For the next fifteen years, without ever seeing a therapist (the group's facilitators did not provide therapy), I was able to obtain chest reconstruction (more commonly referred to as a bilateral mastectomy); a hysterectomy with removal of all internal female organs; the first stage of a failed genital reconstruction surgery (the surgeon convinced me I would not be mutilated); and, sporadically during those first eight years, access to hormones. Although it was very difficult at times to do so, I was living my vision.

The medico-psychological literature and practitioners and, in the early days, other transpeople told us that we must give up our past. So I did for ten years. One thing was certain: I became paranoid and lived in fear that someone would find out that I was a transperson. Every time I applied for a job I worried about a paper trail that would label me "TRANSSEXUAL." It's no wonder that for many years I avoided labeling myself as such. I was in my thirties before I started taking pride in my history.

I chose this chapter's epigraph because even though I do not think we change gender so much as we change how others perceive our gender, it is particularly true that the changes have their own agenda. Had someone told me when I was seventeen that I would not only graduate with a Ph.D. but also write about my journey and try to give voice to others like myself, I would have had a hearty laugh and then run the other way. No one told me anything of the kind, but my undergraduate research questions led me to conduct research on my people and write this book. I discovered through listening to them that there is more to gender diversity than being transvestite or transsexual (although I suspected that all along). I also discovered that there are more than two sexes or genders (I suspected that was the case as well).

CHAPTER 1

Making the Visible Invisible

To stand in the margins is to look through it at other
margins and at the so-called center itself.
—Serematakis 1991:1

Does my experience as a transman, that is, the "standpoint" position
(Haraway 1991) qualify me to produce a better understanding of female-
bodied transexperiences? Does such a position give me insights unavail-
able to those who are not transpeople?[1] Can I (or anyone else) speak for
others? It would be arrogant to think so. Yet being a transman has given
me access to female-bodied transpeople, many of whom are no longer
willing to trust nontransgendered researchers to "get it right." Although
I do not think that such researchers are incapable of doing so, I understand the wariness regarding them. As a research subject, I have seen my
history misinterpreted and distorted.[2] Because I am a transman, many
others so identified were willing to let me hear their stories and use their
voices.[3]

Because the things I have gone through are similar to those of other
transmen and FTMs, I know what kinds of questions to ask; I recognize
the talk we use and what it means within particular contexts; and, as an
insider, I understand what it means to be a female-bodied transperson. But
because my experiences are different, my perspective is really only one
among many.

Nonetheless, my perspective allows me to see and interpret things in a
way that individuals who are not transpeople do not or would not. For
example, I can examine descriptions in the literature about female-bodied people who after their discovery have been turned into lesbians or
passing women through "trans-tinted glasses." With the former, where les-

bians may only see homosexual relationships between two female-bodied people I am able to tender the possibility of a female-bodied man or a transgendered individual in a relationship with a female-bodied woman. Where others may see only economic opportunity and the desire for status I am able to see the possibility of a female-bodied man doing what men do. In either case, I am able to consider another possibility beyond the common interpretations of socioeconomics and homosexuality.

Discourse Analysis and Feminist Theory

My research is framed by discourse analysis and feminist theory. Participant observation, open-ended interviews, and discourse analysis have enabled me to evaluate the meanings attached to individuals' identities. (By identity I am referring to the person's self-concept and how individuals perceive themselves, that is, self-image and the subjective sense of self.) Discourse analysis allows an understanding of what people do linguistically to communicate identities (Moerman 1988). Furthermore, discourse analysis provides a microscopic view of how society is recreated through language usage (Sherzer 1987).

Unstructured interviews allow an individual's "interpretations of experience [to] guide the interview" (Anderson and Jack 1991:24). Anderson and Jack point out that "a person's self-reflection is not just a private, subjective act . . . [and that] reflecting upon and evaluating ourselves come from cultural context" (18). Likewise, Smith advises that "social relations external to [an individual's everyday world] are present in its organization" (1987:188). As such, discourse analysis of interviews attends to the "moral language" transmen and FTMs use as they talk about their lives (Anderson and Jack 1991:19). Because gender diversity—"cultural expressions of multiple genders (i.e., more than two) and the opportunity for individuals to change gender roles and identities over the course of their lifetimes" (Jacobs and Cromwell 1992:63)—stigmatizes individuals, it is necessary to evaluate the relationship between self-identity and the imposition of medico-psychological discourses and their practitioners.[4] By evaluating this relationship, it may be possible to determine how transmen and FTMs self-define and self-validate their lives rather than how society attempts to denigrate them.

Similarly, an analysis of literary materials also must attend to moral language. These materials seldom allow individuals to speak for themselves. Rather, most sources, written by outsiders, treat subjects sensationally and therefore contain moral judgments. The prevailing binarisms "preclude any understanding of [individuals] in their lived reality: as subjects in their own right" (Lazreg 1990:336). Too often the authors of literary sources impose the binary of sex-equals-gender onto female-bodied people and assume motivations that may not obtain for all individuals. Discourse analysis is helpful in teasing out "the social assumptions that [authors] must have made" about their subjects (Gumperz 1982:35).

Female-to-male transpeople constitute a prime subject for feminist thought and methods, if for no other reason than being born biologically female or assigned at birth as female.[5] Feminists should be concerned that male-dominated discourses have made female-to-male transpeople virtually invisible. Until the early 1990s (Blackwood and Wieringa 1999; Nicholson 1994; Rubin 1992; Wieringa and Blackwood 1999), the few feminist theorists who have approached the topics of transgenderism have done so from a male-focused viewpoint (Garber 1989, 1992; Irvine 1990; Shapiro 1991; Tyler 1989). They have largely focused on male-bodied gender transgressors and/or succumbed to "biological foundationalist" arguments (Nicholson 1994). In Stanley and Wise's terms (1990:39), such theorists have capitulated to the "malestream" tendency to ignore, and thus silence, female gender diversity that is not mainstream. A classic example of such thinking is Raymond's statement that female-to-male transsexuals are "tokens" intended to validate transsexualism as a human phenomenon (1978 [1994]:xi). Such a viewpoint not only renders female gender diversity invisible but also effectively silences any voices that might be heard by individuals who are gender-variant, whether transidentified or not. Furthermore, Raymond presumes that FTMs and transmen are not agents in their own lives.

Despite the Raymond-esque feminists (e.g., Hausman 1995; Millot 1990; Woodhouse 1989), other feminist theories and the scholarship resulting from it take the personal narrative as a "genre of social testimony" (Lewin 1991:787). Although this book is not entirely a personal narrative, it derives from the personal narratives of myself and others. In many ways it is a social testimony concerning how I and other female-bodied transpeople have chosen to define ourselves and—to paraphrase Lewin—how we negotiate and validate our identities with ourselves. What interests me is what transpeople themselves "construe as meaningful, and how they construct that meaning" (Povinelli 1991:238).

Coming-out stories for many gay men and lesbians often bring an individual to terms with what "constitutes 'who I am'" (Lewin 1991:787). Because there is little in the way of published coming-out stories for female-bodied transpeople, their identities do not become revealed in that way. Because there are few stories (most of which are either out of print or difficult to obtain), transmen and FTMs do not rely on them to form their identities. Within the frameworks of support groups, conferences, newsletters, and Internet venues, however, such stories have begun to validate and contribute to the negotiation and solidifying of identities.

One of the primary methods of anthropology is participant-observation. By adding the feminist method of reflexivity, I have been able to "reflect upon, examine critically, and explore analytically" the daily lives of individuals and "gain insight into the assumptions" (Fonow and Cook 1991:2) about gender identity, gender roles, and gender performances. Reflexivity as a method takes into account that I am a subject, just as other transmen/ FTMs became the subject of this book as well as a part of myself (cf. Caplan 1993:180). I have studied, as Greed eloquently states, "a world of which I myself am part" (1990:145). I am aware that my inquiries and comments have had some modicum of influence, if only to prompt other FTMs/ transmen to reflect upon their conceptions and ideas of what it means to be transidentified or a man.

In numerous ways, the process of writing this book has been a collaborative project. I have sought help in defining terminology and asked several transmen/FTMs to read portions (and in a few cases all) of the text in its various manifestations. Throughout the course of both research and writing there has been near-constant discussion about our bodies, identities, genders, and sexualities. My research and the process of shaping it into a book have been interactive, and those interactions have resulted in a mutual sharing of personal information. The reflexive turn in anthropology is a recognition and acknowledgment that ethnography is a cooperative endeavor.

For Collins, a key theme to black feminist thought is "self-definition and self-evaluation. . . . self-definition involves challenging the political knowledge-validation process" (1991:37–38). Although mainstream researchers and theorists have refused to hear the voices of female-to-male transpeople, many, because of self-definition and self-validation, see themselves as being normal rather than pathological and therefore challenge knowledge-validation processes of gender constructions and critique the view that their gendered ways of being constitute mental illness. By allowing individuals to describe their personal self-definitions and self-validations, my insights can "reframe the entire dialogue" (Collins 1991:38) of what constitutes legitimate gender expressions and gender identities. A reframing of the dialogue can engender moving from "fixed gender categories as normative" (Scott 1990:144).

The Marginalization of Transmen and FTMs

We are largely invisible because we were born into female bodies.
—Blake, cited in Green 1994b:4

The title of this chapter, "Making the Visible Invisible," is meant to represent the marginalization of FTMs and transmen. That invisibility and marginalization occurs on four levels. First, female-bodied transpeople are signified as invisible by virtue of having been born with female bodies and being assigned to the female sex. As with other female-bodied people in society, invisibility occurs "through the stories not told" (Gilmore 1994:8). Discourses such as anthropology, history, medicine, and psychology, as well as some feminist interpretations of these discourses, render lives invisible by arguing that FTMs and transmen are "really" and "truly" women because the "truth" is in their female bodies.

As Spender points out, discourses are controlled through publication and therefore made legitimate: "The power to decree what is good and what is not, to decide what will be published and become a part of the reservoir of knowledge, is significant power. It is the power of gatekeepers" (1985:313). This gatekeeping authority is one way in which FTMs' and transmen's lives are rendered invisible.

Second, medical and popular discourses make female-bodied transpeople visible as well as invisible as pathological women. Women (because they are females) or homosexuals (because of their sexual orientation) are no longer allowed to be pathologized by medical or popular discourses and practices because doing so constitutes discriminatory treatment. Yet transgendered people continue to be pathologized. At the same time, many people know someone who is transgendered yet not pathological. The politics of definition perpetuate the claims of pathology although doing so contradicts commonsensical knowledge. Thus, as represented here, female-bodied transpeople are unrecognizable given the dominant discursive fields that authorize identities but do not represent lived experiences.

Third, many female-bodied transpeople are or become invisible by living as men. Gilmore provides an astute explanation of how that obtains: "Gender is interpretable through a formalist logic by which the sex one can *see* becomes the sex one must *be*. According to the formalist logic of gender, the binary of sex (which there are only two: male and female) is the 'natural' ground on which gender as a cultural construction is layered" (1994:11 emphasis in original). In spite of transpeople's female bodies, which society insists means that they are women, they become men and in many ways behave like other men in their respective communities. They have lovers and/or mates, marry, raise children, work, and play—their lives and behaviors are indistinguishable from those of others. Because they are, they often become invisible as transgendered people and only visible as men.

Fourth, to be discovered or revealed as FTMs/transmen is often to be treated as less than real or artificial. That can and does result in the loss of jobs, opportunities for advancement, and often the end of relationships, regardless of their duration. Thus, becoming invisible as transmen/FTMs and only visible as men is precarious and dependent upon how "out" someone is. There is always some risk of being found out and marginalized as a result. Often when discovered, regardless of how and irrespective of the duration of their lives as men, they are turned back into women and again made invisible.

Despite such invisibility, by their existence alone transpeople challenge mainstream conceptions, in particular a sex and gender ideology that attempts to dictate that bodies equal genders. Although assigned to be female at birth, they have gender identities that span the categories of man and masculinity. Many, in order to be accepted as men, conform to codes of masculine behavior that are socially enforced. Nonetheless, there are many forms of masculinity and consequently many ways of being men. Even though many within mainstream Euro-American societies would restrict masculinity and subsequently the behaviors of men to a finite definition, both masculinity and the category "man" are amorphous and constantly shifting in meaning. They depend on age, class, occupation, and political affiliation as well as racial, ethnic, and cultural background. What it means to be a man or masculine, for example, is different for African Americans than for white Euro-Americans. In this book, I have not attempted to deconstruct masculinity or problematize the category of man. I assume that readers will bring personal information and meanings to those categories.

The Limitations of This Study

Who can or should represent the experience of those who populate
the accounts we produce[?]
—Lewin 1991:786

Like all studies, this one has limitations. The primary one concerns the fact that only those individuals active in support groups, those who attended conferences, or those active on the Internet have been included. Many female-bodied transpeople never contact a support group or attend a conference or for that matter a clinic. A significant number of participants in this study did not see their transidentities as problematic. Although it might be seen as a limitation that individuals who participated in the study have a level of comfort with being identified by the prefix *trans,* at least among others likewise identified, I believe it is an advantage. Several participants have given more than one public talk about being transgendered. A few are considered to be leaders of the transcommunity because of their level of political and social activism. These levels of publicly acknowledging identities have empowered people by destigmatizing them, and they have proclaimed pride in their identities. That, in turn, has led to the formation of networks that have enabled others to make contact with people like themselves without imparting negative messages.

For clinicians, another limitation of this study is that no battery of tests were given or used. The participants and I saw that as an advantage. Many felt that clinicians had poked and probed their minds and bodies yet still did not comprehend the meaning of their lives. Many who filled out clinical questionnaires and took psychological tests felt they had been insensitively dehumanized as objects of research—treated as numbers as well as a source of income for "helping professionals" who frequently knew less about issues involving the transcommunity than did their clients. Although behavioral data are more easily measurable and lend themselves to ready quantification, it does so at the expense of "identity and subjective meaning" and is fraught with the "methodological biases" of its practitioners (Vance 1991:881).

What might be seen as another limitation was, from my perspective as well as that of a number of participants, a clear advantage: my position as an insider. During my first six years of research I avoided studying female-bodied transpeople because I believed that I could not be objective. I was concerned about interjecting my voice onto those whom I studied. I have realized, however, that all research is not objective, no matter how much it is asserted to be so. Rather, researchers bring personal biases to their studies, and their worldviews distort their data (Devor 1989:1; see also Benjamin 1988:189; Minh-ha 1991:70). Although the biases may be unconscious, as Gould (1981) has demonstrated, they affect what questions are asked as well as what findings are considered significant (cf. Denny 1993a). I believe that gender diversity is not a manifestation of pathology but rather a part of human social life.

This study does not concern itself with etiologies other than in chapters 8 and 9, where medico-psychological constructs are discussed. My research is concerned with feelings, memories, and the lived experiences of individuals who have constructed lives around the gendered category of identity labeled variously as male, men, and masculine. Therefore, another shortcoming from a clinician's perspective might be the fact that participants' memories are suspect as contrived constructions (Blanchard 1985:252–56; Freund 1985:261; Higham 1984:18; Knorr, Wolf, and Meyer 1968:523; Kubie and Mackie 1968:435, 437). However, "Everything we remember is relevant to our identity" (Haug, ed. 1987:52). Individuals construct identities through remembering what has become significant to them. Therefore, this book is an acknowledgment that we are the experts about our personal lives (cf. Haug, ed. 1987:54).

By turns this is a representation as well as an interpretation of others' voices and a self-representation and interpretation. My voice is embedded within the text not only as an anthropologist but also as a transman who, because I am able to live an invisible life (and capable of doing so), represents a marginalized category. One of my goals has been to give participants control over their history and its interpretation and recover and uncover "what has been hidden through silence, neglect, or marginalization" (Hall Carpenter Archives/Lesbian Oral History Group 1989:1, cited in Lewin 1991:788).

Many people who use the word *transsexual* may drop the label itself and go "stealth," "woodwork," or into "the closet at the end of the rainbow" (Denny 1997:39)—that is, they assimilate. For many years assimilation was the enforced mode in which transpersons lived. A long-held belief was that "the better patients [wanted] no contact with other" transpersons (Dushoff 1973:200).

Although times have changed and it is no longer an absolute necessity to assimilate, many transpeople want no one to know that they have ever identified as transsexual or that they are transsexed. I would like to be able to include them in this narrative, but it is not possible to do so. None of them stay around long enough for their stories to be told or heard. That is unfortunate because they have important perspectives to add to the enlarging picture of "transness" (the state or condition of being transgendered).

Therefore, this book does not include the voices of those who mainstream into society. Instead, it is about transmen and FTMs who, in varying degrees, are out as transpeople and live both outside the lines and within them. Being out is context-sensitive and a relative state as well as an ongoing process. Many who know transpeople only know them as men, which is how they present themselves to the world. Others, however, know them as FTMs and transmen, many of whom are out in all aspects of life yet constantly meeting people who do not know that.

Since the mid-1990s there has been a tremendous increase in the numbers of people who have chosen not to assimilate and accept transness as a part of their identities. To paraphrase, Denny (1997:39), they define themselves rather than asking or allowing others to define them. Many are working on forming community via support groups, conferences, the Internet, and other social networks, both public and private.

This book gives voices to individuals who have a transidentity and are out as transpeople in whatever degree—those like myself, for example, and the others who have permitted me to quote them. I offered them all anonymity. Where I have been given permission to use individuals' names, these appear as either a full name or a first name followed by an initial. In the latter case, individuals wanted to retain some, although only partial, anonymity. In most cases they are out, at least within the transcommunity, but may not be so to family and others. Those who wanted even more anonymity use either a first name only or initials. Pseudonyms are used in a few rare cases—those of "David Hughes," "Jack Watson," and "Jack Hyde." Some of my personal experiences and feelings are also included in the text.

The Limitations of Prior Studies

When most people hear or use the word "transsexual" it is understood to mean male-to-female.
—Harrison 1997:131

Anthropological studies of sex and gender diversity have been limited primarily to Native American (Roscoe 1991; Williams 1992 [1986]), Indian (Nanda 1990; Phillimore 1991), and Polynesian (Herdt 1981) societies.[6] With the exception of the groundbreaking studies by Newton (1972) on female impersonators and Bolin (1988) on male-to-female transsexuals, anthropologists have overlooked contemporary Euro-American transpeople. Although both studies have contributed to an increased understanding of female impersonators and male-to-female transsexualism, they are limited in that their focus populations do not consider female-to-males. "The doors are quickly shut" (Lothstein 1983:14) when questions concerning female-to-male gender diversity are raised.

Most studies concerning transpeople have been clinical psychology studies, with Bolin's, Newton's, and Devor's (1997) work being the exceptions. As such, these studies have been limited by the clinical environment and a focus on individuals who see their identity as problematic. Therefore, they are frequently less stable emotionally and psychologically than are transpeople who use the services of private practitioners and support networks. As Irvine (1990) has pointed out, clinical psychologists and other sexologists have been concerned with males who are "sexually dysfunctional," which includes transvestism and transsexualism. Consequently, most studies have overlooked female-bodied transpeople.

The few studies that have considered female-to-male transsexuals have concluded that they are a homogeneous group (Steiner, ed. 1985:3); reported them to have stable identities as men trapped in women's bodies (Lothstein 1983:44; Pauly 1969:86); presented them as androgynous in appearance and behaviors (Fleming, MacGowan, and Salt 1984:52); identified them exclusively as heterosexual (Fleming, MacGowan, and Costos 1985:47–48; Lothstein 1983; Pauly 1969; Stoller 1972); and described them as being obsessed with having penises (Lothstein 1983; Steiner 1985:353).

An Overview of the Book

The remainder of this volume is roughly divided into three parts. The first reviews materials on theories concerning bodies, genders, sexes, and sexualities. Each review is followed by a discussion of how transpeople (with a particular focus on FTMs and transmen) fit or do not fit within the frameworks of these theories. The second part is a review of the cross-cultural data concerning female gender diversity and the Euro-American historical evidence of female-bodied people who have lived as men regardless of duration or motivation. These chapters are not separated to perpetuate the West-versus-the-rest dichotomy. I initially began by dividing the material in a chronological order but settled on the present format for expediency. The third part discusses contemporary transmen and FTMs as constructed by transsexual discourses and how they construct themselves. These chapters provide a perspective on the transcommunity by using individual voices to articulate personal experiences.

Chapter 2 examines the language used to create a transsexual discourse perpetuated by most medico-psychological practitioners as well as some transsexuals. I discuss how transpeople have adapted the limited categories of transvestite and transsexual and expanded their meanings and how that process has led to the development of languages specific to the transcommunity. I also explain my use of the discourse. This chapter also provides a brief comment on the continuum of butches, FTMs, and transmen.

Chapter 3 reviews theories about bodies, sexes and genders, and sexualities as well as the social construction of these categories. It discusses the stigmatization of transpeople and the concept of passing. It also examines these theories from the perspective of the transcommunity, critiques some of the discourses on issues involving that community, and discusses sites of resistance.

Chapter 4 describes female gender diversity as it occurs cross-culturally. Although the phenomenon occurs widely around the world, anthropological and historical literature has largely rendered it invisible. The primary purpose of chapter 4 is to illustrate that there are many ways of "doing" gender, and I hope that its inclusion will broaden the understanding of gender as a social construct.

Chapter 5 presents cases throughout Euro-American history that have involved transgendered females: transvestic opportunists, female husbands and mannish lesbians, and female-bodied men. I follow Weeks's (1977, 1980–81) lead by distinguishing between transgendered behavior that has occurred widely both historically and cross-culturally and transgendered identities, which are specific to the last half of the twenty-first century. I also offer a set of questions for reconsidering female gender diversity.

Chapter 6 considers the default assumptions regarding people assigned as female at birth and the ability to live as men and without medical intervention during the modern era. It focuses on the death of Billy Tipton, who had a female body but had lived as a man for more than fifty years. It also reconsiders Tipton's choices from a transperspective and debunks some of the myths of social privilege.

Chapter 7 ties into the two previous chapters by presenting contemporary female-bodied transpeople's perspectives on cross-cultural and Euro-American historical data. I discuss the androcentrism, homocentrism, and phallocentrism of these categories and argue that such terminologies are inappropriate and have no symbolic meaning or significant relevance for contemporary transmen and FTMs.[7]

Chapter 8 reviews the history of the construction of transsexualism and transvestism as categories. It discusses as well as critiques the transsexual discourses and the medico-psychological practices that do not recognize female transvestites and fail to account for the heterogeneity of FTMs and transmen.

Chapter 9 continues the discussion in the previous chapter by providing a review of medico-psychological practitioners' etiological construction of transmen and FTMs. It examines and discusses identities, bodies, and sexualities with respect to the transcommunity and as subversive within the dominant binaries. It also addresses the use of strategic discourse to reframe how many transpeople think about their bodies, identities, and sexualities.

Chapter 10 addresses how FTMs and transmen are working to form a community, an activism challenging the mental illness model of transness as well as that of other dominant discourses, and the steps they are taking to end their invisibility.

For those interested in numbers, an appendix provides an overview of my fieldwork in a nonsituated population and the methods I used to gather data. It also provides an overview of the results from an anonymous survey as well as formal interview and questionnaire demographics.

One purpose of this book is to examine the paradoxes of female gender diversity and critique the dominant discourses concerning it. Stone notes that polyvocality is needed to develop "a deeper analytical language for transsexual theory" (1991:297). In keeping with that belief, my critiques are delineated by providing multiple voices: mine as an anthropologist who has worked with transpeople for more than ten years and as a transman and other voices from female-bodied transpeople themselves. The voices, in most cases, contrast with the discourses about transpeople and give substance to each individual's "everyday world" (Smith 1987). My selection of voices reveals two assumptions. First, because transpeople, by virtue of being transidentified, do not conform to gender stereotypes they are constructed as pathological. Second, crossing the gender borders is for many individuals normal rather than pathological.

The findings in this book can contribute to research on issues that "will be enhanced by investigating the general sense-making phenomenology and style of adaptation chosen by such individuals. Such research is necessary in order to add depth to the literature which, up to now, has emphasized etiology and psychopathological categorization" (Fleming, Costos, and MacGowan 1984:592). The book can perhaps supply information on gender and sexual identity through a critical analysis of female gender diversity that complements like studies of male gender diversity.

CHAPTER 2

Transsexual Discourses and Languages of Identification

Language . . . can be extraordinarily ambiguous and inaccurate,
especially when describing feelings.
—Blacking 1977:9

Transsexual discourses are those created by medico-psychological practitioners who "diagnose, classify, regulate, and produce transsexed bodies" and the supposed truths about their lives and experiences (Hale 1995:2). These discourses are a "moral discourse" (Mageo 1995:285) that assumes that transbehaviors of any kind are abnormal. Consequently, those who engage in these behaviors need to be cured. That assumption is reflected in the language used to speak about transpeople. Furthermore, these discourses were developed by practitioners who "treated" male-to-female transsexuals and then blithely applied the same discourses to female-bodied transpeople (cf. Hale 1995:2). Such language, touted as being "scientific and neutral" (Birke 1982:77) or merely descriptive, is stigmatizing and seldom descriptive (e.g., gender dysphoria, "wrong body," and "afflicted" or "suffering" transsexuals).

The discussion over whether to spell the word *transsexual* with one *s* or two is, in part, a creation of "strategic discourse" (Mageo 1995:289), which inverts and reframes stigmatized words and meanings. Strategic discourse is a step toward the creation of transdiscourses adapted out of (or created from) trans experiences (chapter 10). Transdiscourses are nonmedical, nonpathological, and noncolonizing. They are affirming, empowering, positive, and reflective of trans experiences and the lives people choose to live. The development of an alternate discourse is necessary because the transcommunity is, as Stryker has astutely observed, "something more, and something other than the creatures our makers [i.e., therapists, endocrinologists, and surgeons] intended us to be" (cited in Hale 1995:20). For some, the use of the single *s* spelling of the word *transsexual* is one step toward ending complicity with transsexual discourses.

Words Spoken about Transsexuals

The words aren't just about identity, or positive and negative value judgments. The words are about danger.
—Christina 1997:34

By clinical definition, a transvestite is a heterosexual male who dresses in women's clothing and is erotically and/or sexually aroused by doing so (Benjamin 1969:2; Blanchard 1985:231; Stoller 1975:143; Stoller, 1982:100). Within the limitations of that definition such behavior is considered to be extremely rare in females (cf. Stoller, 1968, 1975); nonetheless, female transvestites do exist. Just as the clinical definition excludes females, it also excludes males who cross-dress for other reasons.

The third edition of the *Diagnostic and Statistical Manual of Mental Disorders* defines transsexualism as a gender identity "disorder" in which the individual experiences "a persistent sense of discomfort and inappropriateness about one's anatomic sex and a persistent wish to be rid of one's genitals and to live as a member of the opposite sex" (*American Psychiatric Association* 1987:74, sec. 302.50). By its fourth edition, however, the manual had dropped the term *transsexual* as a diagnostic category and replaced it with "Gender Identity Disorder." The criteria remain the same (Bradley et al. 1991; Levine et al. 1991). Although the term did not originate with Benjamin, he has defined transsexuals as individuals who believe they belong to, want to be, and function as the "other" sex (1977[1966]:27).[1] "Transsexual" is used in two ways: first, to describe someone who is in the process of becoming (transitioning) a man (and vice versa); and, second, to describe someone who has completed sex reassignment surgery. As Lynn points out, many postoperative transsexuals no longer consider themselves to be transsexual (1988:30).[2]

From a clinical perspective it is believed that the transsexual's goal is to have sex reassignment surgery (SRS) and ultimately live as a heterosexual woman or man. Rather than "sex reassignment," some transpeople prefer "gender assignment," or "sex confirmation," or "gender confirmation," or "genital reassignment" surgery. Others, however, like myself, do not believe they are changing or confirming genders, nor that changing or confirming sex is possible. For some transpeople, a more appropriate terminology might be "sex and/or gender congruence surgery" (i.e., making gender congruent with sex as much as is possible given current medical technology). Regardless of the terminology, the goal for many transsexuals embedded in the ideology of the Euro-American sex and gender system is surgeries that will result in legally being seen as nontranssexual men or women.

Although transgender has begun to emerge in medico-psychological discourses (Bockting 1997; Cole 1998; Cole and Meyer 1998), it still is not recognized as a diagnostic category. Frequently these discourses read as if "transgender" is the same as "transsexual." An early example is that of Docter, a psychologist, who defines transgender in his own terms without regard to its origins or its definition by transgendered people themselves (1988:21–22). He restricts the usage of the term to those who go "back and forth from one gender role to the other. Without such oscillations, the full-time cross-gender living would qualify in our definition as transsexual behavior. We prefer the term, *preoperative transsexual*, simply to indicate that reassignment procedures are anticipated" (22, emphasis in the original).

The Beginnings of Transdiscourses

More broadly defined, a transvestite is any person, regardless of sex or gender, who cross-dresses (Feinbloom, 1977:16) for social presentations. The term itself was coined by Hirschfeld in 1910 (Karlen 1971:213), who noted that it was derived "from 'trans' 'across' and 'vestitus' 'clothed'"; furthermore, he "readily admit[ted] that this name indicates only the most obvious aspect" of such behavior (Hirschfeld 1966[1938]:187).[3] Some of the transcommunity objects to the term because of its clinical designation as compulsive and sexual behavior and the fact that, by implication, it connotes a perversion.

> It is in itself an innocent term, but it is very easy to understand why so many people who cross-dress do not want to be identified with that word. The initials "TV" for some reason do not carry the same negative connotations the word "transvestite" does. Many people who absolutely abhor the word "transvestite" have no qualms whatever with being called a "TV." . . . Also, the initials "TV" are convenient to use, and readily identifiable.
>
> The only difference between "cross-dresser" and "transvestite" is that "transvestite" implies a psychological condition (compulsion), while "cross-dresser" implies voluntary behavior. Most people who cross-dress would rather be identified with the word "cross-dresser" than "transvestite." (Lynn 1988:28)

In a similar vein, Prince, considered by many male-bodied transpeople as the "grandmother" of the transcommunity, has noted (1992:20) that the term *transvestite* has come "into disfavor because it has a medical and thus an 'abnormal' and pejorative flavor to it. Thus crossdresser, or CD (which simply substitutes English for Latin), has come into common use." Regardless of individual preferences, "transvestite" and "cross-dresser" mean someone who wears the clothing and takes on the behaviors, socially constructed as the proper domain, of the other biological sex: males who present themselves as women (male transvestites) and females who present themselves as men (female transvestites).

Although most people in U.S. society do not recognize three or more sexes and genders, some individuals identify as other than men or women. They may identify as transvestites, transsexuals, transgenderists (Bolin 1994), or "somethingelse."[4] Bolin (1988) discusses the identity shift of male-to-female transsexuals (MTFs) as they make the transition from men to women. Initially, they identify as transsexuals, which gradually gives way to a feminine identity as they learn to be, and become, comfortable as women in society. During Bolin's study the only option available to MTFs/ transwomen was to become as physically female as possible. Since the early 1990s, however, another category has emerged: Some individuals label themselves as "transgenderists." They neither want nor desire sex reassignment surgery, and their gender diversity is not limited to periodic episodes of cross-dressing. They live the majority of their lives in a gender that opposes their biological sex. They may or may not identify as men or women, and they may identify as either/or, neither/nor, or both/and (Bolin 1994).

Some who define themselves as transgendered may go back and forth between gender roles.[5] Docter fails, however, to recognize that some define themselves as transgenderists yet have no intention of having genital surgeries. Furthermore, he does not recognize that many individuals are content to be—and have purposely chosen—an intermediate category. Transgenderists are all too aware of the term *preoperative transsexual* but have rejected it because it does not describe them. Individuals who define themselves as transsexual but have not yet had genital surgery (yet anticipate doing so) often use "preoperative transsexual (pre-op)." Transgenderists who have no intention of having surgery do not view themselves as transsexuals, preoperative transsexuals, or transvestites.

Notwithstanding the emergence of "transgender" in the humanities and social sciences literature (Rubin 1992; Weston 1993), the term and its derivatives arose out of the transvestite and transsexual community (Lynn

1984, 1988).[6] Within that community it is used in two ways. First, it designates individuals who do not fit into the categories of transvestite and transsexual. Transgendered identification offers a more specific reference to people who live as social men or as social women but neither desire nor have sex reassignment surgery. Transgender is viewed as a "viable option *between* crossdresser [transvestite] and transsexual" (Holly 1991:31, emphasis in the original). Second, "transgender" is used as an encompassing term for transvestites and transsexuals as well as for those who do not fit neatly into either category. Bolin asserts that the transgender community

> is in the process of creating not just a third gender, but the possibility of numerous genders and multiple social identities. As such, they challenge the dominant American gender paradigm with its emphasis on reproduction and the biological social body as the *sine qua non* of gender identity and role. As a political movement the transgender community views gender and sex systems as relativistic structures imposed by society and by the privileged controllers of individual bodies, the medical professions. The transgenderist is disquieting to the established gender system and unsettles the boundaries of bipolarity and opposition in the gender schema by suggesting a continuum of masculinity and femininity, renouncing gender as aligned with genitals, body, social status and/or role. Transgenderism reiterates what the cross-cultural record reveals, the independence of gender traits embodied in a Western bio-centric model of sex. (1994:447–48)

Transgender is a move away from a physically based definition (sex of body), and the sexual connotations implied by "transsexual," toward a social definition (gender or gender identity) (Holly 1991:31; Lynn 1984:61; Lynn 1988:30). Many within the transgender community have adopted the terms *transsexual, transgender, transgenderist,* and *cross-dresser* intentionally to distance themselves from the medico-psychiatry and subsequent stigmatization attached to the terms *transsexual, pre-operative transsexual,* and *transvestite.* Consequently, members of the transgendered community are individuals of any sex who are incompatible with and/or beyond specific gender assignments or are preoperative or postoperative transsexuals, cross-dressers, transvestites, and transgenderists.

There are important differences in the use of some terminology. For female-bodied transpeople, for example, terminology such as "the operation," "pre-op," and "post-op" are inadequate (cf. Hale 1995:26). There are no clearcut pre- and post-op statuses for FTMs or transmen. Those who have surgery must have more than one operation. Is an FTM or transman who has had chest reconstruction still pre-op? Would he be post-op if chest reconstruction were his only surgery? Is he pre-op or post-op if, in addition to chest reconstruction, he has surgery to remove female reproductive organs? Or is he only considered post-op if he has chest reconstruction, a hysterectomy (the removal of the uterus), and phalloplasty (the construction of a penis) and/or metoidioplasty (the surgical release of the posthormonially enlarged clitoris)?

Untying the Tongues of Transpeople

Language produces the reality it names.
—Lazreg 1990:331

The vocabulary is only now developing to speak of the experiences of transpeople who do not fit neatly within existing categories. Butler has noted that language constrains what "constitutes the imaginable" (1990:9). In order for people to be coherent and congruent they must fall within "socially instituted and maintained norms." Those who do not are no longer intelligible and thus supposedly cannot exist (Butler 1990:17). If they are found to exist, they are either rendered invisible or considered pathological and labeled as gender failures (gender-confused or disoriented, gender-misidentified, gender-disordered or a gender aberration, and gender-dysphoric).[7]

Transpeople are developing other terminologies, including "transperson," "transpeople," "transmen," "transwomen," and "trans community." They have also devised a number of acronyms: FTM (female-to-male) or F2M; MTM (male-to-men, based on some FTMs'/transmen's belief that they have always been men in spite of being born with female bodies); and (for male-to-females) MTF (M2F) and FTF (with the opposite meaning and belief basis as for MTM). These are "native," insider, or emic terms.

Although the definitions of some terms and their appropriateness for general usage are often the topics of debate, it is important to use the language—trans discourse—to write and speak about the transcommunity. The terms are more accurate descriptors of how people self-identify, and they enable self-recognition. Furthermore, the transsexual discourses that medico-psychological practitioners have made available are too frequently applicable only to a small minority and are agenda-laden. Most practitioners continue to attempt to regulate what transsexuals and transvestites are and are not, regardless of whether they fit within the narrow definitions of those terms. Many practitioners, for example, exclude gay-identified female-bodied transpeople, individuals who flexibly shift from one gender role to another, and those not obsessed with having genital surgeries.

Many female-bodied people do not and have never felt like "a man trapped in a woman's body" or as though they have "the wrong body." Nor have they felt gender-dysphoric (i.e., disassociated or disconnected from their gender). It is inconsistent to feel trapped in a category—woman—when one has never felt like others in that category. Many have expressed confusion over the whole notion of "wrong body." I, for example, have asked on more than one occasion, "If I have the wrong body, whose body do I have and where is my body?" Many female-bodied transpeople have never experienced gender dysphoria yet have felt stigmatized by others' discomfort concerning gender expressions. "Gender dysphoria" is "a term used by nontransexual shrinks who write surgery letters" (Wilchins 1997:225). Many transpeople believe that it is nontranspeople who have gender dysphoria.

Because transpeople are in the process of developing the language to speak of their identities and lives, terms are still under development. Some, such as the various forms of FTM (F2M, FtM, F-t-M), are viewed as being either politically correct or incorrect. In general, although I only have anecdotal evidence, it is male-bodied transpeople who find the term politically incorrect.

I once became embroiled in a heated discussion with Wilchins, who insisted that I was a MTM (male-to-male or male-to-man) transsexual. She insisted that she could not think of me (and others she mentioned by name) as ever having been females—I think she used "women"—and that FTM was derived from the medical and colonizing term *female-to-male transsexual.* I argued passionately that I had every right to turn a medical term into a shorthand that I found descriptive and useful. I asserted, and still maintain, my right to recognize and acknowledge that a personal history includes a female body and its incumbent socialization. Most important, I argued that neither she nor anyone else could label me in a way I found inappropriate. For her to do so is no less restricting than the actions of the medico-psychological people against whom she railed.

Being trans-anything is a self-diagnosis. Female-bodied transpeople identify in varying degrees with masculinity and maleness and with the category labeled "men." Individuals have every right to use whatever terms they wish. Some refer to themselves as transsexuals, others as transgendered, and others as something else. A new discourse is being created by those who articulate their transsubjectivity differently then medico-psychological discourses have allowed.[8] They are, in a real sense, untying their tongues.

Nicholson proposes thinking of the "meaning of woman" in a manner similar to Wittengenstein's use of the word *game:* "We see a complicated network of similarities overlapping and criss-crossing: sometimes overall similarities, sometimes similarities of detail" (Wittengenstein, cited in Nicholson 1994:100). Therefore, the meaning of woman "is not found through the elucidation of some specific characteristic but is found through the elaboration of a complex network of characteristics." Doing so, Nicholson suggests, first acknowledges that for extended periods some characteristics (e.g., "possessing a vagina and being over a certain age") may have been present within a particular network; second permits the use of the word in some contexts in which particular "characteristics are not present" (e.g., transwomen who do not have vaginas but identify as women); and third provides a framework for "all those words into which *woman* is translatable" (100–101, emphasis in the original). Seeing "woman" as encompassing many meanings indicates that the meaning has changed and is changing and recognizes that there are many ways of being a woman. Consequently, the meaning can be a map that illustrates the intersection of similarities and differences (101).

I suggest that we think of words regarding transpeople in the same ways. Whether transexuals or transsexuals, transvestites, transgenderists, butch women, "nelly" men, or other gender nonconformers, transpeople still have characteristics that may be present in some contexts and not in others but have existed in different historical epochs and cultures. Moreover, the prefix *trans* has several meanings, both singular and multiple. According to the *Oxford English Dictionary* it indicates, but is not limited to, outside of; a change from one place, state, or form to another; to pass across or go beyond; to exceed the limits of; to go against; and to be brief. Some transpeople may use these meanings interchangeably, others may use only one, and still others may use them all.

Seeing *trans* as meaning more than one thing allows for acknowledging multiple terms that express transidentities: transgender (TG), transexual, or transsexual; FTM, trans or tranny man, boy, fag, and gay (for MTFs replaced by woman, girl, dyke, and lesbian); masculine or male-identified woman, lesbian man, dyke daddy, drag king and queen, new woman, new man, baby butch, soft butch, butch dyke, tryke, boy chick, and boy dyke; transfaghag, gender-bender or blender, gender fuck, gender outlaw, and gender queer; transqueer, queer, cross-dresser, androgynous, transhuman, transfolk, transpeople, man or woman of transgendered or transsexual experience, and, finally, people.

In every regard such ways of expressing transidentities are "the creation of a new transgender language" (Hemmings 1996:38n3); they are the creation of transdiscourse. Yet some terms may have different meanings, depending on the communities in which they are used. A transgendered lesbian is a butch dyke in lesbian communities, for example, whereas in transcommunities the same term means being a MTF transsexual and a lesbian.

Butches, FTMs, and Transmen

Female-to-male transsexuals appear to share many similarities with lesbian butches.

—Newton 1994:574n41

Outside of surgical contexts it is sometimes difficult to understand the differences among butches, FTMs, and transmen.[9] Jamison Green, a leader of the FTM/transmen community, notes that "many people assume that FTMs are lesbians" (1994b:2). Complicating matters is the fact that many FTMs and transmen have lived as, or attempted to live as, lesbians and have found lesbian communities to be relatively tolerant of masculine identities and behaviors. Some may have even identified as lesbians for a time; Green, for example, "identified as a lesbian for twenty-two years" (2). Most rarely felt that they truly fit in or belonged, however. Their masculinity was often regarded with suspicion and may have been allowed expression only in androgynous ways (Green 1994b:1).

To further complicate matters, several "scientific" studies have compared lesbians and FTMs/transmen (Blanchard and Freund 1983; Ehrhardt, Grisanti, and McCauley 1979; Lyons 1986; McCauley and Ehrhardt 1978; Strassberg et al. 1979) with respect to childhood and adolescent development and behaviors, parental and sibling relationships, mental abilities, sexual functioning and fantasy/desire, and life-style.[10] These studies inevitably conclude that there are similarities as well as differences between FTMs/transmen and lesbians. Paramount is the fact that many butch lesbians have masculine gender identities, but, unlike FTMs and transmen, they do not identify as men. Nonetheless, "Many butches have partially male gender identities. Others border on being, and some are, female-to-male transsexuals (FTMs), although many lesbians *and* FTMs find the areas of overlap disturbing. Saying many butches identify as masculine to some degree does not mean that all, even most, butches 'want to be men,' although some undoubtedly do. Most butches enjoy combining expressions of masculinity with a female body" (Rubin 1992:468, emphasis in the original).

FTM and transman identities are not necessarily clear-cut either, and there are gray areas between trans- and butch identities. Among a minority of butches and FTM/transmen these gray areas have given rise to what

Halberstam (1998) and Hale (1998) term butch-FTM "border wars." In part, those who perpetuate border wars operate from places of misunderstanding; neither side clearly understands the other's perspective. From some FTM/transmen's perspectives, butches are transsexuals in denial; from some butches' perspectives, FTM/transmen are misguided lesbians. It is not always possible to make clear distinctions.

Intersections on a Transmap

More pertinent to this discussion are the differing but also overlapping ways in which the terms *FTM* and *transmen* are used.[11] "FTM" is used in at least two ways: female-to-male and female-toward-male (as in having surgery) or female-toward-man/masculine (as in gender or gender identity). In the first instance FTMs are those individuals who pursue genital surgeries and disappear into society as men. Those who use the term in this sense do so to designate a temporary status and as a transitional definition of the process they are going through. Once through the process (no matter what surgeries they ultimately have), their identities shift from FTM to that of males/men. In a personal communication with me in 1998 Gary Bowen referred to these individuals as "hardcore FTMs." They are also referred to as "stealth" or as "woodworkers." They may already be living as men. Often when (and if) they contact a support group or other support network they do not maintain that contact for long. They tend to obtain the information or resources they need and then disappear again into the woodwork. Some may resurface after five, ten, even twenty years to seek new information and connect with others like themselves. In the second instance, FTMs may retain the label in order to acknowledge their female socialization and history. Some prefer this terminology because they are moving toward male and may not think of themselves as men. Some may prefer the term *FTM* because they identify as female men. Those who use it in this sense may or may not take testosterone and may not have surgeries that would alter their bodies.

In its original coinage, "transman" was intended to be an encompassing term that included anyone assigned female at birth but who identifies somewhere on the so-called continuum between male/female and man/woman. They may or may not take testosterone and may or may not have body-altering surgeries but live either some or all of the time as men (Bowen 1998 personal communication). Some transmen still use "FTM" as a way to reinforce the fact that they have a female socialization and history. Others may use "transman" instead to distance themselves from anything that connotes female or feminine. Still others use the term to distance themselves from their transsexual status.

Transmen and FTMs may also use any number of the other transidentity terms to name themselves. In essence, the terms *transman* and *FTM* are interchangeable. That may be because there is always, at some physical level, an awareness of having a history as female, if for no other reason, than being assigned such at birth. Sex reassignment surgeries (in particular, genital surgeries) are inadequate no matter what techniques are used. Depending upon the technique and the surgeon's skill there is at least one or more physical reminder of once being female in body: scars, an inability to have spontaneous erections, and (for most) a lack of sensation in the penile shaft, the insertion of a prosthetic device for intercourse, and an inability to urinate through the penis.

Nonetheless, some transmen and FTMs who have these surgeries may deny ever being female. But some among both those who do not have genital surgery and those who do may retain a label of trans. That label may be retained, in part, because testosterone does change the shape, yet the genitalia are anatomically still female. Some FTMs and transmen may never identify as transsexuals, contact a support group, or have sex reassignment surgeries yet live out their lives as men. Some who do contact medico-psychological practitioners may only have chest surgery and/or a hysterectomy/salpingo-oophorectomy (the removal of the ovaries and fallopian tubes) yet still identify as men.[12] Regardless of what steps are taken, most FTMs and transmen live out their lives as men.

To encompass all manifestations of transness, I prefer the term *transpeople*. My intention is to move away from "transsexual" because the label implies female/feminine identity (Bolin 1988:77). Transpeople is a change from the sexed connotations of transsexual, which only heightens the confusion between sexual behavior and gender identity. When a distinction is necessary between female-to-male and male-to-female, I have prefaced the term *transpeople* with "female-bodied" and "male-bodied," respectively.

The conceptualization of the term *female-bodied* resulted from conversations with female-bodied transpeople. "Female-bodied man" is akin to but not the same as "man with a vagina," nor is it meant to imply women who became men. Rather "female-bodied" recognizes that the individual was assigned as female or had a female body. Biologically, the individuals' genitalia, chromosomes, and phenotype (although that varies from person to person) are those of a female. Many may have medical interventions that reconstruct their bodies to be more congruent with their identities, yet they never, contrary to what some may believe, have male bodies in the same sense that those born male, phenotypically and genotypically, do. Instead they have transbodies or transsexed bodies, which is not to insinuate that they are imprisoned by or limited in phenotype or genotype. After all, if they were, testosterone would not have the effects it does nor would they be able to live as men.

The designation *man* recognizes that the individual lived (or is living) as a man. Female-bodied men or female-bodied transpeople are also those individuals who acknowledge that their bodies are those of biological females but may or may not identify as either a female transvestite or a female-to-male transsexual. By making that distinction I am signifying female-bodied transpeople's differences from male-bodied transpeople. I intend this signification as a move away from generalizations and toward specificity and the equal marking of females and males.[13]

I use "FTM" and "transmen" as identities, recognizing that not all people who use the label *transsexual* have an identity as FTM or as transmen. One misunderstanding that occurs in the FTM/transmen community centers around the issue of retaining trans terms whatever they may be and identifying as trans. On one hand, many see being transsexual as a temporary status, and many do not understand why transmen and FTMs want to be, in their estimation, anything other than men. On the other hand, many have trouble understanding why some want to deny so vehemently (in many cases) that they were born female and socialized as women. Perhaps part of the misunderstanding is in not making a distinction between an adjective and a noun. "FTM" and whatever "trans" prefix is used are descriptors (adjectives) of the process of going from being seen as female to being seen as men. For the majority of FTMS and transmen, being transidentified is not the sum of all existence any more than being transsexual is for others.

Rather than engage in turf wars, it is important to recognize and acknowledge overall similarities as well as those of detail. Overall similarities occur among female-bodied transpeople, such as being socialized—although in varying degrees—as girls who presumably grow up to be women yet identify as men or with masculinity. There are also similarities of detail, such as whether to live as men and pursue or reject medical interventions. In the former, the similarities intersect on a transmap. In the latter, the differences result in the choice of different paths. Failing to recognize and, accordingly, acknowledge similarities as well as differences and diversity among transmen and FTMs has a coercive and regulatory effect (Bohan 1993:8; Butler 1990).

CHAPTER 3

Bodies, Sexes, Genders, and Sexualities

Knowledge about often gives the illusion of knowledge.
—Minh-ha 1991:65

The terms *sex, sexuality, gender,* and even *bodies* are social constructions, none of which can any longer be taken as natural categories. Even though often treated as distinct entities, they are "deeply interrelated" (Edwards 1990:110, 122). It seems logical to begin a discussion with the construct of bodies, because, as DiGiacomo has stated, "It is through our bodies that we experience and come to know the realities of our worlds" (1992:114).

Bodies

The body is common to us all.
—Douglas 1982[1970]:vii

Although it would seem that not much could be said about the body beyond the fact that everyone has one, the human body has been a problem for philosophers, members of the judiciary, and social scientists as well as for medicine for several centuries. Only since the late 1970s, however, has the body been considered to have a specific history and be viewed as a social construction. That view came out of the realization that not everyone, everywhere, nor even throughout time, has viewed the body in the same ways (Gallagher and Laqueur, eds. 1987:vii).[1]

The body within discourse is viewed, generally, from three perspectives: first, individual body experience (i.e., the phenomenological body); second, as a symbolic system for thinking about culture, society, and nature (i.e., the social body); and third, as an object that is subject to either social or political control (i.e., the body politic) (Scheper-Hughes and Lock 1987:7–8).[2]

An understanding of the phenomenological body can be captured in the following expressions: "my sense of my body" (Young 1989:44); "the self is felt to inhere in the body as a whole, not its parts" (Young 1989:56); "we both are and have bodies and . . . we think and act through our corporeal selves" (Scheper-Hughes and Lock 1991:409); and "it is through my body that I perceive things" (Merleau-Ponty 1982:186, cited in Blacking 1977:1). In theory, our bodies are not only vehicles that provide mobility in various ways but also the location of being.

It is through socialization that our bodies, even specific body parts, "especially the sexual parts" (Young 1989:62), have symbolic meaning. These symbols may seem natural because they "are culturally learned and culturally transmitted" (Douglas 1982[1970]:xiii–xiv). Butler states that "bodies cannot be said to have a signifiable existence prior to the mark of their gender" (1990:8). What we learn about and what is transmitted to us about bodies helps to sustain the status quo of any particular social system (Scheper-Hughes and Lock 1987:19). The social body constrains whatever we may experience through our bodies and "controls exerted from the social system place limits on the use of the body as a medium" (Douglas 1982[1970]:65, 67).

The limits on the uses of bodies, and on what types of bodies are considered legitimate, is regulated through the body politic (judicial, medical, and political systems). The body politic controls what can and cannot be done with bodies (e.g., laws that regulate abortion, surgical reconstruction of ambiguous genitalia, and categorization of disease) (Scheper-Hughes and Lock 1987:25). Furthermore, through the body, the body politic dictates what constitutes legitimate sex and gender, normal sexuality, and even what identities are considered appropriate.

Sexes and Genders

Gender [and sex] categories are learned by all, and are "natural" to none.
—Newton and Walton 1989:245

Sex, until the 1990s, has been assumed to be locatable on and within the body and as such has been considered a biophysical entity determined by chromosomes, gonads, genitalia, and secondary characteristics such as musculature and hair distribution. In general, when I use the term *sex* it is as a biological marker. Because maleness and femaleness are constructed as biological components of sex, the words *male* and *female* are used in that sense also. The term *sex* also is used to refer to acts and practices. Weeks states that it is "through our sex [that] we are expected to find ourselves and our place in the world" (1986:12).[3] Weeks seems to have conflated sex with gender. Although how people present gender leads to assumptions about their sex, the two often are not in agreement. I do, however, agree with Weeks that "we experience sex very subjectively" (1986:11). We also experience gender subjectively.

Sex and gender are often conflated (until the early 1990s, they were considered one and the same thing). Normal, typical males are viewed as masculine men, and normal, typical females are seen as feminine women (Butler 1990). Gender has long been considered a social construction and the social manifestation of sex (cf. Devor 1989; Kessler and McKenna 1985). It is in that sense that I use the terms *man, masculine, woman,* and *feminine* to designate gender. In that both sex and gender are social constructions, the construction of men (gender) is not exclusive to male bodies (sex) and vice versa. It then follows that man and masculine can be signified as male by a female body and vice versa (Butler 1990:6).

Nonetheless, the conceptions of sex and gender have been limited by a Cartesian duality, a binary value that insists there are two, and only two, sexes and genders (Jacobs and Cromwell 1992; Scheper-Hughes and Lock 1987:9). Because of that duality a person can be said to have a true sex and a true gender. Although no unambiguously proven causal links exist among sex, gender, and gender presentation (Butler 1991:25), sexologists, psychologists, sociologists, and medical practitioners—the majority of the medico-psychological discursive fields—have attempted to maintain links to "impose order on the inherently disorderly universe of gender and sexual behavior" (Irvine 1990:267). The imposition of order is most clearly evident in the medical treatment of hermaphrodites and intersexed individuals.[4] Both, although more than one sex or alternately neither sex, are surgically constructed as one or the other (Epstein 1990; Fausto-Sterling 1993; Foucault 1980a, 1980b; Freid 1982; Kessler 1990, 1998).

The imposition of the dominant order does not end with the biophysically ambiguous. Despite individual variations, the sex and gender order mandates standards of normalcy upon everyone. Thus the body politic, by imposing cultural norms, "is always the arbiter of what is 'appropriate,' 'natural,' and, ultimately, 'good.' There is an unarticulated assumption that men should be stereotypically masculine, women stereotypically feminine, and both heterosexually oriented. Deviations from this standard of normality are received with varying degrees of tolerance" (Irvine 1990:237). Those assumptions are clearly articulated. Messages for conforming to stereotypic behaviors bombard transgendered and nontransgendered alike.

There have been two ways of thinking about sex and gender as categories: as essential and as a construct. In essentialist formulations, gender is viewed as being within the person, "a quality or trait describing one's personality, cognitive process, moral judgment, etc." and not necessarily the same thing as biological determinism (Bohan 1993:6). Yet sometimes the two are not readily, or easily, distinguishable (e.g., Raymond 1994[1979]). Most early theorists who wrote about transsexuals viewed sex and gender as essential, and concepts such as "core gender identity" (Money and Ehrhardt 1972), "gender core" (Stoller 1985), "gender identity disorder," and even "cross-gender identity" derive from that viewpoint.

Within essentialist frameworks the phenomenological body, sex, and gender are real and true, changeless and constant substances that "define the 'whatness' of a given entity" (Fuss 1989:xi). If born female, for example, then one must be a woman based solely on genitalia—which seems exceedingly biological determinist. Sex (the body) provides the physical foundation from which gender is constructed (Nicholson 1994:81) so that categories such as man, woman, male, and female "are assumed to be ontologically stable objects, coherent signs which derive their coherency from their unchangeability and predictability" (Fuss 1989:3). In the essentialist model, it is the sexed body that gives the entity its "essence," whether gender or identity, and nothing more need be elaborated. The body is "'real,' accessible and transparent [and] interpretable through the senses" (Fuss 1989:5). As intersexed people and transpeople illustrate, however, that is not always the case, nor is it entirely interpretable through the senses. As such man, woman, male, and female are not stable categories.

In constructionist formulations, sex (somewhat) and gender (particularly) are viewed as not residing within the individual but are found in "those interactions that are socially constructed as gendered" (Bohan 1993:7) such that there is social action and reaction upon gendered subjects (Nicholson 1994:83, 90). Scott has described gender as having "two parts and several subsets [which] are interrelated but must be analytically distinct." It is "a constitutive element of social relationships based on the perceived differences between the sexes, and gender is a primary way of signifying relationships of power" (1991:26). The subsets are: (1) "culturally available symbols that evoke multiple (and often contradictory) representations, [e.g.,] Eve and Mary as symbols of women"; (2) "normative concepts that set forth interpretations of the meanings of the symbols . . . [that] typically take the form of a fixed binary opposition, [and in which] the position that emerges as dominant, however, is stated as the only possible one"; (3) politics, "social institutions and organizations"; and (4) "subjective identity [because] real men and women do not always or literally fulfill the terms of the society's prescriptions or our analytic categories" (Scott 1991:26–27). In other words, gender as lived through the phenomenological body derives symbolic meaning from the social body and is regulated by the body politic. Nevertheless, Scott states (and Butler would likely agree) the necessity of recognizing "that 'man' and 'woman' are at once empty and overflowing categories. Empty because they have no ultimate, transcendent meaning. Overflowing because even when they appear to be fixed, they continue to sustain within them alternative, denied, or suppressed definitions" (1991:31–32).

Embedded within the constructionist formula is a performance theory that says that gender is not something people have but rather something they do. For example, "Gender is a performance with clearly punitive consequences," and "genders can be neither true nor false, neither real nor apparent, neither original nor derived" (Butler 1990:141). Butler likens gender to drag performances, wherein "drag constitutes the mundane way in which genders are appropriated, theatricalized, worn, and done; it implies that all gendering is a kind of impersonation and approximation. If this is true, it seems, there is no original or primary gender that drag imitates, but *gender is a kind of imitation* for which there is no original" (1991:21, emphasis in the original). She contends that gender performances become "naturalized" by being viewed as essential, but "it is always a surface sign" (28). Within performative theory, gender is a process rather than something "naturally" possessed.[5]

Most societies are known to have "some kind of a male/female distinction [and] most appear to relate this distinction to some kind of bodily distinction between men and women" (Nicholson 1994:96). Nonetheless, there is potential for subtle yet great variety in the meanings between the bodily distinction and the classifications of male and female. Furthermore, the subtleties "may contain important consequences in the very deep sense of what it means to be a man or a woman" including how the body is read as male/female (96). Even so, both essentialist and constructionist formulations result in imposing normality onto the behaviors of people. Neither formulation is unfriendly "to arrangements as they are" (Tuzin 1991:869).

Gender diversity is viewed as problematic because neither formulation is unfriendly to the status quo and because of the potential depth of the interrelationships of sex, gender, sexuality, and identity. If societies did not assign "each individual body its place, its social status, and ultimately its destiny" (Scheper-Hughes and Lock 1991:412), then those who divert from these preassigned places, statuses, and destinies would not be subject to social control (i.e., the body politic).

Categorizing people by sex is both a legal and a medical matter in which bodies are made legitimate and normal depending on what genitals they possess. Sex ambiguities are not tolerated because they upset the status quo of dichotomous sexes (Pagliassotti 1993:475). Many still seem afraid of "monsters," even though surgeries purportedly reconstruct as natural both intersexed/hermaphroditic and transsexed bodies.[6] Hermaphrodites and intersexed people are reconstructed and made to fit within one category or another, although most usually it is the category labeled female (Findlay 1995:43; see also Fausto-Sterling 1993). It is more difficult but not impossible to reconstruct and make transpeople fit, especially those who self-identify as being transsexual, a temporary status. It is nearly impossible to reconstruct and make transpeople fit who neither want nor feel the need to be reconstructed or fit within a particular category. Certainly, the latter are sanctioned, disciplined, or punished as gender transgressors, usually by labeling their identities and behaviors as pathological and disordered. Such labeling occurs in an effort to silence "the questions [their] behavior raises" (Pagliassotti 1993:475).

Sexualities

Sexuality lies between things. . . . It is intrinsically ambiguous.
—Dimen 1989:144

As with bodies, sexes, and genders, sexuality also has been framed within essentialist and constructionist theories. In essence, one only need to reread the preceding and substitute the word *sexuality* for the words *sex* and *gender*. Sexuality in essentialist models is viewed as "a fixed essence, which we possess as part of our very being; it simply *is*. And because sexuality is itself seen as a thing, it can be identified, for certain purposes at least, as inherent in particular objects, such as the sex organs, which are then seen as, in some sense, sexuality itself" (Padgug 1990:49). It is considered as essential to one's being, regardless of one's sexuality. Accordingly, sexualities are seen as appropriate to categories of persons: male, female, child, heterosexual, and homosexual. They can also be identified and categorized into types and groups (Padgug 1990:49–50). Davidson underscores these standards by observing, "What we have come to call 'sexuality' is the product of a system of psychiatric knowledge that has its own very particular style of reasoning and argumentation" (1990[1987]:18).

Another essentialist model, although it appears on the surface to be a constructionist model, is the "cultural influence model" (Vance 1991:879). Within this framework, sexuality is viewed as a cultural byproduct of learning specific sexual behaviors and attitudes. It is "assumed—and often quite explicitly stated—to be universal and biologically determined" (878). The model covers everything about sexuality, from sexual acts and practices to gendered roles. Sexuality is "not only related to gender but blends easily, and is often conflated with it." That conflation arises because of "our own folk beliefs that sex causes gender . . . , and, gender causes sex" (879). Furthermore, the model assumes that what is true for one culture or society is true for all others and ethnocentric such that sexual practices labeled "heterosexuality" or "homosexuality" in Euro-American societies are treated as if they are the same historically and cross-culturally.

Constructionist theories do not view sexualities as inherent but rather as inventions of societies that have been given meanings. Within these theories, sexuality is seen as having a history and being situational. In essence, people are what they are sexually because of their social frameworks and historical epochs. As a social construction, heterosexuality is privileged (as it has been throughout history) because it conforms to the ideology (in particular, a reproductive imperative) of the dominant society. "A social construction approach to sexuality would examine the range of behavior, ideology, and subjective meaning among and within human groups, and would view the body, its functions, and sensations as potentials (and limits) which are incorporated and mediated by culture" (Vance 1991:879).

Regardless of the model or the system of knowledge from which it is derived, sexuality is the result of relations among or between individuals and is created by them. "It consists of activity and interaction—active social relations—and not simply 'acts'" (Padgug 1991:55–56). It also varies between participants and within contexts and takes many forms (53). Those on the periphery of culture, such as gays, lesbians, and transpeople, feel less constrained by the limitations placed on their identities, regardless of which identity or identities has resulted in their being marginalized. Appropriately, marginalized people "give rise not only to new ways of organizing behavior and identity but to new ways of symbolically resisting and engaging with the dominant order" (Vance 1991:877).

The Stigma of Transness

> The credibility of people who go through this process is so easily challenged.
> After all, who in his or her right mind would get her or his sex changed?
> —Green 1994b:3

The general public perceives little or no difference between transpeople and homosexuals. It is commonly assumed that if one cross-dresses (sometimes even to a limited extent) then one is either gay, lesbian, transvestite, or transsexual, where the latter categories are known. Many gays and lesbians have been asked whether they did not "really want to be" a woman or a man, respectively. Likewise, many transpeople have been asked whether they are not "really homosexual."[7] Many individuals feel no confusion whatsoever, however, and may never question their gender or sexuality. "I always knew" or "I've always been this way" is a familiar part of retrospective narratives. For these individuals, the labels "gay," "lesbian," or any one of the labels that deal with being a transperson may help explain their feelings and behaviors as well as their alienation and isolation from others unlike themselves (cf. Bolin 1988:73ff.; D'Emilio 1983; Weeks 1989). They usually do not find their "non-normative" identity problematic.

Nevertheless, lesbians, gays, and transpeople have identities that are stigmatized by society. The stigma intersects with the perception of nonconformity to gender and specific sexual practices. Ponse has noted (1976:313) that "the secrecy surrounding gay life in our society is rooted in the stigma which characterizes homosexual acts and persons." Transpeople are similarly stigmatized for their acts and persons. Consequently, depending on context, gays, lesbians, and transpeople may have a "perceived need for secrecy" that results from the "ever-present possibility of stigmatization" (Ponse 1976:315).

"The term stigma [is] used to refer to an attribute that is deeply discrediting" (Goffman 1963:3). Attributes that can cause an individual or groups of individuals to be discredited include physical and mental handicaps, terminal illnesses, class background, education, race, and ethnicity (4–6) in addition to sexual and gender identity. Those who become stigmatized are "reduced . . . in our minds from whole and usual person[s] to tainted, discounted one[s]" (3). One way in which individuals overcome stigma is by passing as normal.

The Concept of Passing

Being able to name a thing and recognizing its presence are two different processes.
—Castendyk 1992:70

In its original usage, "passing" referred to African Americans who passed as whites (Friedli 1987:251n2). Historically, other minorities have chosen to pass from "one group to another, typically one that offers greater advantages" (Glazer and Moynihan 1975:16). Gay men and lesbians may opt to pass as straight, and, not surprisingly, many transpeople attempt to pass out of a stigmatized group and into the mainstream.

Within transsexual discourses, passing means blending in and becoming unnoticeable and unremarkable as either a man or a woman. Blending in as normal means that one has succeeded and become a "real" man or woman. With "realness," an individual is no longer a member of the stigmatized group of transsexuals; she or he has completed "transition" and is now "just a woman" or "just a man." To do otherwise is to fail. Stoller believed that passing is problematic for transpeople and related to the "problems of identity formation" (1965:191). Similarly, "The predicament of the transsexual, especially the preoperative one, provides a rich example of how an individual engages in artful impression management to present a problematic gender identity as beyond doubt and within a totally taken-for-granted world of social action" (Weigert, Teitge, and Teitge 1986:75). Passing within this discourse is only problematic when artful impression management is not successful and the person is read (e.g., as a man in a dress or as a woman in a man's suit).

Within mainstream discourses, passing is the notion that a person dresses in the clothing of the opposite sex "for the purpose of convincing an 'unknowing audience' that one actually is a member of that sex" (Herrmann 1991:179). Although that seemingly reads no differently than the passing of transsexual discourses, there is an implied difference. Consider what happens when female-bodied people who have lived as or who do live as men are discovered. Others read their success at blending in and becoming unnoticeable and unremarkable men as disguise, masquerade, and pretense. The assumption is that a reader knows the meaning behind the behavior and actions and that these involve intentional artifice; the person is something other than what he or she says or does (cf. Drorbaugh 1993:130). Within this discourse there is no transition or passing out of a stigmatized group and no realness, but rather there is the discovery of truth and the unmasking of deception. Both discourses insinuate deception. In transsexual discourses, a person lies to become real (cf. Bornstein 1994:62); in mainstream discourses, realness is the lie.

How are these dominant discourses different from transdiscourse? Many transpeople feel they are passing, "doing drag," and living a lie when they attempt to live in their assigned sex; for them, doing so is a matter of disguise, masquerade, and pretense. Rather than passing, many FTMs and transmen feel they are being seen as their true selves in living, dressing, and behaving as men.[8] Being seen rather than being read is an important distinction. The latter implies an intent to deceive and falsehood; the former is a recognition that there is no deception and that observers see those whom they observe as they see themselves. Fewer and fewer accept the stigma of being FTMs and transmen. Although individuals may look like "normal" men, they feel no need to pass as such. They are transpeople "by choice, not by pathology" (Bornstein 1994:118) and have become integrated and whole. Those who acknowledge and accept transness by claiming existing labels as their own or creating a discourse disempower stigma and proclaim pride in their identities. In essence, they "make a safe land for [their] reality" (Cordova 1992:291) by overcoming the stigma of transness.

A Critique of Discourses on Transissues

The issue being raised here is one of representation.
—Namaste 1994:12

Discourses, misrepresentative or not, are perpetuated at two sites. The first concerns transsexual discourses as practiced within the medico-psychological fields and by transvestites and transsexuals who do not challenge the discourses as they are perpetuated and denigrate those who come out as transpeople. The second are radical feminist theories (and others such as legal and social science theories) that use discourses without consulting the subjects themselves or by misconstruing or reinterpreting what has been said. In the following, I focus on radical feminist theories. Transsexual discourses, in particular medico-psychological ones, are critiqued in chapters 9 through 11, and discussion of the two discourses that occur among transvestites and transsexuals appears throughout the text.

Discursive fields such as sexology, medicine, and psychology have the "status of objective knowledge" (Scott 1990:136). As a result, they maintain the appearance of authority and have been viewed as legitimate truth. Feminists often have challenged the discursive fields and by doing so continue to reveal the subjectivity of so-called objective knowledge. Ironically, however, when it comes to discourses that are not about women (or, more correctly, about one-dimensional women), many accept the discursive fields as objective, authoritative, and legitimate.[9]

While reading Lazreg's (1990) cogent critique of feminist academics' writings on the one-dimensional portrait of Mideastern women, it occurred to me that a significant number of feminists have reduced transpeople to one dimension of life: surgical and hormonal alteration as a reification and reinforcement of dichotomous gender and sex. That is most obvious in the denunciations of transpeople as always already embodying the other. Transmen and FTMs in particular are accused of "betraying womanhood," "joining the patriarchy," "becoming the oppressor," and "only doing this for male privilege" to name but a few of the similarly worded sanctions.[10] Transpeople, for their part, struggle to explain how they are different "from what they say we are" (Nestle 1989:235). What radical feminists often discount is agency in shaping and reshaping the meanings of bodies, sexes, genders, and sexualities in particular and idiosyncratic ways.

Echols argues that "the contradiction of transsexualism is that it both undermines and reinforces gender as a significant category. However, cultural feminists (read radical), especially those who favor biological determinism, find transsexualism troubling because it confounds the boundaries between maleness and femaleness" (1989:61). I am not so sure it is that simple. There is, I think, a deep, underlying fear that there may be little real difference between maleness and femaleness. To acknowledge such a fact would unravel the fabric of biological determinism.

Biological determinists essentialize sexed bodies by equating genitals with gender. In doing so, they deny the existence of gender diversity. Through these discourses the "wrong body" syndrome is invoked as an argument for the essentialist nature of sexed and gendered schemas of understanding. Theory, therefore, is locked into an inadequate model (chapter 9) based on discourses that perpetuate sex and gender differences to essentialize the body and the individual. Biological determinists thus join transsexual discourses and medico-psychological practitioners in attempting to eradicate gender diversity.

Within these kinds of feminist discourses "difference becomes essentialized" (Lazreg 1990:339) and differences become entrenched as hegemonic binaries: male/masculine/men versus female/feminine/woman. There are, however, a "variety of modes of being female" and male (Lazreg 1990:341). If female is used as a sexed category, then being female can mean being a man or masculine and living as such. Likewise, if male is used as a sexed category, then being male can mean being a woman or feminine and living as such.

Transsites of Resistance

The issue is relationship with the larger self, and for transsexuals gender is
the prism.
—Green 1994b:6

Theories are one thing and subjective experiences are an entirely different matter. Too frequently, experience is the "excluded middle" (Tuzin 1991:867) left out of theories. The excluded middle is expressed as feelings and emotions that are catalysts that bring "acquired knowledge into understanding" and they are "the mediator between the body and . . . the mind" (Blacking 1977:5). What most, if not all, theorists do not have is the experience of being, and therefore they cannot know what it is to feel like a transperson. They do not know what it is to experience their bodies "in the first person" (Lingis 1994:47). That is not to say that the only way to understand transidentities is through subjective experience. One does not have to be FTM or a transman to understand the nature of FTM/ transman identity (as gender), although that is likely the case in order to understand depth of feeling. As a consequence, most radical theorists do not have a conceptualization that transpeople's identities are "real, lived, viable" (Namaste 1994:5) in and of themselves.

It may be true that a society tries in many different ways "to socialize its members, to educate its bodies" (Isenberg and Owen 1977:3, cited in Young 1989:44). Yet one is only able to make an "investment of a self in the body insofar as the self is felt to inhere in the body as a whole, not its parts" (Young 1989:56). Socialization and education are doomed when a person's experience of their body does not accord with their sexed body and the symbolic meanings it is supposed to have. Hence, the phenomenological body is a site of resistance to sex and gender ideologies. Not only can there be "experiences of bodily resonance" (Blacking 1977:7) but there also can be experiences of bodily dissonance. Dissonance, however, is too clinical a term to describe what is really bodily resistance. People "do not always or literally fulfill the terms of their society's prescriptions or our analytic categories" (Scott 1991:27). Feelings of this kind, whether called dissonance or resistance, are nonetheless treated as marginal and pathological within Euro-American societies.

The body as a site of resistance for transpeople is manifested by gender expressions. According to performative theory, gender is a "routine, methodical, and recurring accomplishment" by members of society who thus express masculinity or femininity. That people "do gender" in the presence of others (West and Zimmerman 1987:126) may have some validity. Even when alone, however, people have and manifest a gender.

If gender were only important in social situations, then transpeople would not know that their gender is different than what societies dictate they should be according to their bodies. Transpeople do not take off gender as though it were clothing. Contrary to Butler's statement about there being "no gender identity behind the expressions of gender" (1990:25), gender and gendered identity are, and feel, basic to beingness. "Individuals have many social identities that may be donned or shed, muted or made more salient, depending on the situation" (West and Zimmerman 1987:139), but gender identity is not one of them. The gender presentations of transpeople are not drag (although some are known for drag performances), nor do they feel like performances. Performance-based theories of gender cannot account for people "doing gender" outside social interactions. Contrary to some theorists' claims, transpeople do not don and then cast off gender identities.[11] They wear them all the time.

Transpeople can, and do, recognize that gender is an essential part of their beings. At the same time, they acknowledge that it is constructed. On the one hand, transpeople conceive of gender as an internal, persistent identity such that transmen and FTMs have an identity referenced within society as male/masculine/man despite having female bodies and regardless of whether they alter those bodies via hormones and surgery. On the other hand, they recognize that their social identities are constructed through learning what behaviors, mannerisms, and speech patterns are marked for the culturally gendered category "men."

Essentialist cum biological determinist and constructionist theories are nothing more than the old nature-versus-nurture debate cast anew. Like the old debate, neither can stand alone to account for individual experiences. Both sides of the coin contribute to the whole. Rather than viewing bodies, sexes, genders, and sexualities as either essentialist (nature) or constructionist (nurture) and flipping the coin periodically to explain the behaviors of persons, both theories must be taken into account. People do feel that aspects of their being are essential (natural), yet they also know that what they feel is due in part to how the dominant society constructs (nurtures) ideologies seen as pertinent to being an embodied, sexed, gendered, and sexual being.

It is because transpeople recognize the constructedness of essentialism and constructionism that they are able "to say 'no' to [society's] demands or at least to reinterpret them in a way that permits him or her to say 'yes'" (Hewitt 1989:151). What that means is that transpeople can say no to the essentialist construction of bodies, sexes, genders, and sexualities and say yes to or reinterpret the social constructions of those same categories.

Transpeople not only shake the foundations of the biological foundationalist and essentialist theories but also undermine them completely. They are social disruptions and as such are a threat to the social body. They are not like other people. Rather than allowing society to dictate who and what they are, they define themselves.

CHAPTER 4

Visible Yet Invisible:
Female Gender Diversity, Historically
and Cross-Culturally

[People] remain adamantly wedded to identifying sexed bodies and thus
exposing the falsity of the gender appropriated.
—Blackwood 1997:2

There are striking similarities between studies of homosexuality and
transgenderism.[1] First, like the concepts of sex and gender, they become
conflated. Where there is transgendered behavior there is a presumption of homosexuality. Beginning with some of the earliest literature on
Native American gender diversity, individuals displaying transgendered
behaviors have been called sexual inverts (Hill 1938:338) or homosexuals (Devereux 1937:500). Devereux, for example, has stated that "the
Mohave recognize only two definite types of homosexuals. Male transvestites, taking the role of the woman in sexual intercourse, are known
as *alyha*. Female homosexuals, assuming the role of the male are known
as *hwame*" (1937:500). And, "In the literature the term ['berdache'] has
been used in an exceedingly ambiguous way, being used as a synonym
for homosexualism, hermaphroditism, transvestism, and effeminism"
(Angelino and Shedd 1955:121).[2]

In an attempt to clarify the ambiguity surrounding the status of gender
diversity and sexualities Callender and Kochems observe that "its frequent
equation with homosexuality, even by explicitly gay writers, distorts the
sexual aspects of berdachehood" (1983:444). More recently, that remains
the case even when clear evidence is lacking for homosexuality. Roscoe
has concluded, for example, that We´wha, a Zuni "berdache," occupied
"a traditional gay role" (1988:64; see also Roscoe 1991). Fulton and Ander-

son infer that the attribution of homosexuality is a result of "a tendency to conflate gender and sexuality" (1992:608).

Second, for both homosexuality and transgenderism it is assumed that what was and is true for males was and is true for females. Concerning lesbianism, McIntosh notes, "The assumption always is that we can use the same theories and concepts for female homosexuality, and that, for simplicity, we can talk about men and assume that it applies to women" (1981:45). That is also the case for male-to-female and female-to-male transpeople. Devor has observed that "by definition, a transsexual is a person whose physical sex is unambiguous, and whose gender identity is unambiguous, but whose sex and gender do not concur" (1989:20).

Note the clear lack of sex or gender-specific pronouns. Frequently, when such markers are noted they quickly disappear once discussion is underway. Nanda has stated, for example, that "gender identity refers to the inner psychological conviction of an individual that *he* or *she* is either a *man* or a *woman*. The concept of gender identity allows transsexuals to maintain that, in spite of a *male* body, they are and always have been *women*" (1990:137, emphasis added). Again note the use of sex or gender markers, from those that include male and female to those that gloss over the female-to-male case. Just as researchers once assumed that lesbianism was "the mirror-image of male homosexuality" (Blackwood 1985:6), many now assume that female transgenderism is the mirror image of male transgenderism. To paraphrase Blackwood (1985), it is time to break the mirror.

Female gender diversity as a phenomenon occurs cross-culturally and historically yet has been rendered largely invisible in anthropological and historical literature. Notwithstanding a flurry of literature since the 1990s, females who have lived as males, or taken on the roles and statuses of males within their cultures are discounted as "pretenders," "masqueraders," and "fake men." That nomenclature occurs because of androcentric, biological determinism and homocentric biases and results in female gender diversity being made invisible.

Biases in the Literature

To "commit" a homosexual act is one thing: to *be* a homosexual is
something entirely different.
—Padgug 1990:58–59, emphasis in the original

Many of the cases cited in this chapter are biased in three ways. First, they are less than objective in that "the researchers' own social norms tend to make their way into the interpretations of the behaviors and responses they have observed or collected. This has the effect of imbuing behavioral data with social meanings, but the meanings are those of the researchers, not the [individuals] they study" (Miller and Fowlkes 1980:784). One way the data are imbued with social meanings is through language that psycho-pathologizes both individuals and societies manifesting gender diversity. Much of the data contain words such as "aberrant," "pathetic," or "peculiar," and occasionally individuals are referred to as "it."

Another way in which the data are endowed with social meanings occurs through language that denies the validity of individual claims. Consequently, even when female-bodied transpeople identified themselves as men, their identifications were discounted or ignored. One researcher, for example, insisted upon referring to these individuals as "women," "she," "her," and other female markers. Another consequence of this tendency is that females who live as men are often said to be homosexuals or lesbians. Sexuality and gender (as well as sex) are separate entities.

> In anthropological literature, gender [diversity] traditionally was interpreted as homosexuality since individuals who change gender roles generally form sexual relationships with persons of the same sex. Moreover, in [Western] culture femininity in males and masculinity in females are seen as "symptoms" of homosexuality. Recent studies, however, have shown that a same-sex relationship is not necessarily also a "same-gender" relationship. Such relationships may be homosexual on the level of biological sex, but not on the level of gender. (Lang 1991a:1–2, see also 1996:188 and 1997:104)

Work activities or religious roles for Native Americans and for many other cultural groups are more significant than sexual relationships in indicating a change in gender status (cf. Lang 1991a:2, 1996:187).

The second bias in data also involves language and arises out of the Western binary. Not surprisingly, as Fulton and Anderson have noted, "Western chroniclers coined the terms 'man-woman' and 'halfman-halfwoman'—hybrids of the only words they had at their disposal to translate such terms as nadle, winkte, heemaneh, et al., into English. . . . these terms refer to a distinct gender—one separate from 'male' and 'female'" (1992:607). Yet Fulton and Anderson continue to use the terms *man-woman* and *men-women* throughout their article.[3] Given that, it should not be surprising that they fall into another linguistic trap and refer to female-bodied "berdaches." Rather than reverse the usual "man-woman" to "woman-man," they add a modifier: "female." Consequently, female "berdaches" become "female men-women." Such designations are the result of androcentric and phallocentric biases and Eurocentrism in cultural constructions.

Third, the data are biased in that most are from the period of colonization and are thus written in language that perpetuates colonial images. It is not my intention to continue this practice, although some statements will be cited in entirety to preserve their context. Nor is it my intention to separate "the West" from "the rest."

Until the mid-1970s, as feminist studies have demonstrated, females have been overlooked in most cultural research. "Since all early data come through the writing of Western male explorers, military men, or missionaries, [and male anthropologists], . . . it is woefully incomplete" (Lamphere 1987:23; see also Medicine 1997:150–51). These early observers operated under the mistaken belief that what females did was unimportant and so limited their observations to males.

The phallocentrism, androcentrism, and heterosexism of most of the literature concerning Native Americans frequently overlooks or only mentions in passing the existence of females who have histories and life-styles similar to male gender diversity. "Evidence for a cross-cultural examination of the 'berdache' status is scanty, fragmentary, and often poor in quality" (Callender and Kochems 1983:443). That is even more the case for female gender diversity. As Whitehead has stated, "The vast majority of reported cases are ones of anatomic males assuming aspects of the status of women. For these the term 'berdache' (from the French word for male prostitute) has come down to us in the ethnographic literature. Female deviations into aspects of the male role were far from infrequent, but in most areas . . . these excursions were not culturally organized into a named, stable category comparable to that of 'berdache'" (1981:86). "Observers," notes Blackwood, "seem to have been unable to recognize the cross-gender role. Indeed, no nineteenth-century reports mention cross-gender females among the western tribes, although later ethnographers found ample evidence" (1984b:38). Consequently, a great deal of data concerning female gender diversity has been overlooked if not entirely lost.

Still, it is a worthwhile endeavor to make female gender diversity visible.[4] I assume that not all females identify as or consider themselves to be women (some identify as or consider themselves to be men) and not all female-bodied people are women (some are transsexuals, transvestites, transgender, or something else). Therefore, contemporary female-bodied transpeople are in need of a history. This chapter is a first step in reclaiming a historical legacy made invisible by androcentrism, biological determinism, and homocentric biases, particularly appropriations by lesbians.[5] By examining the cross-cultural record it is possible to consider gender more broadly.

Female Transvestites? Female Men?
Cross-Gender Roles?

People everywhere learn to attach culturally constructed labels
to subjective feelings.
—Lock 1993:139

It is unclear why the female-to-man category has never been studied or
reported upon or why there is also under-reporting of the many cases that
do appear in the literature. In 1887, for example, John Perham wrote that
Iban males and females in Borneo could become *manang bali* (1887:102).
The word *bali* means "changed," and a *manang bali* is one who has changed
gender (Gomes 1911:180). It is the only reference I have found which
indicates that Iban females change gender. Although several observers
(Gomes 1911:179; Haddon and Start 1936:45; Low 1848:175; Roth, ed.
1892:119) have described the behavior of males who were *manang bali*,
none have done so for females. Similarly, Adriani and Kruyt have reported
that among the Celebes Toradja people, females who "behaved like men,
occurred only rarely" (1950:361). In Java, both males and females who
cross-dress are referred to as *wandu* (Blackwood and Wieringa 1999:44).
Zulu girls and unmarried females herd cattle in clothes borrowed from
their brothers in the belief that a change in outer appearance ends
droughts (Bullough and Bullough 1993:17). An Ibo woman who dresses
like a man, however, is considered an abomination and sold into slavery
(Meek 1937:225). The Basongye people of the Congo have been noted
to include male as well as female *kitesha* (transvestites). Although the males
wear women's attire, females are not known to wear men's clothing but
refuse to do women's work (Merriam 1971:95). The Mangaian people of
Polynesia "supposedly" include females who like doing the work men do
(Marshall 1971:161).[6]

In the latter cases there are no indications of "cross-gender" roles nor
explanations of how refusing to perform women's work or doing men's
work equates with transvestism. The examples illustrate the paucity of
detailed descriptions involving females cross-culturally. Much of the data
consists of brief statements such as the following, which concerns the
Cubeo of northwestern Brazil: "I learned of no case of persistent male
homosexuality, and only one of a woman. This woman developed strong
male characteristics and eventually, it was said, she grew a penis" (Goldman
1963:181). Goldman also states, "I heard of only one woman who became
a shaman and she was a transvestite who made such a nuisance of herself

bothering women that the shamans who had prepared her stripped her of her powers" (264).

Among the Fanti of Ghana, a heavy spirit is said to be characteristic of males whereas females have a light spirit. But an "extroverted female, or one with homosexual tendencies" is said to have a heavy spirit and is referred to as *obaa banyin* (female man) (Christensen 1952:92). Christensen provides no indication of which behaviors an extroverted female might exhibit or what indicates that the person may have homosexual tendencies. It is possible that what being an *obaa banyin* entailed or meant will never be known. I have found no other references to that status. Slightly more details are available concerning Amhara females of Ethiopia, however:

> When a woman consistently acts like a man . . . it is believed that there is some biological "mistake of God." [The individual] is likely to be blamed and even insulted, called "mannish" (*wandawande*). This term is used if she acts independent, takes interest only in masculine weapons and activities, and speaks in hard, insubordinate ways. If she is physically a tall, powerful virago [manlike woman], she is called *"wandagrad"* (lit. male-female), a female with too much masculinity. Male-transvestites are more often pitied than blamed, for the populace feels even more certain that this is a biological "mistake of God." For, they argue, *a woman might try to fool people and assume male prerogatives,* but what male would want to surrender the privileges of being a man? (Messing 1957:550–51, emphasis added)

It is difficult to determine how much of the passage is a projection of the writer's cultural values. According to Gilmore, however, the Amhara masculine ideal termed *"wand-nat* . . . involves aggressiveness, stamina, and bold 'courageous action' in the face of danger; it means never backing down when threatened" (1990:13, citing Levine 1966:18). Females who display such behaviors are called "mannish" (*wandawande*) or "male-female" (*wandagrad*) and assumed to be taking on male privileges.

De Gandavo reported in 1576 that females among the Tupinamba Indians of Brazil "determine to remain chaste: these have no commerce with men in any manner, nor would they consent to it even if refusal meant death. They give up all the duties of women and imitate men, and follow men's pursuits as if they were not women. They wear the hair cut in the same way as the men, and go to war with bows and arrows and pursue game, always in company with men; each has a woman to serve her, to whom she says she is married, and they treat each other and speak with each other as man and wife" (de Gandavo 1922:89, as cited in Williams [1992]1986:233).

In New Guinea *waneng aiyem ser* have a special status not available to other Bimin-Kuskumin females: "The adult, married woman largely 'appears' to be disvalued in stereotype, disenfranchised political and economic power, disassociated from religious matters and relegated to the domestic domain of children, gardens, and pigs in a manner long enshrined in the Highland Papua New Guinea ethnography. Yet, *waneng aiyem ser* is respected, powerful, wealthy, and prominent in male ritual" (Poole 1981:116–17). The *waneng aiyem ser* "is a transvestite, an androgynous being, and an image of the hermaphroditic ancestors Afek and Yomnoke, with who she is identified" and "represents the male-in-female and female-in-male in everyone" (153, 157). Poole has also described the *waneng aiyem ser* as "female ritual elders [who] are old, post-menopausal women" who once they have gone through a rite of passage are then ritual leaders (1996:209). There are scant details concerning this gender status other than the mention of some rituals that involve transvestism.

Gender-Transformed Social Men

One of the best-documented examples of female gender diversity concerns the Chukchi (Chukchee) of Siberia, who consider themselves to have seven gender categories not counting the usual female and male ones: three for males, three for females, and an additional category for transformed individuals. Each category varies from the others only by degree. Jacobs and I have conjectured that the categories are nearly the same for males as well as females (Cromwell 1987:26–28; Jacobs and Cromwell 1992:50–53), and an overview of the three male categories is necessary because no details are available for females other than for the fully transformed category.

The first and second male categories are used for "shamanistic or medico-magical purposes" (Bogoras 1975[1904–8]:450; Cromwell 1987:26; Jacobs and Cromwell 1992:50). In the first, the individual changes the "manner of braiding and arranging the hair of the head" (Bogoras 1975[1904–8]:450; Cromwell 1987:25). In the second category, the individual not only changes hairstyle but also adopts female dress. These categories are invoked so the spirits will not recognize the individual (Bogoras 1975[1904–8]:450; Cromwell 1987:26; Jacobs and Cromwell 1992:50).

The third category involves a more complete transformation. The individual gives up all male pursuits as well as all male behaviors and takes "up those of a woman" (Bogoras 1975[1904–8]:450; Cromwell 1987:25). In general, he becomes a woman with "the appearance of a man" (Bogoras 1975[1904–8]:451). Further, it is said that some "even acquire the organs of a woman" (Bogoras 1975[1904–8]:451; Cromwell 1987:26). Bogoras does not profile the female categories but describes one individual:

> She cut her hair, donned the dress of a male, adopted the pronunciation of men, and even learned in a very short time to handle the spear and to shoot with a rifle. At last she wanted to marry, and easily found a quite young girl who consented to become her wife.
>
> The transformed one provided herself with a gastrocnemius from the leg of a reindeer, fastened to a broad leather belt, and used it in the way of masculine private parts. After sometime the transformed woman, desiring to have children by her young wife, entered into a bond of marriage with a young neighbor and in three years two sons were really born into her family. According to the Chukchee interpretation of mutual marriage, they were considered her own lawful children. (Bogoras 1975[1904–8]:455; Cromwell 1987:26; Jacobs and Cromwell 1992:51)

Although Bogoras seems surprised by these transformed individuals, he reports that the Chukchi accept them (Bogoras 1975[1904–8]:448–55; Cromwell 1987:26; Jacobs and Cromwell 1992:53). The seven-gender category system allows room for individual gender expression without stigma (Cromwell 1987:26; Jacobs and Cromwell 1992:53).[7]

Grémaux (1994:242) reports having found "some 120 cases" in the ethnographic literature for females living as men in the Balkans (Albania, Serbia, Croatia, and Montenegro) and has written two different (although similar) articles concerning transgendered females in that area. In the first (1989), Grémaux proposes to explicate "to what extent they actually identify themselves with the male gender" (144), yet gender markers obscure individual identities. The article is an excellent example of the androcentrism, heterosexism, phallocentrism, and biological determinism found in writings on gender diversity. Throughout, Grémaux insists upon the femaleness of individuals' bodies as constituting "true sex." Regardless of what he was told by (or about) these "gender-transformed" (Herdt 1991:483) females, he insists they are women. In a later article (1994), however, Grémaux uses male markers for three of the four cases in which individuals clearly express that they identify as men.

Reports begin during the 1800s and continued into the summers between 1985 and 1988, when Grémaux conducted interviews with two "masculine sworn virgins" as well as with others about individuals "now deceased" (1994:243). Two distinctive "social" male types are described: those who have been reared as such from infancy and those who "reconstruct" themselves later in life. Both groups "abstain from matrimony and motherhood" and are referred to in native terms as virgins. Some native terminology, however, stresses their manhood, such as the South Slavic "muskobanja" which is translated as "manlike woman" (244). Dickemann (1997:249) has provided other emic terms: "Albanian *vergjineshe* (virgin, unmarried); Serbo-Croatian *haramabsa* (woman-man); *tybeli* or *tombelije* (from Turkish, one bound by a vow); [and] *ostajnica* (one who stays, i.e., in the natal household)."

Grémaux presents four case histories. The first concerns Mikas, who was legally "registered under" a male name and since childhood had lived as a man; he referred to himself in male terms and in 1934 at his death was "buried like a man" (1994:250, 247, 251, 253). The second case history is that of Tonë, who reportedly "decided" to become a man following the death of two brothers. He did not, however, adopt a "masculine name" (1994:253, 254).

> [Tonë] succeeded in changing her voice, her way of speaking, her posture and manners to such a degree that it was hard to distinguish her from a male. Her tribe recognized her as a man.
>
> The acceptance of Tonë as a male within the family seems to have been so complete that some members, at least, were ignorant of her female sex. "It was only after his death that I realized that Uncle Tonë had in fact been a woman," a young man of about twenty-five years told me. (Grémaux 1989:150–51)

In 1971, like Mikas, Tonë was buried in male clothes (1994:256). At the time of Grémaux's research, Stana, the third case history, was "fifty years old" and had been "encouraged by the parents to adopt the male role" at a very young age (1994:256, 257). Like Tonë, Stana did not adopt a male name (1994:261) but "consistently used the male gender while talking about herself" (1989:155). "Most of all I detest being a female," Stana declared, "nature is mistaken" (1989:155; 1994:262). Durgjane, the fourth case history, is the only individual to refer to herself in female terms (1994:263). "At first glance, it was not quite easy to discern a female in Durgjane, wearing grey trousers and a white shirt, and with a short hairstyle. The person's voice, bearing, and movements further strengthened the masculine image" (1989:156–57). Durgjane claims that no one had encouraged her, but rather "I wanted it that way I started to dress and behave like a boy. As far as I remember I have always felt myself more like a male than a female" (1994:263, 265). Despite Grémaux's use of female markers, Stana's and Durgjane's comments are like those of Euro-American female-bodied transpeople.

Nonetheless, there are "regional" as well as individual variations in enactments (Dickemann 1997:249–50) of this social role. Grémaux argues that the Balkan practice is unique in relation to other cultural areas where female men have lived. It has resulted in a "more permanent and institutionalized social crossing . . . [and] . . . concerned crossing gender identities rather than merely cross-dressing, since the individuals assumed the male social role with the tacit approval of the family and the larger community" (1994:242).

Despite Grémaux's claim, however, many Native American tribes as well as the Siberian Chukchis have institutionalized social roles for females as men. Furthermore, females have lived as men throughout history and continue to do so.

Another institutionalized form of female gender diversity occurs in contemporary Japan. Some members of the all-female Takarazuka Revue ("founded in 1914") act the parts of men on the stage (Robertson 1989:50; see also Robertson 1998). As Robertson explains, "[They] must, through technologies of gender such as clothing, speech, gestures, and ambience, signify 'male' gender. . . . However, unlike the *onnagata* [male actors who act as females], [they] must not, at the same time, be 'completely transformed' into [their] secondary gender" (1989:53). Nevertheless, individuals subvert male gender in ways not intended by the founder of Takarazuka by taking their roles outside the theatrical arena and into daily life (Robertson 1989:55, 58–63). After the 1930s a term was coined (*das´no reijin*) to refer both to Takarazuka females who play males and masculine women who dress in men's clothing and wear short, cropped hair (Robertson 1992:429). Not surprisingly, the term is from the title of a fictionalized story about the life of Kawashima Yoshiko (1906–48), a woman who "passed as a man" during part of her life (429).

Cross-culturally, Blackwood has reported forty-four cultures in which there are instances of what she initially termed "cross-gender" behavior in females, including Native American tribes, South America, Africa, Polynesia, and Melanesia (1984a:112–15).[8] The earliest of these cases was reported in 1901 (114).

Many Native American cultures accept gender diversity and even believe that some individuals are destined to transcend or mix genders. Both males and females can assume the dress, mannerisms, and labor activities of different genders. Although males are reported far more often, females are also reported.

The number of tribes that accept gender diversity among their female members is debatable. The discrepancy can be attributed to a lack of data and a lack of consensus over what constitutes gender diversity. The number of Native American groups varies from nineteen (Jacobs 1968:34) to sixty-three (Roscoe 1987:169). Lang divides female gender diversity into two categories of individuals: those in relationships with women and those who have either lived alone or do not have sexual relationships with men (1994:4). Callender and Kochems (1983:446) have the number of categories at thirty, whereas Blackwood (1984b:29) has determined that there are thirty-three. Contributing to the lack of data is some theorists' resistance to the concept that females can and do transcend gender roles. Some theorists may consider only those tribes that have a tradition of institutionalized roles; others may include any female perceived to have stepped out of a particular culture's gender boundaries; and still others may incorporate idiosyncratic cases as well.

One component in institutionalized roles concerns the naming of a status. In this regard, Roscoe (1987:138–53) supplies only twenty-one Native terms from the sixty-three tribes he considers to have female gender diversity. He acknowledges that for determining "alternative sex and gender" statuses he has employed "an inclusive definition" ranging from institutionalized forms recognizable by specific terminology to nonspecialized or nonformal roles (82–83). It is unclear what criteria or definitions other theorists have used, but it is clear that they have included cases without Native terms and formalized roles as well as institutionalized forms for female gender diversity in data.

Popular writers such as Grahn (1984) and Feinberg (1992, 1996) have the tendency to include any individuals who have stepped out of a proscribed cultural gender boundary, for example, "manly-hearted women" and the Crow called Woman Chief.[9] Grahn embraces "manly-hearts" under the rubric of "dyke," which, borrowing from Allen, she defines as a woman "who bonds with women" (Allen 1981:81; Grahn 1984:61) as well as "a woman who cross-dresses at least to some extent and is often found doing work, sports, games, and other activities that have formerly been the exclusive preserve of men" (62). Feinberg uses Woman Chief as an example of "the most notable of all 'berdache' Native Women" (1992:7; see also 1996:24). By definition, "berdache" represent "the high incidence of transgendered men and women" in Native American cultures (7).[10] Grahn and Feinberg, however, have taken manly-hearted women and Woman Chief out of cultural context.

The role of manly-hearted women is restricted to mature (older than fifty) married women who have wealth and high social status (Lewis 1941:175–76). Furthermore, the term *manly* does not refer to male appearance or masculine behavior or lesbianism but rather to "aggressiveness and boldness," which are "characteristics considered more appropriate to men" (Lewis 1941:183). Clearly, based on Lewis's account manly-hearted women do not qualify as dykes as defined by Grahn.

Not only does Feinberg's accounting of Woman Chief force Western terminology on a Native person but it also elides the fact that Woman Chief did not engage in transvestism and was known to wear women's clothing throughout her life (Schaeffer 1965:225). Although the idea of females engaging in hunting and warfare pushes Western cultural boundaries (especially those of the nineteenth and early twentieth centuries), it neither betokens transgenderism or warrants the "berdache" rubric. Within their respective cultures, manly-hearted women and Woman Chief retained their statuses as females (Forgey 1975:1; Lewis 1941:187).

As Blackwood has argued, because of "the presence of variety of socially approved roles" for females within Native cultures there is no need to connote acceptable female behaviors as other than normative. "Warrior women were not a counterpart of the male 'berdache,' nor were they considered cross-gendered. Ethnographers' [as well as popular writers'] attributions of masculinity to such behaviors [is] a product of Western beliefs" (1984b:37). Similarly, Lang asserts (1996:193) that within cultures in which more that two genders are recognized it is inappropriate to label members of these groups as exhibiting "gender reversal." Such phraseology "implies exchanging one gender for the other," however within such cultures individuals may grow up being "neither 'man' nor 'woman' from an early age." They are not moving from one gendered category to another.

The inclusion of idiosyncratic cases may be an attribute of a single observation by eyewitnesses as well as a solitary occurrence, for example, Woman Chief (Schaeffer 1965:227). Such accounts may explain the brief mentions that occur in the literature along with nonspecific details. What follows are several examples of such cases.

While Forgey (1975:1) contends that a "berdache" status did not exist among Plains Indian females, Schaeffer (1965:224) reports that "occasional instances of transvestism" did occur. He does not, however, provide specific data to back that statement. The discrepancy may be explained in Angelino and Shedd's position: "While a 'berdache' is a transvestite, a transvestite is not necessarily a 'berdache'" (1955:125). Even so, as Callender and Kochems have noted (1983:447), although transvestism was a mark of the "final stage of gender transformation" and a prevalent and notable attribute of the role, it was neither "universal nor invariable." Among the Klamath, for example, "a woman named [Co'pak] lived like a man although she retained women's dress. She married a woman who lived with her a long time and finally died. She observed the usual mourning, wearing a bark belt as a man does at this time to prevent the back from growing bowed. She tried to talk like a man and invariably referred to herself as one. Another woman still living has had relations with women and men. She never adopted men's garb but told them she was a man" (Spier 1930:53). Spier also notes that "she was never married to a man" and was known to have had several female partners. As Wheeler-Voegelin reported information from her Klamath informant, "'In early days [we] didn't have any [transvestites],' [but the] informant knew of only two hermaphrodites" (1942:228). Among the Cherokee, at least one female-bodied person assumed a warrior/hunter status and was referred to in emic terms as *Ghigau,* which meant 'Beloved Woman'" (Richmond 1996:4; Woodward 1963:34). Around 1785, one *ghigau* was familiar to settlers and known among them as Nancy Ward (Richmond 1996:4). Yet according to Woodward (1963:35), being a warrior and a hunter were occupations "enjoyed by both the sexes"; it is therefore erroneous to assume that *ghigau* were transgendered.

"One Plateau group, the Kaska, manifests the anomaly (perhaps an artifact of poor reporting) of having had only female-to-male crossers, not the more usual male-to-female" (Whitehead 1981:85). The Kaska found it acceptable for a female to be raised as a male in lieu of having no male child in a family group. Further, Whitehead reports the incidence of at least one female cross-dresser among the Kutanai, another Plateau group: "This transvestite woman was definitely an idiosyncrasy among the Kutenai who seem to have lacked even male 'berdaches,' and it is likely that she adopted the idea of switching her sex from the example of male 'berdaches' in neighboring groups (she was known among the Flathead)" (112n5).

There are cases that are documented more thoroughly. For example, in 1811, David Thompson, an explorer, wrote in his journal:

> A fine morning; to my surprise, very early, apparently a young man, well dressed in leather, carrying a Bow and Quiver of Arrows, with his Wife, a young woman in good clothing, came to my tent door and requested me to give them protection; somewhat at a loss what answer to give, on looking at them, in the Man I recognized the Woman. . . . [she told me that] the Kootenays were also displeased with her; she left them, and found her way from Tribe to tribe to the Sea. She became a prophetess, declared her sex changed, that she was now a Man, dressed and armed herself as such, and also took a young woman to Wife. (Schaeffer 1965:203–4)

Based on Schaeffer's ethnohistorical account it seems reasonable to assume that this person was a female-bodied man.

Devereux documented the case of Sahaykwisa, a Mojave female considered to be a *hwame,* which he considered to be "female homosexuals" (1937:500). He reports that Sahaykwisa was "feminine in appearance and had large breasts" and, as was Mojave tradition, was referred to with male pronouns and was married to a number of women (523). Despite stating that Sahaykwisa did not wear the attire of Mojave men, Devereux repeatedly refers to her as "the transvestite" (523ff), which may indicate the confusion between homosexuality and transvestism.

A number of other native North American tribes allow and encourage gender diverse expressions by females in attire as well as social roles. A child or adolescent who shows a propensity toward the characteristics of the "opposite" sex receives reactions ranging from "mild discouragement to active encouragement . . . but, there was seldom any question as to the meaning of certain opposite-sex-tending behaviors. They [assume that these are] signals that the youth might be destined for the special career of the gender-crossed" (Whitehead 1981:85–86).

Many anthropologists are familiar with the *hijras* of India, male-bodied transgendered individuals (Nanda 1990). Nothing had been reported concerning females who become social men, however, until Phillimore (1991:332) documented the occurrence in northwestern India of *sadhins,* individuals who renounce marriage, adopt men's clothing, and keep their hair close-cropped. "Becoming a *sadhin* has to be a girl's own choice. . . . Once a girl has become *sadhin,* the decision is seen as irreversible" (335). In one case a *sadhin*'s father told Phillimore that from the age of six "she preferred to wear boy's clothing and had wanted her hair cut like a boy's. He and his family had interpreted these preferences as indicative of her choice to become a *sadhin*" (335). Even though acting in "characteristically male ways. . . . despite her male dress and appearance, a *sadhin* is never classified socially as a male. Being a *sadhin* is unambiguously a female gender" status (336). Thus, "a *sadhin* is tacitly thought of as a female who is a surrogate, or 'as if' male. Her [sex] may not be in question, but she can nevertheless operate socially 'like a man' in many situations" (337).

An example of another contemporary gender-transformed status is that of the West Sumatra *tomboi.* Some identify as men, bind their breasts, and behave in culturally specific masculine ways, whereas others identify as lesbians (Blackwood 1999:185–89). One *tomboi* "felt like a man and wanted to be one" (186). Even though some *tombois* may insist on being treated as men, they are not allowed to participate in their culture as men. Nonetheless, Blackwood reports that in a village near her fieldwork site at least one was rumored to live as a man and be married to a woman; the individual operates a store, wears loose clothing, and binds his breasts in order to pass. "Gender transgression" is produced differently in different historical and social contexts (199).

Thus far I have described examples of female gender diversity that involve total or near total changes of gender role and status. Female-bodied persons assume the dress, work, and other social accoutrements of men and in doing so change their sociocultural designation from women to men. The next few examples will involve different forms of gender transformations or transgressions.

Ritual Female Transvestism

The following examples are provided to illustrate the scarcity of information available, and it is impossible to determine what meaning they may have for each specific culture. For example, Sotho (South African) females are initiated wearing men's clothes (Bullough and Bullough 1993:17); female transvestites in Bali perform temple rites (Blackwood and Wieringa 1999:44); and Gond (in Central India) females wear men's apparel before the start of the hunting season (Bullough and Bullough 1993:18). The Kom of Cameroon have a traditional ritual—*anlu*—that is a form of discipline for offenses such as beating or insulting a parent, beating a pregnant woman, seizing a person's genitals during a fight, and abusing elderly women. During the ritual the women of the village dress "in vines and bits of men's clothing, with their faces painted" (Ardener 1987:116).

A similar ceremony is performed at marriages among the Serea of Somoa. The old women of the village "are called upon to publically display the masculinity concealed within their own being. As ceremonial transvestites, they dress up in men's clothes and feign to poke imaginary phalluses into imaginary orifices. Unconstrained laughter erupts and flows at this ridiculous manifestation of biological maleness teased out of female bodies" (Abramson 1987:211). Abramson, the anthropologist who observed this behavior, reports that when the audience laughs at the females it does not laugh at "what is clever make-believe but at the dramatic starkness of the truth. The starkness of this truth is its contradiction. Serean women have, in fact, two genders, yet the logic of producing viable 'humanity' through the kinship system and its rites decrees that they have just one" (211).

Although the Serean example is clearly ritually contextual, other reports of female transvestism are not always so apparent. Basden has noted, for example, that among the Ibo of Nigeria "the women have their own clubs or societies. On one occasion I had the opportunity of watching a crowd of women making preparations for a meeting. The peculiar feature about it was the fact that they were dressed up as men; they wore men's hats and, in some cases, coats; the breasts were bound down close to the body by crossover straps and each member flourished a cutlass in her hand, and in every way they could they imitated men" (1921:94). It is possible, although doubtful, from this description that a ritual was about to take place. Basden also states that "a woman may not wear an article of male attire nor in any way act as a man; severe penalties follow the infringement of this rule" (271). That may be the result of British colonial law and perhaps explains why Basden's observation of the Ibo females was unusual. Alternatively, Simon Ottenberg has suggested in a personal communication (1990) that the event was a ritual reversal. Ritual reversals are most familiar to Westerners as they occur in Mardi Gras and Carnival in Latin America—and most often involve male transvestites. But it also could have been a matter of transgenderism in females and thus something Basden would not have recognized.

Making Cross-Cultural and Historical Female Gender Diversity Invisible

> The importance for me is the depth and breadth of evidence underscoring
> that gender and sex diversity are global in character.
> —Feinberg 1996:47

Although most cultures view gender as dichotomous, gender diversity is (and has been) openly recognized in some. Whether recognized or not, gender diversity has occurred throughout time and in nearly all societies that have much to contribute to contemporary understanding of the concepts of gender. What ties the preceding cross-cultural and historical examples together is the lack of data available, which results in female-bodied transpeople being made invisible. Several factors contribute to this invisibility: language usage, androcentrism, biological determinism, and homocentrism (specifically, lesbian-centered perspectives).

Many accounts of gender diversity are rife with phraseologies that may reveal more about author than subject. Implying that female-bodied transpeople are fakes, masqueraders, and pretenders by labeling their behaviors as "deceit," "disguise," "concealment," or "indulging in cross-dressing" and considering their female bodies as "their hidden nature" pathologizes gender diversity and contributes to its invisibility.

The problem with such language is its reliance on Western binaries. It reveals the authors' belief in biological determinism in two ways. First, such phrases as "hidden nature" imply that there are only male men and female women. Yet anyone familiar with hermaphroditism and intersexuality will see the error of that supposition. Words such as "deceit," "disguise," and "concealment" hinge on that premise and also reveal the author's gross assumption that somehow he or she is privy to an individual's identity. Is it deceit or disguise, for example, when an individual wears clothing considered appropriate for their identity? Dickemann (1997:250) asserts that Grémaux wrongly uses the term *male disguise* because Balkan people are fully aware of the female-bodied social men among them; consequently, no deception is involved.

Second, there is no way to know the biological sex of those described in historical and cross-cultural literature, especially the earlier sources. Some were perhaps hermaphrodites or intersexed. Even if their sex were known irrefutably, their identities would still be unknown based on the prejudicial accounts that have survived. The use of phrases such as "indulging in cross-dressing" potentially trivializes their lives. It assumes that the individual is wearing clothing inappropriate for their biological sex although it may have been appropriate for their identity and status or role within their culture.

Not only has androcentrism resulted in females being overlooked in anthropological data until the late 1970s, but it has also obscured the motivations of those who have transcended gender boundaries. With a few rare exceptions, whenever and wherever females have been found to have taken on male roles their motivations have been rationalized in androcentric terms. The anthropological literature generally focuses on one of several rationales: first, unwillingness to marry, as for the Balkans and northwestern India (Clover 1986:44; Dickemann 1997:250–52; Lang 1991b:11, 20); second, a family's need for a surrogate son, as in the examples of Durgjane's statement and the Kaska (Clover 1986:44; Dickemann 1997:251; Lang 1991b:20); and, third, the pursuit of male privileges or status—as indicated by my emphases in the Amhara example (Callender and Kochems 1983:456; Lang 1991b:20; Roscoe 1987:164). As Dickemann points out, there are probably "half-truths" in these rationales, but none considers individual agency (250). With the exceptions of the Balkan and northwestern Indian examples, individual self-identity is lost along with the motivation for assuming male roles.

What is most questionable about these rationales is their positioning within the dominant ideology, which even now results in the motivations of contemporary female-bodied transpeople's lives being rationalized by the same androcentric arguments. Contemporary transpeople are rendered invisible, as are their historical and cross-cultural counterparts. Positions invoking biological determinism also render female gender diversity invisible. Theorists "resist the idea of a complete social reclassification because they equate gender with biological sex" (Blackwood

1984b:29). Yet several of the preceding examples demonstrate that females were accepted as men (in varying degrees) within their societies.

Frequently, invisibility results because transbehaviors are subsumed under the rubric of homosexuality or lesbianism. That position is also one of biological determinism; where females have transcended or transgressed gender boundaries and had relationships with women, by virtue of their morphology they are viewed as lesbians. For example, Blackwood (1984a, 1984b, 1985) discusses ninety-five societies in which lesbian behavior occurs. Nearly half ($n = 44$) contain what she labeled "cross-gendered females." Sexual relationships between female-bodied men and women, however, "can not properly be termed 'homosexual' or even 'lesbian' since one of the partners involved did *not* have a woman's gender status" (Lang 1991b:16, emphasis in the original). Recognizing that fact, Blackwood no longer classifies cross-gender females as lesbians and in a personal communication in 1998 told me that she has ceased using the term *cross-gender* because it is inappropriate.

Although most anthropological literature treats female gender diversity as an afterthought or has completely overlooked it, females have transcended or transgressed the genders of their cultures (Blackwood 1984b). Given the scant data available, it is difficult to determine what the motivations may have been for particular individuals, but it is clear (with the exception of those cases found within a ritual context) that such people were accepted within their societies as social men (Dickemann 1997:250) or as a part of an institutionalized alternate gender.

The preceding cases should not be construed as anything more than reflections of gender diversity. They are by no means examples of the history of female-bodied people. To argue such would ignore not only cultural differences but also the different meanings of gender within different cultural contexts. Furthermore, gender transgressions cannot be equated with contemporary transgendered people because the meaning of "gender transgression" is also variable and depends upon cultural context. Nonetheless, insights gleaned from transgender studies may apply to the puzzles and complexities of the gender diversity and sexualities of other cultures. It is also necessary to transcend a mindset that insists upon classifying individuals based on their bodies and learn to recognize that some cultures allow individuals to go beyond the usual categories. Cases of female gender diversity that have occurred in Euro-American societies have been treated in similar ways (chapter 5).

CHAPTER 5

Transvestite Opportunists, Passing Women, and Female-Bodied Men

> They are made visible only in so far as . . . deceivers and manipulators, as individuals whose "true" sex must be uncovered. What their own experience or identity is remains invisible.
>
> —Blackwood 1997:1

Throughout Euro-American history, like the cases in the previous chapter regarding cross-cultural data, female-bodied people who have lived as men are often erased by androcentric, phallocentric, and biological-determinist arguments and subsumed under the rubric of lesbianism.[1] This chapter provides a number of cases and analyzes the arguments that have and continue to make female-bodied men invisible. In addition, the cases provide an opportunity to consider historical Euro-Americans' behavior (as well as that of contemporary people who may not choose surgical routes) from a different viewpoint.

Most researchers conclude that female-bodied individuals who have lived as men did so for one of two primary reasons. The first concerns socioeconomic factors such as better-paying jobs in addition to adventure and male privilege (Faderman 1991:43, 45; Friedli 1987:234; Newton 1984:558; Perry 1987:96; Vicinus 1992:473; Wheelwright 1990:19). Pagliassotti has observed that "females were so restricted by social institutions that they had to stop 'being' female (by dressing—and thus becoming—male) to achieve certain goals" (1993:486; cf. Fraser 1985:468). A second reason given for living as men is to provide a cover for lesbianism (Friedli 1987:235; Newton 1984:558; Vicinus 1992:474; Wheelwright 1990:19). "Many of the cross dressers . . . were lesbian" (Bullough and Bullough 1993:164). That statement comes after their caution that "lesbianism does not in itself explain cross dressing" (162). Nonetheless, the conjecture seems to be that if a person lives with a woman the relationship must be a lesbian one.

The histories of the categories "homosexuality," "transvestism," and "transsexualism" are inextricably entwined and to many seem to be one in the same. That should not be surprising because transvestism and transsexuality were embedded within the category of homosexuality (Bullough 1976:24; see also Whittle 1993). Despite the entwined history, many theorists are perplexed by female-bodied people who continued to live as men after the end of their service during war or upon being "discovered." "More troubling, because more difficult to place," as Vicinus states, "were those women who either appeared 'mannish' or continued to cross-dress after the wars were over" (1992:474).

The basis for the conundrum is an inability to conceive of another possibility: female-bodied people who identify as men. Although it is impossible to make clear lines of demarcation, there are several types of female-bodied people who have done that. Transvestic opportunists may identify as men for short-term gain or adventure (i.e., socioeconomics); passing women and female husbands do so for love (i.e., they are lesbians); and female-bodied men do so because they identify as men, whatever that may mean for their particular culture and historical era.

It is not always possible to make tidy distinctions between FTMs/transmen and butch lesbians; there is much overlap and many similarities between the types. By leaving out categories, however, or by subsuming them within others, the forerunners of contemporary female-bodied transpeople are made invisible. At the very least their motivations are obscured by socioeconomic arguments and the presumption of lesbianism. If categories are limited, then those who do not fit are considered perplexing and become unauthorized beings (Magee and Miller 1992:69).[2]

Transvestic Opportunists: Soldiers, Sailors, and Criminals

> To be a soldier, to wear a uniform, to bear arms. That is the only reward which you can give me, Sovereign.
>
> —Durova 1988:72

Dekker and van de Pol have documented "119 'women living as men' in the Netherlands between 1550 and 1839" (1989:xi). The majority (eighty-three) were female soldiers or sailors (1989:9), another twenty-two joined the "land army," and the remainder were civilians (1989:10).[3] Such individuals were able to enlist because physical examinations were not required (Wheelwright 1990:120). Furthermore, certain clothing styles such as the "cassock coat and breeches of the average soldier was at once *dis-*

guise and protection" (Fraser 1985:200, emphasis added) and aided female-bodied people in passing as men. Too, before the mid-twentieth
century females did not wear pants, and someone who did so was "assumed
to be male" (Faderman 1991:41). Nonetheless, the possibility of discovery while in the military was extremely high.

Dekker and van de Pol (1989:3) also observe that "many archives have
been lost and many others have not been researched. Moreover, we do
not know how many cross-dressers left no trail behind them in written
source-material. We can make a guess that this especially concerns those
women who transformed themselves so successfully that they were never
unmasked. For these reasons, we presume that our 119 cases are only the
tip of the iceberg." In a similar vein, Wheelwright (1990:6) has concluded
that "it is impossible to know how many women actually chose to live as
men by adopting male clothing and assuming a 'masculine' occupation
throughout British history. Only those women whose identity was discovered or who, for various reason, publicly surrendered their masquerade
have come to light."

Exactly how many female-bodied people may have lived as men is unlikely
to ever be known, regardless of duration or motivation, because their objective was "anonymity rather than publicity" (Fraser 1985:197). Various
authors have noted a number of anonymous persons discovered only after
death to have been female-bodied—a mark of their success (Hirschfeld
(1966[1938]:220).

Those discovered during life provided various motivations (some were
presumed) for living as men: a desire to remain with their husbands, to
search for them, or to avoid detection while traveling in dangerous areas;
encouragement by other people; poverty; patriotism; adventure; and a belief that it was their "nature" (Dekker and van de Pol 1989:25–27). "Not
all women who cross-dressed wanted to be soldiers or pirates," Ramet asserts
(1996:10). "Some wanted to sign on board a ship bound for the Dutch East
Indies, and make their fortune there; others cross-dressed in order to engage in a life of crime, or alternatively, in order to elude the police, who
might be searching for a female offender." Regardless of motive, "The decision to start dressing as a man was never for one reason alone" (Dekker
and van de Pol 1989:27).

In the discussion that follows I will use pronouns as well as names appropriate to the individual's role rather than ones determined by their
presumed biology. Consequently, male markers will be used for those living as a man and female ones for those living as a woman. The combina-
tions his/her, she/he, and her/him indicate that the person either lived
a dual role or was known to others as being female-bodied. I recognize

that such usages are unusual and often difficult to follow yet employ them out of respect for personal life-styles and to acknowledge the purposeful-ness of individual choice.

Wheelwright (1990) has documented twenty cases (and referred to thirty-five others) of females living as males in Europe (primarily England), Russia, and the United States. As the title of her book—*Amazons and Military Maids*—indicates, the majority were soldiers or sailors. Some kept their secret, and others acknowledged that they were females throughout their military lives.

An example of the latter is Flora Sandes (1876–1956), who attained the rank of captain in the Serbian army during a nationalist uprising. Sandes, born in England, originally signed on as a nurse at the age of thirty-eight but within a few years was a soldier (Wheelwright 1990:34, 35). Following retirement from the army, Sandes, wearing a military uniform, lectured on her experiences throughout Great Britain, Australia, New Zealand, France, Canada, and the United States (103–8).

Cases abound of female soldiers and sailors who kept their secret or revealed it only when doing so became absolutely necessary. Among them are Christian Davies/Christopher Welch, Hannah Snell/James Gray, Mary Ann Talbot/John Taylor, Mary Read, Anne Bonny, Valerie Arkell-Smith/Col. Victor Barker, Mary Frith, Emma Edmonds/Franklin Thompson, and Loreta Janeta Velazquez/Lt. Harry T. Buford.

Christian Davies (1667–1775) was born in Dublin. It has been conjec-tured that she was impressed by her father's friend Captain Bodeaux, a Frenchman who was mortally wounded in battle and subsequently "dis-covered" to be female (Thompson 1974:54; Wheelwright 1990:25). Davies reportedly inherited a urinary device from Captain Bodeaux—a "silver tube painted over, and fastened about her with leather straps" (Wheel-wright 1990:25).

Before serving as a soldier, Davies married Richard Welch and gave birth to two children (Thompson 1974:55). Following her husband's sudden, unexplained disappearance, Davies, leaving her children with her mother, dressed in his clothes to search for him and joined the British army as Chris-topher Welch (Fraser 1985:200; Thompson 1974:56–57). During his ser-vice Welch was wounded by gunshot; captured by the French along with sixty others, all of whom were exchanged for French prisoners; and engaged in a duel in which he wounded his opponent and was jailed for the offense (Thompson 1974:58–62). In 1703 Welch was seriously wounded in the leg and nearly discovered during treatment (63).

After twelve years in the army, Welch finally found Richard Welch (64–65) and asked that he keep her/his secret and treat her/him as a brother

(Thompson 1974:66; Wheelwright 1990:14). Shrapnel struck Welch while they fought side by side and caused a skull fracture. During the period of unconsciousness that followed she/he was discovered to have a female body (Thompson 1974:67). She and Richard were reunited as husband and wife after a set of "suitable" clothes were found (67–68). She traveled with him in the army until his death and then returned to Dublin. Once home, she gained notoriety for having been a female soldier. Davies was 108 when she died; she had a ceremonial burial with military honors (69).

Some female-bodied soldiers—Hannah Snell, for example—turned their notoriety into profitable stage and business careers. Like Davies/Welch, Snell (1723–92) donned men's clothing to go in pursuit of her husband, who had abandoned her while she was pregnant with their first child (who died seven months after birth) (Thompson 1974:98–99; Wheelwright 1990:14). After running out of money, Snell sought employment and eventually joined a regiment of soldiers as James Gray (Thompson 1974:99). Fearing discovery, however, Gray deserted and then enrolled as a marine on a ship headed for the East Indies (Thompson 1974:100, 101).

After arriving at the Cape of Good Hope, the crew marched as soldiers and engaged in several battles. Gray was wounded in both legs and the groin. Not wanting to be discovered by the company surgeon, Gray told his "secret [to a] negress whom [he] had befriended" and who aided in treating Gray's wounds (Thompson 1974:102). After Gray ascertained that his husband had been killed, he returned to London. During a drunken moment he "revealed the secret of [his] sex" to a former crew mate, who spread "the story" despite promising not to do so. In need of money, Snell/Gray decided to use the notoriety to her/his advantage and went on the stage (103). After tiring of performing, Snell/Gray again took up men's clothes and bought a "public house . . . for which [she/he] had a signboard painted . . . [and] inscribed: The Widow in Masquerade or the Female Warrior" (105). Snell/Gray died after a period of physical and mental ill-health (106).

Another female-bodied soldier who gained a modicum of fame was Mary Anne Talbot (1778–1808) (Thompson 1974:84). In 1792 her guardian, a Captain Bowen, was ordered back to his regiment and insisted that Talbot accompany him dressed in men's clothes. Calling her John Taylor, Bowen "compelled" her to enroll as a drummer in his regiment (Thompson 1974:85, 86; Wheelwright 1990:47). Taylor was wounded in the chest and back during a siege but, fearing exposure, treated himself. Captain Bowen was killed during battle, and Taylor, who was determined to escape, secured a sailor's uniform and deserted.

Unable to secure other work, Taylor shipped out on a French ship in 1793 (Thompson 1974:86–87). The ship and crew were captured by the British, and when Taylor told the ship's admiral his/her tale he put him/her on another ship bound for England. The admiral kept the "secret," and Talbot sailed as a "powder-boy" and later became the captain's "principal cabin-boy" (88). Taylor was wounded in the thigh and hip during an engagement but, because there were many injured, escaped detection during a cursory medical examination before being shipped to a hospital. After four months' recuperation Taylor "was drafted as a midshipman." When that ship was attacked by French pirates, Taylor and others were captured and imprisoned for more than eighteen months (89).

In 1776, following his release, Taylor shipped out yet again—this time as a steward on an American merchant ship destined for New York (90). After returning to England, Taylor was accosted by a press-gang for being without proper papers. Wanting to escape, she/he revealed his/her sex (91) and returned to the ship to confess to the captain, who wished to retain Taylor's services. Taylor declined, however, and then debarked and returned to London.

Although Taylor/Talbot was advised to "wear female dress and give up masculine habits," she/he continued to wear sailors' clothing and began to gain notoriety for having been a female sailor (Thompson 1974:92). She/he also worked as a jeweler and joined "a lodge of the Odd Fellows [none of whom] knew their new member was a woman" (93–94). When another woman began passing as John Taylor in 1797, a magistrate who knew of Taylor/Talbot's whereabouts (a hospital) sent for him/her to confront the impostor, who was duly imprisoned. After being discharged from the hospital Talbot began to wear women's clothes and took up acting for a time (94). She then became a domestic servant after being imprisoned for debt.

Not all females who lived as men received accolades for their deeds. Mary Read and Anne Bonny, for example, were female pirates.[4] Mary Read (?–1720) was raised as a boy in order to deceive her paternal grandmother, who provided money for the child's maintenance (Thompson 1974:70). At thirteen Read was put into service as a footboy for a Frenchwoman. When he reached the age of maturity, he became a "hand on board" a war ship and later enlisted in a foot regiment in Flanders. After failing to gain a commission, he transferred to a horse regiment. While with that regiment he fell in love with, and revealed her/his sex to, a Flemish comrade (71). When the campaign was over, Read returned to wearing a dress. The couple married and opened an "eating house," prospering until the husband died.

When money ran out Read took up men's clothing again and joined a foot regiment in Holland. Unable to gain a promotion, he "took [his] discharge from the regiment" and boarded a ship bound for the West Indies (72). During the voyage, pirates boarded the ship and Read was captured and taken to the Bahamas, where he settled for a time. He later joined a ship under the command of a Captain Rackham on an expedition to rout Spaniards from the West Indies. At this point Read met Anne Bonny (1697 or 1698–1720) and "confided the secret of [her/his] sex" (73). Read also revealed her sex to a young prisoner with whom she/he had fallen in love. They later married and continued to sail with Rackham (74).

Anne Bonny was Rackham's lover, and he felt threatened by her friendship with Read. To appease him, Bonny revealed the truth about Read, which Rackham "carefully kept secret" (Thompson 1974:73–74). Bonny had been born in Ireland and when a child had emigrated to America with her family. Her father had disowned her after she fell in love with, and secretly married, a sailor. The sailor, in turn, had abandoned her after realizing that she would not inherit her father's money and property (75). Bonny met Rackham and agreed to accompany him to sea but to do so "was obliged to dress in men's clothes so as to keep her sex concealed" from the crew. When Bonny became pregnant, he put him/her ashore, to rejoin Rackham after giving birth (76). In 1720 the ship was attacked by the governor of Jamaica's "armed sloop," and Bonny and Read were captured along with the rest of the crew. All were tried for piracy and sentenced to death. Read died before the execution "could be carried out," and Bonny was spared execution after revealing that she/he was female but died in prison nonetheless (Thompson 1974:77).

Beyond piracy, other female-bodied people who lived as men seem to have done so for other dubious motivations that sometimes included fraud. A twentieth-century example concerns Valerie Arkell-Smith/Col. Victor Barker (1895–1960). Barker never joined the military but seems to have chosen the appellation of colonel to gain status. Barker successfully lived as a man for six years, whereupon (as Barker) he was arrested on a bankruptcy charge during the late 1920s and remanded to prison (Wheelwright 1990:1, 3). Upon release, Arkell-Smith/Barker resumed masculine attire. Wheelwright maintains that Barker had lesbian relationships, and Barker had told his/her wife, Elfrida, that "there could be no normal relations" because of an injury obtained during the war (4). In addition to being a consummate liar, Arkell-Smith/Barker freely admitted that the primary reason for the male disguise was to make a living (5). Even so, she/he wrote, "I feel more a man than a woman" (cited in Bullough and Bullough 1993:162). She/he lived as a man until death (Wheelwright 1990:165).

Preceding Arkell-Smith/Barker by four centuries was Mary Frith (1584–1658), also known as Moll Cutpurse because of her penchant for picking pockets (Thompson 1974:19). She/he had careers as an astrologist and fortune teller, petty thief, pickpocket, and fence and also was somewhat of a Robin Hood who would visit jails and "feed the prisoners out of her haul" from thievery (Fraser 1985:153–54). She/he abandoned female clothes during youth and in a self-published book in 1662 claimed to be a hermaphrodite (Thompson 1974:20). The wearing apparel she/he devised consisted of a man's jacket and a woman's skirt, with the occasional addition of men's pants (21). Despite such clothing, Frith was arrested for "wearing man's apparel" and sentenced to "do penance" during a Sunday sermon (24). In later life she/he ceased wearing a jacket (27). Ellis considered Frith "to have been the subject of sexo-aesthetic inversion" (1937:8). An acrostic has been based on her/his name:

> Merry I lived and many parts I played,
> And without sorrow now in grave am laid.
> Rest and the Sleep of Death doth now sure ease
> Youth's active sins and old ag'd increase.
> Famous I was for all the Thieving Art,
> Renowned for what old woman ride in cart;
> In pocket and Placket I had part.
> This life I lived in Man's disguise;
> He best laments me that with laughter cries.
> (Thompson 1974:28)

Although no ditties were composed in the honor of Civil War soldiers such as Emma Edmonds/Franklin Thompson and Loreta Janeta Velazquez/Lt. Harry T. Buford, their many exploits included participating in battles and spying on enemy troops. A Canadian, Edmonds (1841 or 1842–1898) was born Sarah Emma Evelyn Edmonson (Hall 1993:74) and was influenced to join the army after reading *Fanny Campbell, the Female Pirate Captain: A Tale of the Revolution,* which had been given to her by a "grateful peddler" (Hall 1993:75; Wheelwright 1990:14). In her autobiography, Edmonds wrote that the book "inspired! . . . each exploit of the heroine thrilled me to my fingertips. I went home that night with the problem of my life solved" (cited in Hall 1993:76). While she was very young, her father decided to "marry her off" to an older man. Although she agreed, she did so only from obedience and before the wedding executed an escape with the help of a friend of her mother. In 1858, informed that her father had learned where she was, she cut her hair, put on men's clothing, and began to call herself Franklin Thompson and live as a man (Hall 1993:76; Wheelwright 1990:14).

Before enlisting in the Union army in 1861 Thompson was a successful traveling bookseller (Hall 1993:77). Two years later, afflicted with a serious case of malaria, Thompson deserted in order to avoid "being exposed as a woman if placed in hospital" (83). After recuperating, Edmonds resumed wearing dresses. She wrote *Nurse and Spy in the Union Army,* a partly fictionalized account of her war exploits, in 1865 (83–84).

Loreta Janeta Velazquez (Lt. Harry T. Buford, 1842–?) dressed as a Confederate soldier, with a heavily padded coat, a wire mesh undershirt he had devised, and an "artificial beard and mustache" (Hall 1993:107; Wheelwright 1990:26).[5] An "opportunistic" soldier who was not assigned to a regiment, Velazquez/Buford "sought combat assignments or commissions" (Hall 1993:107–8). As Buford he was accompanied by a black servant who was unaware of his employer's identity (108). Velazquez/Buford recalled being inspired by Joan of Arc and wishing to be a man (Hall 1993:109). She/he later decided, however, that "to be a second Joan of Arc was a mere girlish fancy, which my very first experiences as a soldier dissipated forever . . . convincing me that a woman like myself who had a talent for assuming disguises . . . [and] had it in her power to perform many services of the most vital importance, which was impossible for a man to even attempt" (113–14).

Resuming women's clothing, she embarked on a career as a military spy. Following a successful foray to Washington, D.C., Velazquez put on her soldier's uniform and was assigned to a "detective corps" (Hall 1993:114). When "arrested on suspicion of being a spy" he protested vehemently in order to prevent detection of his physical sex. He was successful in his efforts and released. The following day, however, he was again arrested "on suspicion of being a woman." He tried to maintain through several interviews that a mistake had been made, but a confession eventually followed, as did conviction and a short jail term (119).

Following release, he enlisted as a soldier and obtained a transfer as a commissioned officer but was then badly wounded in the right arm while performing burial duties (120–22). After recuperation, she resumed female dress and once again became a spy before "documents were traced back to her [and she was] arrested" (123). When Velazquez/Buford was released, she/he once again resumed wearing a uniform and went to Richmond, only to be arrested yet again "on suspicion of being a woman in disguise." The prison's superintendent, made a confidant during Velazquez/Buford's confinement, championed her/his cause, "interceded," and she/he was officially assigned to "the secret service corps" (124). On a return from an assignment, Velazquez/Buford "was again arrested on charge of being a woman in disguise." By this time tales of her/his exploits had become known, and "crowds gathered to see the Confederate heroine" (125).

After things settled down, Velazquez/Buford resumed spying for the Confederacy, exchanging women's clothing for a uniform as situations dictated, and eventually became a double agent (126–42). In part these exploits were for self-protection from Union pursuit (143). By chance, the Union had provided "instructions on a general plan for capturing the female agent"—that is, Velazquez/Buford, who was surprised by the extent of the Union's knowledge of the spying expeditions. Coincidentally, her/his brother issued an invitation to accompany him and his family to Europe.

It was a chance to escape. Velazquez/Buford accepted both the Union's assignment to catch the female spy and the invitation to Europe. Under the pretense of pursuing the spy, she/he went to New York and waited for the brother. They then sailed to England almost immediately (149). Upon return, Velazquez traveled through the devastated South and then went to South America (1993:152). In 1876 her memoirs were published, and during the 1880s she disappeared. There is no record of her death (153).

Although hundreds of female-bodied people have served in wars, most either escaped detection or died on the battlefield, only to be "discovered" in death. Like other female-bodied people who lived as men, whether temporarily or for the majority of their lives, their motivations for doing so are not always clear. Some, such as Davies/Welch and Snell/Gray, joined armies and navies in search of lost husbands; others, such as Bonny, to accompany a lover; and still others, such as Read, Talbot/Taylor, Edmonds/Thompson, and Velazquez/Buford, did so for adventure.

Many of the tales of female-bodied men seem fantastic. Those who served in the military often suffered wounds so severe that they led to death, and many individuals were captured and imprisoned. Both wounds and capture frequently lead to discovery. Although cross-dressing ended for many following either the end of military service or discovery, some dressed as men throughout their lives. Such was the case with Angélique Brulon (1771–1889), who served in the military for seven years, received three wounds, was awarded the Cross of the Legion of Honour of France, and wore her uniform in civilian life until death (Gilbert 1932:87–97; Wheelwright 1990:91).

For others, dressing as men indicated a life-style choice. For example, Queen Christina of Sweden (1626–89), who abdicated in 1654, declared her independence and "to demonstrate [it] she abandoned the female, and adopted a male, attire . . . [and] took the name of Count Dohna" (Gilbert 1932:95). Until death, she/he was "always strangely attired, partly as a man, partly as a woman, sometimes completely as a man, but never entirely as a woman" (101).

Charlotte Charke's choice of clothing also may have been a life-style choice. Her life "narrative" was first published in 1755 in London. In addition to acting on stage in both female and male roles, Charke (1713–60) also lived as a man for much of life (Bullough 1976:490). As Charke wrote, "My natural propensity [is] to a Hat and a Wig, in which, at the Age of four years, I made a very considerable figure" (1827[1755]:216). Friedli has remarked, "What is unusual [about Charke] is her determination to live as a man in spite of repeated obstacles and difficulties" (1991:4). Charke's narrative has frequently been discounted as being less than truthful. The anonymous editor of the second edition proclaimed, "Ungrammatical, insanely inconsequent, braggart and fantastic, the *Narrative* is not literature. . . . If the swagger has a quaver in it, it is against her will: barefaced beggar that she is, it is your purse she asks, never your pity" (1827[1755]:10). The denouncement of truthfulness, however, may be because the narrative challenged the status quo of the era (Friedli 1987:241).

Female Husbands and Passing Women: Women Who Posed as Men for Love

This disguise also helped me to protect my chum as well as myself.
—Cora Anderson, cited in Katz, ed. 1976:256

Sometimes female-bodied people have lived as men in order to have relationships with women. They take on male roles not only for better-paying jobs but also to live with lovers without being subject to public scrutiny and scorn. The literature abounds with examples, although I will discuss only three.

During the 1730s Mary East (1715–81) met a woman and formed a relationship with her (Katz, ed. 1976:226; Thompson 1974:78; Vicinus 1992:477). They decided to cast their lot together and that one would assume a male identity. By drawing lots it was decided that Mary would be the man, James How (Katz, ed. 1976:226; Thompson 1974:79). The couple ran several successful businesses for eighteen years until a woman recognized How/East and began blackmailing him/her (Katz, ed. 1976:226; Thompson 1974:79–80). How's wife died in 1764 or 1765 (Thompson 1974:80–81). No matter what motivated its origin, the relationship endured for thirty-five years. Following How's wife's death, the blackmailer increased her demands and threatened bodily harm. How/East told a friend about being blackmailed and "how she had posed as a man for many years." With the friend's assistance, the blackmailer was arrested.[6] How/East then resumed wearing female clothes and using her birth name.

On October 30, 1883, the *Milwaukee Sentinel* headlined a short article "Disguised as a Man: An Illinois Wife in Masculine Attire Woos, Wins and Marries a Wisconsin Maiden—An Extraordinary Story." Thus began the newspaper's coverage of the story of Frank Dubois.[7] Dubois's birth name was Delia, she had been married for fourteen years to S. J. Hudson, and they had two children ("Romance and Reality"). The October 30 story said she left because of marital differences. The husband pursued her and, through an acquaintance of both, located her in Milwaukee. When she saw him approach, however, she locked him out, refused him entry, and run away after he left.

During the eight months they were separated she/he had posed as a man, been employed as a handyman and laborer, and married one Gertrude Fuller, who had joined Dubois a few days after his disappearance ("Disguised as a Man"). According to one news account, "There is some unknown bond of sympathy which tempted them to their marriage and subsequent actions" ("The Mysterious Husband"). For two days the press carried stories about the pair not being found ("The Dual Personage"; "Strange Stories"). By November 4, Gertrude Dubois had been located. Frank, however, upon learning that men had come to see him, abandoned her ("Found at Last"). Short stories appeared on the next two days ("On the Warpath"; "Returned Home"), but Dubois was not found until the end of the month, when she/he was arrested and confessed ("Gertie's 'Husband'!").

The outcome of Dubois's case is unknown. It is difficult to surmise from newspaper accounts exactly what Hudson/Dubois's motivations were for her/his male disguise. She/he had been "courting" Gertrude for several months (while still living with her husband), however, before the marriage ("Romance and Reality"). Thus it seems likely that the ruse was for love.

Thirty-one years later another case of two married women would also be a sensation in Milwaukee newspapers ("Presto!"; "Sex Concealment Revives Memory"). Cora Anderson had gone by the name Ralph Kerwineo (also Kerwineio) and passed as a man for thirteen years ("Man-Girl in a Legal Tangle"). She twice lived with women as husband and wife, both of whom knew that she was posing as a man ("Girl Masquerader"). The first, Mamie White, stated that they had married "in a spirit of fun," and she had been fully aware that Cora was a woman (ibid.). Cora said that part of her decision to pose as a man had to do with being part Potawatomie-

Cherokee and feeling that she could make better money as a "dark-skinned man" than as a woman (ibid.). Another reason involved her love affair with Mamie White ("Milwaukee 'Man' Clerk Proves Girl"). "We wanted to be together, so we rented a room and the people with whom we lived never doubted that we were man and wife," White said.

Cora had met someone else, however, and White wrote that she was "dumbfounded when [Cora] told me that she had proposed marriage to her new found friend" ("Milwaukee 'Man' Clerk Proves Girl"). Marriage to the new friend and White's jealousy were the cause of Ralph's discovery as Cora; White had informed the police that Cora was masquerading as a man ("Presto!"). Anderson was charged with disorderly conduct, but charges were dropped after Anderson promised to return to female attire ("Girl-Man Is Free Again"). She also turned her career as a man into opportunity by writing a series of newspaper articles about her adventures, as well as commentaries on men's social behaviors ("Man-Woman Writes for the *Journal*"; "Girl-Man Says"; "Man Displays His Conquests"; "Young Woman Differs from Man").

Female-Bodied Men: "By Nature and Character, a Man"

Clothing is a necessary condition of subjectivity—that in articulating the body, it simultaneously articulates the psyche.
—Silverman 1986:147, cited in Wilson 1990:69

According to Dekker and van de Pol, in at least one case history it is possible that the individual was a transsexual "before the introduction of the word by modern science" (1989:69). Like contemporary female-bodied transpeople or Grémaux's examples of Stana and Durgjane (chapter 4), Maria van Antwerpen (Jan van Ant or Machiel van Antwerpen [1719–69(?)]) stated when asked to what sex "she" belonged, "By nature and character, a man, but in appearance, a woman. . . . It often made me wrathful that Mother Nature treated me with so little compassion against my inclinations and the passions of my heart" (68).

Another who seems to have followed his heart was Catalina de Erauso (1592–1650), who was put into a convent at an early age.[8] At fifteen, de Erauso fled from the convent (Gilbert 1932:148; Thompson 1974:29). After "planning and re-planning and cutting myself out a suit of clothes," he wrote, "I cut my hair and threw it away" (de Erauso 1996[1829]:4). Dressed in this manner he was variously employed as a valet, a cutpurse (briefly), and a page before enlisting to serve on a Spanish galleon bound for the Americas (Gilbert 1932:149–51). Once there, he joined the Spanish army as Alonso Diaz Ramérez de Guzman (Thompson 1974:29). De Erauso served for a number of years until being wounded severely "and seeing as how I was about to die, I told [a priest] the truth about myself" (de Erauso 1996[1829]:56). In 1624 he returned to Spain and continued to wear his military uniform until being granted permission two years later by Philip IV and Pope Urban VIII "to continue to wear men's clothes" (Gilbert 1932:169; Perry 1987:86; Thompson 1974:36, 37). He later returned to America and became a carrier until his death (Thompson 1974:37).

While he was in Spain, de Erauso's story became known and he was treated as a curiosity (Perry 1987:86). Given the century in which he was born, he could only "construct for [him]self a male persona that would completely obliterate [his] identity as a woman" (Perry 1987:94). De Erauso is said to have left the convent because he "wanted to live as a man" and found a way to "dry up [his] breasts" (89). Although Perry declares that de Erauso's "life suggested that anyone with a choice would choose the adventure, the freedom, the exhilaration of being a man" (96), another possibility is that de Erauso identified as a man. He had a clear preference for male clothing and was unable to give it up, even upon threat of torture. Too, he only engaged in masculine occupations, and his values were those of the other men with whom he interacted (de Erauso 1996[1829]:xxxix–xli).

The detailed account of de Erauso's life seems to be the exception rather than the rule. Although many female-bodied people, including Deborah Sampson as Robert Shurtliff, fought in the Revolutionary War (Friedli 1987:243, 1991:5; Medlicott 1966:xv; Wheelwright 1990:52), records are scarce and not well documented. Beginning in the 1850s, however, extensive histories exist of female-bodied people who lived as men. One of the most famous was Calamity Jane (1847–1901), who in 1877 was reported to have abandoned "the society of women forever, and joined the male sex" (Horan 1952:176). "She was completely devoid of a female figure. Her body was slim and hard [but] it is difficult to obtain a reliable physical description of Jane. Her pictures show her to be more of a man than a woman" (172–73). Although Horan seems doubtful about many of Jane's exploits, he does state, "There is no doubt that Jane was tragically miscast by nature in sex. There is little doubt she should have been a man. [Men] accepted her as one of their own kind" (172). Yet that does not mean Jane was a female-bodied man or a female transvestite. She may have been a woman ahead of her time.

A less famous case that has been brought to light by a fictionalized film account concerns Little Jo Monaghan (1857–1903). Monaghan arrived in a small Idaho town in 1868, where he staked a mining claim, herded sheep, broke horses, and became a homesteader, working a sawmill and horse ranch on his property. When he died thirty-five years later, it was discovered that Monaghan had a female body (Horan 1952:305–10).

It was only at their deaths that many others were likewise discovered to have a female body. James Barry, James Allen, Nicholas de Raylan, and Murray Hall are notable cases. James Barry (née Miranda Barry, ca. 1795–1865) enlisted in the military and in 1819 became a staff surgeon in the British army. In 1827 he was promoted to surgeon-major (Ellis 1937:6; Thompson 1974:115–16). In 1851 Barry was made deputy inspector-general and seven years later became inspector-general of the British army hospital in South Africa (Ellis 1937:6; Thompson 1974:121). Although he was brusque and aloof, Barry had a successful career (Ellis 1937:6; Thompson 1974:115–16; Wheelwright 1990:69). He was not known to have had sexual relationships of any kind (Ellis 1937:6). Because of his diminutive size and beardless appearance some acquaintances speculated about Barry's "true sex," concluding that he was either a woman or a hermaphrodite. Those who knew Barry used both male and female pronouns to refer to him. Some clearly suspected his identity, whereas others, including his man-servant, did not (Thompson 1974:117–21). An autopsy determined that Barry was female-bodied (Gilbert and Gubar 1988:348; Thompson 1974:121).

James Allen (1787–1829), too, was not discovered to be female-bodied until his death. He had been married for twenty-one years to a woman named Mary (Thompson 1974:133). Together they bought and ran an inn successfully "for a time" until they were robbed. They then sold the inn and moved to London (Thompson 1974:134). Allen (whose birth name is unknown) died because of an on-the-job accident (Thompson 1974:135). His wife stated that she had come to believe that James was a hermaphrodite yet swore that she did not know he had a female body. When she had made attempts at intimacy, he feigned excuses such as illness. He also bound his chest and always wore layers of underclothing, supposedly to protect himself from catching cold (Duberman 1986:24, 27–28; Thompson 1974:136). Upon examination of his body, it was found that his "breasts, which were moderately full, were forced, by the compression of the bandages, under the armpits" (Duberman 1986:28).

Nicholas de Raylan (1873–1906) died from tuberculosis (Katz, ed. 1976:250–51). He had been a private secretary "to the Russian Consul" and fought in the Spanish-American War (de Savitsch 1958:6). He was "married twice," divorcing his first wife after ten years. His second wife was devoted to him. Both wives "were convinced that their husband was a man and ridiculed the idea" that he was female (de Savitsch 1958:6–7; Katz, ed. 1976:250). He wore self-constructed genitalia consisting of a "penis and testicles made of chamois skin and stuffed with down" and held in place by a waistband (de Savitsch 1958:7; Katz, ed. 1976:251). De Savitsch considers Nicholas de Raylan to have been a homosexual because of his female sexual-object choices (1958:10).[9]

Murray Hall (1831 or 1841–1901) lived as a man for more than thirty years ("Lived as a Man"). He held memberships in "the General Committee of Tammany Hall, . . . [and] the Iroquois Club" and was a friend of a prominent New York senator and an active worker in his political district (Katz, ed. 1976:232). He owned an "intelligence office" in New York City ("Lived as a Man"). Hall "married twice," and his last wife "kept [his] secret" until his death. Hall was not discovered to be female-bodied until dying from breast cancer, for which he refused medical treatment from fear that the secret would be discovered (Katz, ed. 1976:233). Even his adopted daughter did not know (236).

Hall's acquaintances and friends, shocked to learn he was physically female, continued to use male pronouns in speaking about him: "During the seven years I knew him I never once suspected he was anything else than what he appeared to be"; "Suspect he was a woman? Never. He dressed like a man and talked like a very sensible one"; and, "If he was a woman he ought to have been born a man, for he lived and looked like one" (Katz, ed. 1976:234). His death certificate gives his age as seventy, although his friends thought him to be in his fifties (235). During the inquest, one witness, after referring to Hall as "he," was asked, "Wouldn't you better say she?" "No, I will never say she," was the reply. The coroner ruled that Hall was female and that his death was from natural causes (Katz, ed. 1976:237). The response to Hall's life and death is reminiscent of the 1989 death of Billy Tipton (chapter 6).

Death was not the only event that exposed female-bodied men. Sometimes, as was the case with Albert Cashier, Charley Wilson, and Johann Bürger, it was accident, poverty, or wrongdoing. Cashier (née Jennie Hodgers, 1844–1915) was born in Belfast and had arrived in the United States as a stowaway. He was eighteen when he enlisted in 1862 in the 95th Illinois Infantry Regiment (Hall 1993:20; Wheelwright 1990:140). During his three-year military career, Cashier participated in "forty battles and skirmishes and was never wounded."

Following the war, Cashier returned to Illinois and worked as "a farmhand and handyman" in several places. In 1890 Cashier applied for a soldier's pension but refused a required medical examination and was denied the pension. A pension was eventually granted in 1907 (Hall

1993:23, 24).[10] In 1911, after living as a man for more than fifty years, he sustained an accident in which his leg was broken close to the hip. A doctor's examination revealed that Cashier was female-bodied.

Cashier prevailed upon his employer and the doctor to keep his secret. They agreed, and Cashier was admitted "to the Soldiers' and Sailors' Home in Quincy, Illinois, taking the commandant into their confidence" (Hall 1993:21; see also Wheelwright 1990:146). The admission papers referred to Cashier's "'senility' and 'weakened mental facilities'" rather than his broken leg (Hall 1993:21). The secret finally leaked out in 1913, two years after his accident. That same year he "was judged 'insane' and consigned" to a state mental hospital (Hall 1993:24; see also Wheelwright 1990:146). The commitment seems dubious at best, considering that his symptoms included memory loss and times of noisiness, insomnia, and feebleness.

Cashier's story was picked up by numerous U.S. newspapers (Hall 1993:24). Former comrades referred to Cashier without apparent hesitation as a man and "stressed his bravery and fortitude." One comrade who visited Cashier at the hospital reported that he had "found a frail woman of seventy, broken, because on discovery, she was compelled to put on skirts" (Hall 1993:25; see also Wheelwright 1990:147).

In 1915 Albert Cashier, seventy-one, died six months after being confined to the mental hospital (Wheelwright 1990:147). He was buried "with full military honors, wearing [his] Union uniform, and [he] was buried in a flag-draped casket. The inscription on [his] tombstone . . . reads: ALBERT D. J. CASHIER, CO. G, 95 ILL. INF." (Hall 1993:26). Cashier is among the Union soldiers listed on the Vicksburg "monument to Illinois soldiers who fought there" (22).

Charley Wilson (née Catherine Coombes, 1834–87?) worked "for over forty years" as a man in various trades, including dockworker, sailor, printer, decorator, and painter (Thompson 1974:147–48). In 1887 "a little, old, grey-haired man dressed in a neat suit of clothes, wearing a black bowler hat, and carrying a small bag, walked into the Rochester Row Police Station" to seek help (147). Wilson was eventually taken to the men's ward of the poorhouse, where he was instructed to undress for a bath in the presence of two others. He asked to speak with a doctor and ward matron and revealed to them that he was physically female. The confession resulted in his being moved to the women's ward and being provided with a woman's dress (148).

As his story unfolded, he revealed that he had been married for a short time to a man who abused him. Wilson assumed men's clothes and sought work as a painter, a trade learned from his brother (148–49). While living in the poorhouse, Wilson said, "If I had the money I would get out of here in men's clothes and no one would detect me, but at present I cannot work on account of my fractured ribs." He "never reconciled to living and dressing as a woman" during the remainder of his life (150).

Johann Bürger (née Anna Mattersteig) was arrested in St. Louis during 1908 "on charge of abduction and as being a woman." He declared in court that it had not been his intent to break the law as it regarded his manner of dress and his "abduction" of a companion. He further declared that he "felt [himself] wholly like a man" and was certain that nature had made a mistake (Katz, ed. 1976:252).

Another individual convinced he was a man was Alan Hart (née Alberta Lucille, 1892–1962), who was born near Portland, Oregon. He graduated from college in 1912 and went on to medical school, graduating in 1917 (Katz, ed. 1976:258). His medical school diploma gives his name as Alan Lucill Hart (Brown and Morris 1995:1). After Hart's repeated requests, a doctor performed a hysterectomy on him around 1916, and a year later he married a woman, Inez Stark, who was "fully cognizant of all the facts" (Katz, ed. 1976:276, 277). Stark left Hart in 1923, however.

Hart had a successful career as a roentgenologist (X-ray technician) and developed a method for early detection of tuberculosis (Katz 1983:517). He also was a successful novelist (*Dr. Mallory, The Undaunted, In the Lives of Men,* and *Dr. Finley Sees It Through*) and wrote a medical book, *These Mysterious Rays,* about "X-rays, radium, and ultra-violet therapy" (517).

The Undaunted is semiautobiographical. One of its characters, Sandy Farquhar, "included some elements of Hart's own experience" (Katz 1983:518). The doctor who treated him, for example, recalled that Hart "was recognized by a former associate. . . . Then the hounding process began" (Katz, ed. 1976:276). Farquhar is described similarly:

> He had been driven from place to place, from job to job, for fifteen years because of something he could not alter any more than he could change the color of his eyes. Gossip, scandal, rumor always drove him on. It did no good to live alone, to make few acquaintances and no intimates; sooner or later someone always turns up to recognize him. . . . [He] went into radiology because he thought it wouldn't matter so much in a laboratory what a man's personality was. But wherever he went scandal followed him sooner or later. (Hart 1936:521, 522; cited in Katz 1983:522)

Farquhar also is described as having what transmen and FTMs recognize as body dysphoria: "He remembered the first entry in the little book, made when he was twenty. 'My body is an incubus [nightmare] and my fears are born of it. But it is possible for the possessor of a defective body to remain unbroken by the disasters that overcome it because he has it always in his

his servitude, his subjection, to his body'" (Hart 1936:196, cited in Katz 1983:520).

Unlike his character Sandy Farquhar, who commits suicide, Hart had a successful and happy life. Two years after Inez Stark left him, he married Edna Ruddick, and they lived together for thirty-seven years until his death (Brown and Morris 1995:2). Although Katz has insisted that Hart was "clearly a lesbian, a woman-loving woman" (1976:277), he seems surprised that Edna Hart refused his attempts to contact her (1983:522). Perhaps she did so because she was familiar with his earlier work and his conclusion that Hart was a lesbian rather than the man she knew him to be.

Reconsidering Female Gender Diversity

We are not defined by who we are but by what we do.
—Reich 1992:113

Albeit quite fuzzy, some tentative distinctions can be made among the types discussed in this chapter. Transvestite females have lived temporarily as men and engaged in cross-dressing and cross-living episodically. Eventually they return to women's apparel and life-style. Where possible, an individual's statements about personal motivations should be taken into account. Sometimes, however, such statements must be taken with a grain of salt, not only because the person may have been trying to protect herself from possible prosecution but also because of the reporter's possibly skewed perspective.

Female husbands and passing women have tended to take on more permanent statuses of living as men for periods ranging from a few years to a lifetime. Statements by both parties involved in a relationship are also important in establishing whether they are lesbians. Ideally, denials of sexual intimacy must be weighed with caution, especially as society's awareness of lesbianism became more acute and the chances of condemnation and prosecution became more significant for all parties involved.

It is at this point that even tentative distinctions between lesbians and female-bodied men become unclear. First, it is common for female-bodied people to have relationships with women. Second, it is common for female-bodied men to not engage in sexual relationships with their female partners. Furthermore, although it would seem that sexual intimacy between a couple would indicate a lesbian relationship, that is not the case for individuals who did not (or do not) identify as women.

The following questions can be useful for researchers who may be trying to determine how an individual has identified:

1. Did the individual state that (contrary to their physiology) they are men or always felt themselves to be men (e.g., van Antwerpen, de Erauso, and Bürger)?

2. Were attempts made at body modification, such as wearing padded clothing, binding breasts, and using devices in place of male genitalia (e.g., de Erauso, Allen, and de Raylan) and did the individual pursue or obtain whatever surgeries where available (e.g., Hart)?

3. Was there an attempt to live a better part of their lives as men or an undertaking of a lifetime of living as men and were there efforts to take the secret of their female bodies to the grave? If discovered, did they try to arrange a means for the secret to be kept (e.g., de Erauso, Monaghan, Barry, Allen, Hall, Cashier, and Bürger)?

The answers to these questions can be useful in explaining seemingly perplexing behaviors. Also important to consider are what it meant to be a man and what constituted masculine behaviors or masculinity during a specific historical period and within the particular culture in which the individual lived. "Man" is no more a universal category than is "woman." "Living as a man" or exhibiting masculine behaviors is culturally and historically specific. As a consequence, it cannot be assumed that the behaviors considered masculine and the expectations for men have been or are the same everywhere.

It is often difficult to conceive of a person who is female-bodied yet does not identify as a woman. It follows that such behaviors are perplexing. Being perplexed, however, does not justify making assumptions based on gynocentrism or androcentrism, using biological-determinist arguments, and subsuming relationships under the rubric of lesbianism. "Human beings . . . are intentional agents whose consciousness of themselves and the world they live in form an inextricable feature of everything they say, think, or do" (Lorraine 1990:3). Discounting, ignoring, and misinterpreting individuals' statements about themselves or their actions over the course of their lives may render them invisible. Yet it does not mean that they identified as women, were lesbians, or were motivated by socioeconomics.

Beyond Isms

It's time for a fresh look at history.
—Feinberg 1996:59

History is important to understanding Native American, Balkan, early Euro-American, and contemporary FTMs and transmen within gender and queer studies. As Kochems has suggested it is necessary to unpack "the system of gender related categories, statuses, roles and features and [to] examin[e] how they stand in relation to one another" (1993:13). Clearly, within certain Native American cultures and in the Balkans, as well as in Europe from the fourteenth century onward and during the early years of the United States, female-bodied people took on the statuses, roles, and features of men, as is the case with contemporary female-bodied transpeople. Individuals in all of these systems of gender have been seen as men, albeit sometimes only socially, even though they have female bodies (cf. Dickemann 1996:16). Thus studies of contemporary female-bodied transpeople and their historical and cultural predecessors have much to offer in understanding gender systems.

Contemporary transpeople have their own terminology that allows them to live within specific gendered systems. As Bolin has observed, the trans-community is creating a number of gender and social identities that challenge dominant paradigms. Gender-transformed Native American females and contemporary female-bodied transpeople, for example, have created numerous genders and identities. Although some may find both disquieting, it is time to move beyond the androcentrism, phallocentrism, heterosexism, and homocentrism that has rendered female gender diversity invisible.

CHAPTER 6

He Becomes She:
Making Contemporary Female
Gender Diversity Invisible

Clothes play a key part in our acts of self-representation, whether we
like it or not—or recognize it—or not.
—Wilson 1990:67

According to newspaper accounts and the few books that have been published on the subject, female-bodied individuals who assumed men's ways
did so in order to increase their chances of employment and drawing
better wages, for adventure, or to travel unfettered as well as "marry"
women—like the rationalizations of contemporary theorists. Yet seldom
have the individuals been allowed to speak for themselves; therefore, with
the exception of a few rare cases, it is difficult to say what motivated them
to assume the statuses, roles, and life-styles of men. For some, the motivations may have been as the news accounts reported; others may have believed themselves to be men, albeit with female bodies.

When Sullivan planned to publish the Jack Garland story in the late
1980s (chapter 10), "the straight presses said it was a gay story. The gay
presses said it was a woman's story. The women's presses said it was a man's
story" (1989, personal communication). Why was there confusion over a
straightforward biography? Because Jack Garland, like so many before him
and so many since, was a female-bodied individual whose social and personal identity were those of a man. Sullivan persisted and finally found a
publisher for the biography, but had he not done so a story would have
been lost. How many others like it have also been lost? How many voices,
subtly and not so subtly, have been silenced?

After discussing these issues in an earlier article (Cromwell 1998), I
received the following comment from an anonymous reviewer for a prominent feminist journal: "This seems a bit female-to-male centric." Another

reviewer found it "awfully" so. I do not believe that either reader intended to silence me, but such comments might have resulted in or led to silence. Silencing takes many forms. For example, an article by Anne Bolin, an anthropologist, that discussed MTFs in a positive light was rejected by a sociology journal that prefaced the rejection with the words "the author must be a transsexual" (1992, personal communication). Similarly, an article criticizing individuals who go public either in print or on talk shows stated: "In my opinion the release of this type of information serves no practical purposes, nor any reasonable service to the public" (Julie G. 1991:3). Silencing contributes to the construction of binary oppositional sex and gender discourses and effectively obfuscates the rich potential of multiple voices that can be located in individual experience (cf. Stone 1991:295–97). It also leads to inappropriate labeling of individual's lives.

It is erroneous to assume that all females who lived as men were merely "passing women" as a means to economic survival or as a cover for lesbianism.[1] Some were, indeed, female-bodied men. For example, Jack Garland found the notion that he passed as a man in order to have sexual relationships with women ridiculous. "Has love had anything to do with my present mode of living?" he remarked tersely. "Such a question to ask!" (Sullivan 1990a:154). In fact, he had no intimate relations with women (143–45). In Sullivan's well-documented biography it is clear that Garland lived as a man because he was conscious of being a man (154–65).

Neither men nor women claim Christine Jorgensen, Renée Richards, and other male-bodied transpeople as part of their histories. They are considered separate, part of transpeoples' history. Female-bodied transpeople regardless of self-identification are invalidated and dispossessed of a history because they have a female body. The death in 1989 of Billy Tipton and the switch in pronouns used to discuss his life provide excellent examples of how female gender diversity is made invisible.

Default Assumptions; or, The Billy Tipton Phenomenon

Human emotion may at times be devoid of representation.
—Lock 1993:139

Ironically, Katz has stated that "too often, academics act as if to name something is to know it" (1976:211).[2] Not only does Katz misidentify Hart as a lesbian but he also includes Johann Bürger, Nicholas de Raylan, and Murray Hall under the rubric of "lesbian transvestites" based on their dress, life-style, and female partners. He acknowledges that Bürger may have thought of himself as a man and that such an identification "is commonly labeled a[s] transsexual" today (252). Yet he states that the label "is so loaded with traditional assumptions connecting gender and 'masculinity' and 'femininity' as to render it of the most controversial and doubtful character" (252). Furthermore, in a footnote concerning another reference to "transsexualism," Katz (1983:662) refers to Raymond's *The Transsexual Empire* as "the most profound, extended critique of the medical concept."

The failure of Katz's argument, like those of other critics (Garber 1989; Raymond 1994[1979]; Tyler 1989), is in relying on "eminent" authorities rather than consulting transpeople themselves, who even as early as his published works (in 1976 and 1983) were rejecting and bypassing the so-called medical empire as well as rejecting the sexist demands it makes (chapters 9, 10, 11).

Katz, like others (Faderman 1991; Friedli 1987, 1991; Middlebrook 1998; Vicinus 1992; Wheelwright 1990), is also guilty of operating on what Hofstader (1982:18) has called "default assumptions," which are defined as something that holds true in the "simplest or most natural or most likely possible model" concerning any particular topic or subject. "The critical thing about default assumptions is that they are made automatically, not as a result of consideration or elimination." To one degree or another, everyone makes default assumptions. For example, an effeminate man or a butch woman are assumed to be gay or lesbian, respectively.

There are a number of default assumptions about contemporary female-bodied transpeople and their forebears—that females do not become men, for example. Others are that (1) females become men only to take advantage of male privileges or as a cover for their lesbianism; (2) females ceased assuming male identities in the mid-nineteenth or mid-twentieth centuries (depending on an author's perspective); (3) females who live as men cannot accept their lesbianism; (4) females cannot become men; and (5) cross-dressing/living is equivalent to homosexuality. These are biological-determinist assumptions wherein genitals equal sex which equals gender.

The default assumptions can be illustrated through newspaper articles concerning *The Ballad of Little Jo*. Maggie Greenwald, the film's director, states, "I stumbled upon some information about the real Little Jo Monihan, about whom almost nothing is known except that she lived as a man and nobody had *discovered* the *truth* about her until she died" (Kahler 1993:17, emphasis added). The default assumption here is that "the truth" is that

Monaghan was female and thus really a woman. Greenwald reveals another such assumption when she concludes that "women discover themselves—and this is so much a part of feminism—that they don't have to be *fake men;* to be strong; to be powerful. . . . Jo becomes a woman not a man. She passes through a phase to survive, ultimately to be a woman" (20, emphasis added). Still another default assumption is that "it would only be extreme incidents that would make a woman decide to live her life as a man" (17).

These "extreme incidents" always involve socioeconomic explanations. In the case of Monaghan, an out-of-wedlock child was born, and Monaghan was disowned by family. According to one male movie reviewer, "With no family to depend on, Josephine [note the use of "Josephine" instead of "Little Jo"] had to find either a husband or a pimp. Instead she decided to pass for a man and live on the edge of Western society" (Ulstein 1993:11).

One article accompanying a review of *Little Jo* was headlined "Women Posing as Men Pursued Better Opportunities" (Lee 1993:11). Quoted in the article is Julie Wheelwright, who states, "Very often it was a pattern of women in working-class occupations who would take on male attributes to further their careers" (11). The television series *Dr. Quinn, Medicine Woman,* for example, features a title character who is clearly a feminine woman but employed in a male occupation. Indeed, many females pursued so-called male careers without changing their sex (e.g., Elizabeth Blackwell, Angie Debo, Elsie Clews Parsons, and Dr. Mary Walker as well as all of the Protestant missionary women).

I call this default assumption "the Billy Tipton phenomenon." Lee uses Tipton as an example of career opportunism: "In 1989, when Billy Tipton died in Spokane, it was revealed that the American jazz pianist and saxophonist—who had married and was the father of three adopted children—was *in fact* a woman. She apparently began appearing as a man to improve her chances of success as a musician" (11, emphasis added).

Another default assumption is that females cannot be men. Concerning Billy Tipton and others, one writer has stated, "One look usually convinces viewers that these people were quite clearly women" (Lee 1993:11). Yet after he fully assumed living as a man and had moved from those who had known him, no one in Billy Tipton's life knew him as anything other than a man (Middlebrook 1998).

Those who live as men are always considered to be "posing," or living "a charade," or "masquerading." They are not taken seriously. After stories were published about Christian Davies, Hannah Snell, Emma Edmonds, and Loreta Janeta Velazquez, these individuals were discounted as impostors and liars (Wheelwright 1990:27, 123, 137–40). Excuses and rationalizations are made about why they lived as they did. As Bonnie Cromwell has observed in a personal communication (1991), "People say they can understand a woman wanting to be a man because of the cultural privileges that males in our society have. But they cannot understand a man wanting to become a woman. Therefore, a male who becomes a woman must have a *real* need and a *condition* that is treatable. A man who becomes a woman is a transgender and/or transsexual issue. A female who becomes a man is a socio-economic issue and feminists will rally to 'her' cause and, in doing so, deny FTMs their reality."

Concluding that a female lived as a man for economic and social reasons or that a relationship with a woman constituted a coverup for lesbianism constitutes making a default assumption, as is also the case when assuming that Billy Tipton posed as a man in order to be a musician. The assumption obscures the history of women as jazz musicians as well as the fact that Tipton generally formed his own bands (Chin 1989:95; Gossett and Johnson 1980; Middlebrook 1998). Ironically, the assumption is so ingrained that Middlebrook arrives at it despite having provided several examples of women—Marian MacPartland among them—who have been successful jazz musicians (163).

Other default assumptions are illustrated in the following statements from Wheelwright (1990):

> 1. "During the course of their entry into the masculine world many became so immersed in their male identity that women became 'the other' in their eyes" (10).
> 2. "Cross-dressing for women often remained a process of imitation rather than a self-conscious claiming of the social privileges given exclusively to men for all women" (11).
> 3. "Women who entered male occupations, passing as men or known to their workmates, often coped with the contradictions of their position by developing a strong male-identification" (11–12).
> 4. "It is, however, clear that women expressed a desire not for the physical acquisition of a male body but for a male social identity" (12–13).

Two assumptions lie behind the statements. First, Wheelwright presumes, as do many others, to know what was in the minds of these individuals (as Middlebrook does in her "biography" of Tipton). Second, Wheelwright (and Middlebrook) assumes that none of the people she discusses could have possibly conceived of themselves as men (i.e., she leaves out the third possibility). From that perspective they (1) should not have seen women as the other; (2) could only imitate men and so were unconscious of their claim to social privilege; (3) developed a male identification, which had to be a conflict, because they entered male jobs; and (4) did not clearly express a desire for physical transformation.

To rephrase Katz, to name something is not necessarily to know it. Moreover, to refuse to name something may effectively render it invisible but does not make it impossible. Looking at some of these individuals as females who identified as men explains their "troubling behavior." Women would be the other. It was not imitation, and (whether seen as sexist or not) they believed they had a right to male privilege just as other men did. They did not develop a male identification as a result of entering male occupations but entered them because of being male-identified. And, finally, many expressed a desire for physical transformation in the only language they had, which has been discounted, ignored, or reinterpreted as a desire for male power and privilege.

On the latter point, Wheelwright interprets Davies's urinary device and Velazquez's wire mesh shirts as a sign that their "masculinity was only artificial" (1990:59). Likewise, Middlebrook conjectures that Tipton bound his chest because of his attachment to his father (1998:19). These actions can also be interpreted as aids to enhance their masculinity and affirm their identities as men, however, at a time when they had no other choices.

Reconsidering Tipton's Choices

This has been my choice.
—Tipton, cited in Middlebrook 1998:256

The continuing response to Tipton's life poses many questions. If, as Middlebrook insists, everyone knew early in his career that he was female, what was the point of "dressing left"? Why adopt masculinity to such an extreme? Why not be a cross-dressing woman? If he were only passing, why did he so adamantly keep his body a secret? It would have been simpler to have his wives' complicity, as have other passing women. If he was only impersonating a man in order to be a musician, why keep the secret after his career had ended? At the very least, making his secret known to others could have been an interesting inside joke. If he was really a lesbian, why did he marry straight women? Why do women continue to refer to him with male pronouns and insist that they cannot think of him as other than a man? Why lie about his genitals being crushed in an accident? Why did he adopt three children, and why do his adopted sons continue to insist that he was a man and also their father? "He did a helluva job with us," one has said. "He was my dad" (Chin 1989). Does his life as a man have no meaning?

Middlebrook attempts to answer such questions by proclaiming that Tipton's life was the supreme "performance" of an actor "impersonating a common man with an ordinary life in an ordinary place in Middle America" (211). Middlebrook's random usage of male and female pronouns and dismissal of Tipton's life-style as mere performance denigrate Tipton (and irritate readers). She tentatively suggests that Tipton may have been transgendered and may have identified as a man yet dismisses both possibilities (216).[3] In any event, her arguments fall short and are nothing but dubious conjecture. She admits that her account is, at best, speculative when she states, "We will have to substitute imagination for the absent documentation. Perhaps what happened went something like this" (49–50). From that point on the text becomes little more than fiction.

It is difficult to know whether Tipton made any statements about identifying as a man or feeling himself to be a man. He left no written explanation for his choices or actions (Middlebrook 1998:49). Yet there are hints that he may have identified as a man. Although the statement is at best only hearsay, he is said to have told a cousin, "Some people might think I'm a freak or a hermaphrodite. I'm not. I'm a normal person. This has been my choice" (278). According to Middlebrook, he tried living as a masculine woman and, although considered eccentric by some, had success doing so (chapters 4–6). Tipton did attempt to modify his body. He padded his waist, bound his breasts, and used a prosthesis both to assimilate a more malelike crotch and for sexual activities. Tipton did not have surgery to alter his sex, although he lived during a time when it was possible to do so. That is the case for many transmen and FTMs, however. The surgery is expensive, and its results, especially for genital surgeries, are risky and often unacceptable aesthetically. Finally, Tipton attempted to live as a man and did so successfully for more than fifty years. He also made efforts to take his secret to the grave.

Was living as a man the only option that felt normal? Billy Tipton's life speaks for itself. The male privileges that accrue from living as a man do not justify spending fifty years living in fear, hiding from loved ones, taking extreme measures to make sure that no one knows what their body is or looks like, and then dying from a treatable medical condition (a bleeding ulcer). When someone like Tipton dies or is discovered, they are discounted as having been "not real men" or "unreal men." Despite having lived for years as men, the motivations of these individuals are read as being wrought of socioeconomic necessity or the individuals are considered to be lesbians.[4]

Does this mean that "anatomy is not destiny" while one is alive but "anatomy is destiny" after death? That seems to be the case. Why else would people begin to use female pronouns after Tipton died and his body was discovered to be female? At the end of the play *T.S./Crossing* the narrator asks the audience, "What happens when Terry Smith dies? When his soul has left his body? Will you insist that he may have lived his life as a man, but died a woman?" (Finque 1989). Is this insistence a biological-determinist argument, or are female-bodied transpeople rejected as men and claimed as women because they embody the fearful other (chapter 9)? The answers lie in the paradoxes of those individuals who possess a female body but live as men.

Social Hierarchy and Otherness

I certainly didn't change my body because I thought I'd get special privilege.
I changed because it was the only way I could be seen as myself.
—Dominick, in Green 1994b:7

Some theorists claim that male-bodied transpeople move down the social hierarchy whereas the reverse is true for female-bodied transpeople (Irvine 1990:240; Shapiro 1991:270). Green (1994a:51) has made four important points in this regard: (1) because of socialization as female-bodied people, transmen and FTMs are "not prepared to become captains of industry"; (2) hormones do not change a person's socialization, and therefore FTMs and transmen may not know how to "play male hierarchy games"; (3) transmen and FTMs generally do not have the education needed for occupations that require "success as men"; and (4) if they are known as FTMs or as transmen they are subject to job discrimination. Consequently, although it may be more acceptable to advance upward, and although it would seem that female-bodied individuals who live as men automatically elevate their status to that of men, doing so depends on their preparedness to take advantage of the possibility. But even that is a conditional and precarious status that only lasts until the discovery that the man has a female body or was assigned female at birth. Once the discovery is made, then the man is again either an "artificial man" or "less than a man." Like Billy Tipton, he becomes she.[5]

By insisting on the body as the essential signifier of sex and subsequently gender, the switch in pronouns from he to she reifies the body as the ultimate determinant of sex and gender. Shifting pronouns constitutes an appeal to biological determinism. Anyone who steps outside of the sex and gender order is perceived as dangerous and consequently threatening.

FTMs, transmen, and butch lesbians are often threatening to some men with respect to defining what it means to be a man. If female-bodied men can be "men with vaginas" or men with differently shaped genitalia, then men who believe that their penis is what makes a man a man must rethink that position or reject them. To acknowledge their validity would be to admit that men as well as women could resist (and thus subvert the social order) by approximating but never fully becoming the other.

"They Are a Part of My History": Transperspectives on Cross-Cultural and Historical Data

It's not so much that there have always been transgendered people; it's that there have always been cultures which imposed regimes of gender.
—Wilchins 1997:67

Nearly all transpeople in searching for their identities turn to the past. Some may even look to other cultures. Unlike male-bodied transpeople, very few FTMs and transmen identify with the concept of Native American "berdache." Nor do they identify with its linguistic cousins: "female berdache," amazons, cross-gender females, manlike women, manly women, or female man-woman. Such terminology is inappropriate and renders female gender diversity invisible. Although the ethnographic and historical descriptions of these categories may strike an initial chord, that quickly dissipates. Consequently, terms such as *"berdache"* have no symbolic meaning or significant relevance for contemporary female-bodied transpeople.[1]

The initial research for this chapter began when Sky Renfro, a Cherokee/Caucasion FTM, said to me, "FTMs don't have a history." "What about 'female berdache' and passing women?" I asked. He replied: "As I understand the term, 'female berdache' is a complete misnomer. 'Berdaches' were males who were labeled 'berdache' by outsiders. From what I've read, 'berdache' means 'kept-boy' or 'male prostitute.' How, then, can there even be such a thing as a 'female berdache'? What would that be? A female 'kept-boy'? A female 'male prostitute'? I can't identify with such a term. First, because I'm not female, except biologically. Second, I'm not a 'kept-boy' or a 'male prostitute.' 'Passing women' also seems like a strange term. We're talking about females, right? Why did they have to pass as women, they already were women, weren't they? Whatever their reasons were, they were females passing as men. Why aren't they called 'passing men'? I guess that somewhat I can identify with passing women, but I'd identify more strongly with them if they were called passing men. I'm a man who was born female, in this sense, I pass as a man not as a woman."

These are legitimate questions, and some are worth reiterating. How can there be such a thing as a "female berdache"? What would that be? Why aren't they called "passing men"? More to the point, why are the female-bodied counterparts to "berdache" given androcentric terms such as *man-woman* rather than *woman-man* or *female-man*? The answer may be as simple as Mike Hernandez's statement: "'Female berdache' is an oxymoron, and it seems like a means in which to make FTMs or an FTM counterpart invisible. For most people, the bottom line is that a man has to have a penis."

Given such comments I was prompted to ask why transmen and FTMs rarely mention "berdache" or passing women when discussing the historical evidence for female-bodied men. That question also arose from my observation that male-bodied transpeople often turn to the word *"berdache"* as a symbol of affirmation and historical image that lends credence to their modern-day identities. It is common, for example, to hear a male-bodied transperson express the sentiment "there was a time when people like us were revered," yet I have rarely heard a similar sentiment expressed by FTMs and transmen. In fact, there is no mention of Native American traditions in *Information for the Female to Male Cross Dresser and Transsexual* (Sullivan 1990b), which until the mid-1990s was the primary published source for female-bodied transpeople. Yet all the historical cases discussed in the previous chapter, in addition to others, do appear in it. Initially, I thought that might be because females are rarely mentioned in cross-cultural literature as manifesting transbehavior. That turns out not to be the case. Rather, it is an instance of FTMs and transmen not relating to the few cases mentioned.

Issues of Nonidentification

What is a "self" that it can be represented?
—Gilmore 1994:17

It is common in the literature for an entry to consist of nothing more than a statement that says, in essence, "Oh, by the way, females have been known to do this also" (chapter 4). As Blackwood has noted, "Most anthropological work on the cross-gender role has focused on the male 'berdache,' with little recognition given to the female cross-gender role. Part of the problem has been with the much smaller data base available for a study of the female role. Yet anthropologists have overlooked even the available data. This oversight has led to the current misconception that the cross-gender role was not feasible for women" (1984b:29).

In spite of such oversights or lack of data, as well as the still current misconception that female-bodied people cannot or do not manifest trans-behavior, female-bodied people have transcended and transgressed gender boundaries—and continue to do so. As Mike Hernandez explained to me, "It is possible FTMs or what might be our counterparts were overlooked. Given the rugged life-style and the [physical] similarities between men and women in Native cultures an FTM person who worked the fields or was a hunter/warrior [in nomadic tribes] would not have stood out. In cultures where males did not have heavy beards and might have only a few whiskers, females who took on male tasks would not stand out. To an outsider such a person would have passed as a man without question. I imagine this would be like what happened with Billy Tipton. No one knew until he died that he had a female body. Those who lived within the tribe would have known but would an outsider? I doubt it!"

Schaeffer seemingly affirmed Mike's observation when he concluded that a Kutenai female who dressed in male clothing "seems to have had little or no difficulty adapting herself to the new garments, since she evaded detection in such garb at Fort Astoria for an entire month" (1965:197). It is likely the Kutenai female would have continued to pass as a man had a former acquaintance not returned to the fort and revealed her. Male observers seemed to be acutely aware of the male in woman's dress but likely would not have noticed the female who appeared as a "small boy or young man" participating with the other boys or men in tribal societies.[2] Given the Euro-American consciousness wherein what females do is unimportant, why would female gender diversity be noticed?

Ironically, when such people have been noted they are often described as "physically large, tall, and robust . . . and matched this size and strength with assertive personalities" (Miller 1982:281). The Kutenai female "was said to have been quite large and heavy boned"; although she was not a trans-vestite, "Crow Woman Chief [was] taller and stronger than most women" (Schaeffer 1965: 195, 226). Gifford stated that "such females [do] not menstruate or develop large breasts. Like men in muscular build, but external sex organs of women" (cited in Katz, ed. 1976:327). Not surprisingly, nearly all published cases of female gender diversity report that female-men were "outstanding hunters" and providers who did "all the work a husband is supposed to do (Williams 1992[1986]:235; Devereux 1976[ca. 1850–95], cited in Katz, ed. 1976:305).

Yet Brown concludes that few female hunters existed because game animals react adversely to menstrual blood and hunting is incompatible with child care (1983:457; cf. Whitehead 1981:86). When I asked FTMs and transmen about menstruation and reproduction, most thought the issue was irrelevant. As Mike Hernandez stated, "Females don't bleed all the time. So what, they didn't hunt for one week out of the month." Concerning reproduction, Sky Renfro concluded, "Granted there was the need to reproduce, especially so, for females. But children weren't the property of individuals, they belonged to the community. So after giving birth, a female would not be restricted to 'mothering' activities and could take on so-called male tasks. You know, many Native cultures did not have strict social roles."

The assumptions that female-bodied transpeople were incapable of hunting, of being warriors, or prevented from being men within their societies because of mothering activities are biological-determinist (cf. Blackwood 1985:7) and heterocentric. That position is not surprising given the sources of these writings. "The discussions are neatly ordered according to middle-class white views about where [females] fit into social schemes. It is clear, I think, that the ground we are exploring is obscure: [females] in general have not been taken seriously by ethnographers or folklorists, and explorations that have been done have largely been distorted by the preconceptions engendered by a patriarchal worldview in which lesbians are said not to exist" (Allen 1992[1986]:252).

Those remarks apply to female-bodied transpeople as well as lesbians. Although much of the literature contends that gender-transformed females did not exist, other accounts are nothing more than hearsay. "Most accounts are retrospective," Callender and Kochems observe, "based on memory or tradition and describing phenomenon no longer subject to observation" (1983:433). For example, much of Pedro de Magalhaes de Gandavo's description of the so-called amazon warrior is not firsthand information (chapter 4). Williams, however, sees matters differently: "Because I have some disagreements with the concept of gender crossing, and also because 'cross-gender female' is linguistically awkward, I prefer the word *amazon* [for Native American female gender-transformed people]" (1992[1986]:234, emphasis in the original). David Hughes, a Cherokee/African American FTM, has told me, however, that he finds Williams's use of the term *amazon* (234) disturbing: "There is no parallel. Amazons were females who identified as women. Cutting off a breast in no way negates an identity as female. Nor does it imply a male identity. He's way off base. I also think that to name Native American FTMs amazons which were probably mythical somehow implies that we are too. It negates the validity of our existence. What does he mean when he says that 'amazon' isn't 'subservient to male definitions'? He's a man. He decided these folks were amazons. In my mind this makes amazon subservient to his definitions."

Although some transmen and FTMs may identify with powerful females or amazons, others clearly do not. Nor do they identify with the terms *cross-gendered females* (Blackwood 1984b) or *manlike women* (Williams 1992[1986]:239). P.B., a Blackfoot/African American FTM, put it this way: "When I was younger and had to wear girl's or women's clothing I felt cross-gendered. That kind of clothing made me feel odd. People reacted to me as though I was a girl, but I knew I wasn't. I only felt normal when I wore boy's or men's clothes. I may be physically female, but I'm not cross-gendered when I wear men's clothes. Nor am I manlike. I am a man."

Although terminology is central to contemporary female-bodied transpeople's lack of identification with Native American gender-transformed females, it is not the only factor. Most FTMs and transmen do not identify with the "berdache" female counterpart because the available literature (largely written by men) insists on feminine pronoun usage. In addition, such roles have either been described as being temporary or involving gender-mixing or gender-blending or they do not involve complete change-overs. If an individual does not engage in temporary cross-dressing or mix or blend his gender and has made a change-over (i.e., he lives as and is perceived by others to be a man), then identification with such roles is unlikely. Mike Hernandez stated, "Although I haven't had any surgery and probably won't, I don't mix or blend my gender. What I am is a man with a female body. A lot of people really get hung up on that. But I can't see having surgery for something that is so inadequate."

Another factor concerns the conflation of homosexuality with transbehavior. "In Western societies where gender inversion theories of homosexuality prevail," Weston notes, "heterosexuals often confuse homosexuality with transgender identification. Popular stereotypes continue to associate lesbianism with masculinity and male homosexuality with effeminacy" (1993:6). Unfortunately, many lesbians and gay men also misinterpret transbehavior as homosexuality; consider, for example, the discussion regarding Grahn and Feinberg in chapter 4. Almost all references to and discussions of female gender diversity equate it with lesbianism. The argument goes something as follows: If an individual adopts the behaviors, manners, and dress of the other sex and also has a relationship with persons of the same biological sex, then they must be homosexual. Not only does that argument conflate sex and gender but it also shows transphobia and a homocentric bias.[3]

Bolin has observed that the transcommunity is creating a number of gender and social identities that challenge the dominant paradigms. What is missing is the individual's personal sense of identity. When viewed from a contemporary transperson's perspective, identity is key to understanding. Transmen and FTMs may identify as men, as transmen, as FTM, or as something else. Although the partners of most FTMs and many transmen are female, they may or may not identify as lesbians. They may also identify as straight, bisexual, or something else altogether (chapter 10). Linking transvestic behaviors with homosexuality obfuscates the intricacies of identities and makes transpeople invisible.

It appears to be beyond most people's imaginations to envision females as men. Some have even gone so far as to state that "it is impossible" for females to assume male roles "because such behavior poses a threat to the gender system and the very definitions of maleness and femaleness" (Blackwood 1985:14). Although it is true that such behaviors are a threat, that attitude is rooted in androcentrism and phallocentrism. It is androcentric in the relentless assumptions that females cannot possibly live as men, thus they are described as passing women or in other related terms. Second, the attitude is phallocentric because it holds that a person without male genitalia cannot be a man. What is a man without a penis? Mercly a passing woman, an amazon, a cross-gendered female, or a manlike woman. Yet female-bodied transpeople make the impossible a daily reality, and many do so for years without surgical or hormonal intervention. As Jack Watson recalled, "When I started out living as a man I was only eighteen. I tried but couldn't find a physician to prescribe hormones for four years. I didn't have any problem 'passing' except people assumed I was younger than I actually was. I even got carded for cigarettes until I was twenty-five, but no one doubted I was male. Heck, people thought I was male long before I started living as a man."

Most FTMs and transmen find the terms *"female berdache," amazon, cross-gendered female,* and *manlike woman* inappropriate and lacking in significance for their identities. Furthermore, such terminology denies the existence of female gender diversity by assuming that all females who manifest trans-behaviors are lesbians. "I have no doubt that some females who had relationships with other females were lesbians," Carlos has said. "But some were also simply men."

Some theorists have concluded that transpeople could not have existed before medical technology had the ability to transform individuals surgi-

cally. As Raymond, for example, observes, "Without its sovereign intervention, transsexualism would not be a reality. Historically, individuals may
have wished to change sex, but until medical science developed the spe-
cialities, which in turn created the demand for surgery, sex conversion did
not exist" (1994[1979]:xv). Raymond contends that "sex changes" did not
occur until the 1950s, conveniently ignoring that the first recorded surgical effort was in 1882 and, significantly, done on Hermann Karl, a female-bodied person (Bullough 1976:662).

To acknowledge that surgeries undertaken to alter sex have occurred
for more than a hundred years and concede that the first attempt was on
a female-bodied person considerably undermines Raymond's argument
that transsexuals are a creation of the "medical empire." Nonetheless, she
is not alone in that view. As Bullough notes, "The subject of transsexualism
poses special problems for a historian since it raises the question of whether
it is possible to look to history for a phenomenon that was not described
until a few decades ago" (1975:561). Although it is true that terminology
surrounding transsexualism did not come into being until the early 1950s,
it is erroneous to assume that transpeople did not exist before the terminology—as attested to by Hermann Karl—or before available medical technology (Cromwell 1987).

Denying the existence of transpeople is akin to denying the existence
of homosexuality before 1892, when the term came into being (cf. Halperin 1990). As Weeks (1977) has pointed out, homosexual identity (and,
by extension, community) did not exist but homosexual behavior did
occur. The same holds true for transbehavior. Furthermore, from an anthropological perspective, medical intervention was not necessary for an
individual to transcend gender boundaries. All that was required was social recognition. At least one society, the Siberian Chukchi, recognized
gender-transformed females as true men (Bogoras 1975[1904–8]:455;
Cromwell 1987:27; Jacobs and Cromwell 1992:51). Throughout history
and across cultures, transpeople have existed and continue to exist.

Trans as a Third Gender

Discourses are ways of knowing that . . . bring into being the
object of knowledge.
—DiGiacomo 1992:113

There has been some question about whether transpeople constitute a
third (or fourth) gender or some other and whether the word *"berdache"*
should be equated with transgenderism. For example, Williams states,

"What is most noticeable in all the outpouring of new research is that gender studies scholars basically agree with the thesis of *The Spirit and the Flesh:* that berdachelike traditions in other cultures should not be defined as 'transvestites' or 'transsexuals' but as an alternative or intermediate gender. That is, scholars now agree that berdaches are accepted by their societies as being distinct from both women and men" (1992[1986]:xiv).

On one level I agree with that position. We must be cautious in our assumptions concerning the status of "berdache" as well as the status of gender-transformed females. As Fulton and Anderson note, "Imposing Western labels (such as 'male' and 'homosexual') on the aboriginal 'man-woman' imbues the role with Westernized meanings for which, we suggest, there was no context in aboriginal society" (1992:608). That also applies to "female berdache." But on another level, one must ask what transvestites, transsexuals, and transgendered people are if not part of alternative or intermediate genders. Transvestites fall into the alternative category in that they alternate between male and female. By at least one definition, transsexuals constitute an intermediate gender in that the label obtains only while an individual is in transition from female to male (and vice versa). Transgender is an intermediate gender category by virtue of morphology coupled with gender presentation (which is usually in opposition to their biology).

All three categories are distinct from both women and men. That is, they are marked as other. Western ideology insists that sex and gender correspond such that bodies are considered part of gender. Therefore, trans-people, because they mix bodies and genders, have intermediate genders and obfuscate the Western view of two and only two genders. To maintain the myth of only two genders, however, transvestites and transsexuals are considered abnormal, deviant, and of a "nonconforming gender" and as such are considered pathological. They are rendered invisible by trans-sexual discourses and the refusal of medico-psychological practitioners to acknowledge individuals who maintain an intermediate status.

Williams's statement and others like it are examples of cultural blindness. It is like looking at two apples and calling one an orange. "Berdache" (transbehavior), normalized in other cultures, is considered deviant in Euro-American culture. Because of cultural biases we refuse to call another culture's accepted alternative genders by our stigmatized terms of transvestite and transsexual. One could argue that transvestite and transsexual are different than "berdache" and other multiple genders that are constructed. But if not constructed genders, what are they? Defining "berdachelike traditions" as transvestites or transsexuals means admitting the existence of more than two genders and the fact that all genders are constructed. Furthermore, it is necessary to admit a willingness to accept those in exotic cultures as normal yet not those in Euro-American culture. Finally, to refuse to recognize transbehaviors for exactly what they are (i.e., transcending or transgressing gender boundaries) in every culture and in every time is to stigmatize transpeople in contempory culture.

Sabine Lang wisely discusses the "female berdache" tradition as encompassing at least four categories: "berdaches," independent women, alternative feminine gender roles, and lesbians (1991a:9–17). Even so, these categories may not be enough, at least for many contemporary female-bodied transpeople. Yet the actions of individuals persist beyond the obfuscation of androcentrism, phallocentrism, heterosexism, and homocentrism. As Carlos stated, "I've been rethinking what I said before. I still can't identify with the terms but I can identify with how they lived their lives. I take pride in what they did and how they lived their lives as men in their societies without hormones or surgery. In this sense, they are a part of my history."

CHAPTER 8

Fearful Others: Transsexual Discourses and the Construction of Female-Bodied Transpeople

> To date the literature reflects the male-female discrepancy in the sex ratio of this population and consequently a much greater body of information is available on male-to-female transsexuals.
> —Bolin 1988:3[1]

> (I will consider female-to-male transsexuals in another paper).
> —Stone 1991:284

> Transvestism in women . . . is so rare it is almost nonexistent.
> —Stoller 1982:99

> [F]emale-to-male transsexuals . . . are a relatively homogeneous group.
> —Steiner, ed. 1985:3

These comments are a only few examples of the marginal treatment of female-to-male transsexuals and female transvestites.[2] Perhaps, at least in the vast literature concerning transsexuals, transvestites, and gender diversity in general, Raymond is correct in her estimation that FTMs/transmen are "tokens" designed to validate transsexualism as a human phenomenon (1994[1979]:xxi). Often women, children, racial and ethnic minorities, gender, and sexual minorities are constructed as others by those in power. Individuals become a group or a class of people, as in all women are . . . , children are . . . , and certain races are . . .

Like the epigraphs for this chapter, such statements deny the lived experiences of individuals as a result of discourses that construct them. Transvestism and transsexualism are constructed from a male perspective and are most often about male gender diversity. Analogous to early sexologists' construction of female sexuality in general and lesbianism in particular, female gender diversity has been viewed from a male perspective. But as women, whether feminists or not, have illustrated, the constructed discourses create a paradox "of a being that is at once captive and absent in discourse, constantly spoken of but itself inaudible or inexpressible, displayed as spectacle and still unrepresented or unrepresentable, invisible yet constituted as the object and the guarantee of vision; a being whose existence and specificity are simultaneously asserted and denied, negated and controlled" (De Lauretis 1990:115). Although De Lauretis addresses the "nonbeing of woman," her statement applies to the paradox of female gender diversity.

Incoherent Subjects

Dichotomizing pathologizes (and pathology dichotomizes).
—Blacking 1977:14

Smith-Rosenberg comprehends that "the fearful project onto the bodies of those they have named social misfits their own desire for social control" (1989:103). Thus, in the early nineteenth century a female individual who cross-dressed to reject the traditional female role would be constructed by sexologists as an "unstable, incoherent subject, the embodiment of disorder, the fearful Other" (110). That early studies focused on behaviors and physical appearances (113) is germane to transsexual discourses.

Although Smith-Rosenberg's discussion is limited to a specific historical period in Western culture, many still fear those who do not conform to the sex and gender order. Fearful others are feared precisely because observers do not have control over the signs of sex and gender. Without being aware of it, observers can be "fooled" by outward signs. Although some individuals are comfortable with ambiguity and even play with it, nonconformity (being a fearful other) frequently has its costs. One is ridicule. Another, extreme and brutal, is violence or even murder, as in the case of Brandon Teena (née Teena Brandon), who was viciously raped by the two men who eventually murdered him and two of his friends (Konigsberg 1995; Minkowitz 1994; "Woman Who Cross-Dressed Found Dead" 1994).

Although an individual may perceive of himself as a man, observers may perceive of him as a lesbian; social identity and personal identity may not match. Some men and women fear lesbians because they are a threat to both the heterosexual order and gender norms. Most people link behavior with sexual identity. Social norms insist that men are males who have masculine behaviors and a sexual preference for women and women are females who have feminine behaviors and a sexual preference for men (Irvine 1990:231).

Gay men, lesbians, transvestites, transsexuals, and others who live in "gender borderlands" challenge the traditional concepts of man, woman, masculinity, and femininity. In doing so, they become fearful others.[3] Because they challenge traditional concepts, often attempts are made to eliminate them through internalized fear of "being different, being other, and therefore lesser, therefore sub-human, in-human, non-human" (Anzaldúa 1987:18).

One way in which to brand a category of people as less than human is to label those who compose it as failures. FTMs and transmen are often represented in the media as well as in transsexual discourses as "failed heterosexuals" (Cahn 1993:343) or as failed butch lesbians (Person and Ovesey 1974:6; Stoller 1973:387; Stoller 1985:15). They are also portrayed as failed women who because of these presumably failed statuses are "want-to-be men." They are branded as failed heterosexuals because in social presentation, dress, talk, and behavior in what is constructed as the purview of men they are supposedly uninterested in and not attracted to nontransgendered males (that is, they are failed women). They are branded failed butch lesbians because they take on too much masculinity. In doing that they threaten the femaleness of lesbian identities. On both heterosexual and lesbian fronts, female-bodied men violate "gender as well as sexual codes" (Cahn 1993:350). By asserting their masculine identities and refusing to accept the inherent femaleness of their bodies as equal to femininity, they become lesbians by heterosexual (gender and sexual) codes and men by lesbian gender codes.

Like gay men and lesbians, transpeople, regardless of their particular identities, who do not affirm the primary categories of gender are feared and consequently ignored, disavowed, discounted, discredited, and frequently accused of not being a true person. In order to be treated as real they must be cured and thus reaffirm the primary sex and gender categories. When the mind does not agree with the primacy of the body, a discourse must be constructed for the "wrong body."

The Construction of the Wrong Body

> What gives psychiatry the right to define transsexuality, to set the diagnostic criteria to which transsexuals must respond.
>
> —Namaste 1994:12

In the late 1890s homosexuals were in the wrong body—at least their souls were confined in the wrong body: *Anima muliebris viruli corpore inclusa* [a feminine soul confined by a masculine body] (Ulrichs 1975[1898], cited in Kennedy 1981:106). Men in female bodies. Women in male bodies. In the early 1950s transsexuals became trapped in the wrong bodies.[4] As sexologists (in particular Krafft-Ebing, de Savitsch, and Gutheil) delineated differences among categories of homosexuals, it became clear that some individuals were insistent about being women in male bodies and men in female bodies (cf. Heidenreich 1997:268–74; see also Rosario 1994).

One of the paradoxes of transsexual discourse is the notion of having a wrong body. Despite Money's claim that the concept of being trapped in the wrong body was "adopted by transsexuals as their own" (1990:xiv), the idea has been imposed upon transpeople by those who control access to medical technologies and have controlled discourses about transpeople. Some individuals may believe or may come to believe that they are in the wrong body or at least use language that imparts the same meaning. As one transsexual told me in a personal communication, "When a man *is a man in every way* [except] the lower part of his body, *he is trapped,* and I mean *trapped,* in a woman's body" (emphasis in the original). For many transsexuals, once the wrong body has been surgically altered they no longer consider themselves to be transsexual.

> About the question of whether or not I consider myself a transsexual. I don't but . . . that is what I would be classified as by a health professional. (Paul T.)

> I was a transsexual. Now I'm just a man. (James E.)

Their wrong body (a biophysical entity of sex), now "corrected," becomes a gendered body of woman or man. Such individuals are insisting on the right to declare a gender, thus overruling and subverting society's biological designation of sex.

In the preceding paragraphs I emphasized two phrases: wrong body and surgically altered. My intent is twofold: to problematize the definition that has come to embody the transsexual syndrome (i.e., the "wrong body," Stone 1991:297) and to problematize the concept of surgical correction.

For whom is the body wrong and for whom is the surgery corrective?[5] As Stone notes, "In pursuit of differential diagnosis a question sometimes asked of a prospective transsexual is 'Suppose that you could be a man [or woman] in every way except for your genitals; would you be content?' There are several possible answers, but only one is clinically correct" (297). The correct answer, of course, is "No, I would not be content." To answer yes or maybe is to be rendered a diagnosis—at best of nontranssexual, at worst of pathology. Shapiro comments that "transsexuals' fixation on having the right genitals is *clearly less pathological* than if they were to insist that they are *women with penises* or *men with vaginas*" (260, emphasis added).[6]

To conceive of oneself as either a woman with a penis or a man with a vagina is considered pathological because "under the binary phallocratic founding myth by which Western bodies and subjects are authorized, only one body per gendered subject is 'right.' All other bodies are wrong" (Stone 1991:297). According to the imposed order one can only be one or the other, not both and certainly not neither, regardless of choice. Yet the order does not prevent individuals from challenging, and thus subverting, it. Jack Watson observes, "If I didn't have the label transexual I'd probably think of myself as a man with a female body. I belong to neither sex, yet I'm both: I have a beard and a deep voice, I've had a mastectomy but I still have a vagina. I don't have a problem with that, neither does my wife, but society does."

The phrase *wrong body* inadequately describes the feeling that one's body is not a part of one's self. The body's experience is incongruent with the mind's. The insider within the body does not recognize the outside of the body as belonging. Attempts to describe this phenomenon, because of the limitations of language, seemingly lead back to the concept of wrong body. "Wrong body" connotes surface understanding rather than depth of feeling. Using a language that cannot accurately hear or adequately interpret the individual experience of transness results in the discourse of the wrong body.

In part, the answer to the question of for whom the body is wrong and for whom the surgery is corrective is embedded in the sex and gender ideology of what constitutes femaleness and maleness (or woman and man) within Western societies. Furthermore, the concept of wrong body may be appropriate for male-to-female transsexuals if for no other reason than the fact that hormones do not greatly modify male physiology, which is not the case for female-bodied transpeople. Many transmen and FTMs, however, do not identify with this terminology. Many are dissatisfied with having breasts and menstruating, neither of which accounts for the entire body.

The majority of FTMs and transmen do not have gender dysphoria; it is the rare FTM or transman who does not know from an early age what his gender identity is. What many experience, however, is body-part dysphoria, which focuses on elements such as breasts and menstruation that are quintessentially female. Those who do talk about having breasts do so with feelings that range from revulsion and denial to matter-of-fact acceptance. Yet I have never met an FTM or transman who did not want chest surgery. Because breasts are the primary sign of female woman and, by implication, femininity, to reject them acknowledges that fact (Money and Brennan

1968:496). If breasts were defined as male, transmen and FTMs would not be dysphoric about them or have them removed. Because breasts are a sign of feminity, however, chest reconstructions are requested.

Breasts are hated more than genitals, which the majority of people in one's life do not see. Props fill in for male genitalia. Ironically, transmen and FTMs are accused of imitating men when in fact they are improvising and using the available language to communicate personal identities on a social level. More ironically, they are accused of doing so unconsciously. They intentionally communicate the signs of masculinity and maleness, however, because those signs demonstrate their personal social identity. They reject the fact that having breasts and female genitals mandates being women and feminine. They also reject that female equals woman equals feminine. Instead, they are masculine, which equals men, which equals male (at the social level) in spite of having the signs (female genitals, breasts, and menstruation) that dictate being female. Many transmen see their bodies as containers but feel they are not confined to their bodies in expressing their beings.

What Is a Transsexual?

What gives critics . . . the right to represent transgender, with virtually no understanding of transgender specificity?
—Namaste 1994:12

Many seem unable to grasp the concept that transpeople have not identified with their bodies or have done so only superficially. It seems unfathomable to them that an individual can be born with one body and identify as a person who has a different body; that is, a person born with a female body can identify as a man or vice versa. "Sure I was born female," Dave agrees. "But I don't know what it is to be a woman, or for that matter, what it is to be a girl. While it's true I was raised female, I don't know what it *is* to be female. I practiced and put on a face that the world saw as being female. But locked inside was a child (I say child, because there is no concrete image of either a boy or a girl), who knew that irrespective of how I was treated I was *not* what everyone thought" (emphasis in the original).

It is also difficult for many to understand that individuals can identify as men with vaginas or women with penises: "I consider myself a *man* (social gender)," Charles says, "who happens to be *female* (biological sex)" (emphasis in the original).[7]

Garber asks, "But what *is* a transsexual? Is he or she a member of one sex 'trapped' in the other's body? Or someone who has taken hormones and undergone other somatic changes to more closely resemble the gender into which he (or she) was not born? More pertinent to this inquiry, does a transsexual *change subjects*? Or just bodies—or body parts?" (1989:151, emphasis in the original). These are biological-determinist questions that equate gender with genitals. In particular they are essentialist in that they express "a belief in the real, true essence of things, the invariable and fixed properties which define the 'whatness' of a given entity" (Fuss 1989:xi).

Although Garber argues that transvestites and transsexuals essentialize their genitalia (1989:143), she essentializes their entire being and imposes the belief that men are born with male bodies and women are born with female bodies. Underlying Garber's question of whether transsexuals change is a mistaken belief that they identify as either a man or a woman in the first place. "I've been accused of 'betraying womanhood,'" relates Sean. "How can I betray something I've never identified with?"

For most female-bodied transpeople there is no shift from conceiving of oneself as female to as a man or to a variation on the theme. What needs to be understood is that the individual may have never identified as a woman but rather may have always identified as a man or as something else. In spite of messages from family, peers, and society in general, and in spite of biological evidence (in particular, genitalia) to the contrary, most female-bodied transpeople have always had the self-concept of being male and/or man, although the degree varies. The self-image (and belief) of many is that they are boys who will grow up to be men. As I have written elsewhere, "When I was young I did not think of my body and my mind as belonging to two very different people. My name, if shortened (which I preferred) could be androgynous. It was easy to believe that I was as I saw myself. But when I reached puberty the girl-turning-woman caught up with my image of the boy-turning-man" (Taylor and Taylor 1983:13).[8]

What shifts once transition is initiated is social identity, that is, how others perceive these individuals. In spite of transsexual discourses to the contrary, surgery is not the ultimate destination for many. Some elect not to have it for reasons of health or finance or even because the results are viewed as less than adequate if not outright horrific. They choose to live instead as men with vaginas. "I am able to pass as a male 98 percent of the time just as I am," David Hughes told me. "I am 6 foot, 150 pounds, have a deep baritone voice, look and pass as male. With all of this in my favor, I see no reason at this time to invest money and health issues into hormones and surgery. If I could change my name legally, it would probably be all that I would need to live out my life as male. Perhaps if treatment were safer and cheaper, I would invest in transition as an option."

The Construction of Female-to-Male Transsexualism

Discourse becomes oppressive when it requires that the speaking subject, in
order to speak, participate in the very terms of that oppression.
—Butler 1990:16

The discourses that have constructed transvestism and transsexualism have
two elements: a disproportion of male-to-female transsexuals to female-to-
male transsexuals and a nonexistence of female transvestites. The answer
to how these discourses have become "truths" is rooted in the definitions
of transvestism and transsexualism as well as a sex and gender ideology
whose mechanisms attempt to "cure" male-bodied transpeople and ignore
those who are female-bodied.

> The essential features of the disorder [transsexualism] are stated to be
> a persistent sense of discomfort and inappropriateness about one's ana-
> tomic sex and a persistent wish to be rid of one's genitals and to live as a
> member of the other sex ([American Psychiatric Association] 1980, pp.
> 261–62).
>
> The preceding definition is all one really needs to approach the litera-
> ture on female-to-male transsexuals, who are a relatively homogeneous
> group. Male gender patients, on the other hand, present with a wide range
> of clinical signs and symptoms, and it is mainly in regard to gender-dis-
> turbed males that authors vary in their terminology. (Steiner, Blanchard,
> and Zucker, 1985:3)

It is because FTMs and transmen are treated by medico-psychological
practitioners as a homogeneous group that there appears to be disproportion in numbers. By assuming that transmen and FTMs are homogeneous,
clinics are able to ignore and disregard the wide range of signs that individuals may exhibit. Yet that is not the only reason there appears to be a
prevalence of MTFs/transwomen over FTMs/transmen. Other contributing influences are the focus of most researchers on the so-called sexual
dysfunction of men; transmen's and FTMs' ability to pass more easily; their
awareness of the reality of the quality of genital surgeries and frequent
rejection of them; and the fact that transmen and FTMs have primarily
sought care from private physicians and therapists.[9]

Furthermore, while many clinics insisted on phalloplasty as a necessary
part of the "rehabilitative" process (Dushoff 1973:203), other clinics have
excluded FTMs and transmen "categorically because of the greater com-
plexity in surgical technique" (Ehrhardt, Grisanti, and McCauley 1979).
It is the clinics and hospitals affiliated with universities that have kept close

account of the numbers. If fewer transmen and FTMs go to these types of centers, then many are left uncounted. Therefore, several factors go into the counting, including who goes to the research facilities and/or clinics; whether phalloplasty is required or even available; what transmen and FTMs expect, especially regarding surgical outcomes; and what clinicians expect concerning who qualifies as an FTM/transman.[10]

In what ways are transmen and FTMs constructed to be a homogeneous group? Although Steiner does not clearly define what is meant by a "homogeneous group," a careful reading of the medico-psychological literature points to three stereotypes concerning female-bodied transpeople, specifically FTMs/transmen: androgyny, particularly in behavior; heterosexual object choices; and an obsession with having penises.[11] Minh-ha asserts that "the stereotype is not a simplification because it is a false representation of a given reality. It is a simplification because it is an arrested, fixated form of representation" (1991:163). Therefore, although some female-bodied transpeople may have fit into these stereotypes, others have been required to conform to the arrested and fixated ideas put forth by medico-psychological practitioners.

The Androgyny Stereotype

FTMs/transmen are more androgynous than other groups of men. They are also more flexible in their behaviors and comfortable expressing a range of behaviors (Fleming, MacGowan, and Salt 1984:52). Transmen/FTMs "do not adhere strongly to stereotypically masculine roles [nor do they] reject stereotypically feminine characteristics. . . . [they] incorporate aspects of their former roles into their new roles and do not totally reject them" (Fleming, MacGowan, and Salt 1984:56). "I feel all men and women (whether genetic or transsexual) have elements or aspects of both, male and female," Dave says. "I have feminine aspects which do NOT embarrass me at all!" Although some FTMs are flexible and have a large repertoire of behaviors, others strongly adhere to masculine stereotypes. "I have known since age fourteen that I was masculine except biological[ly]," recalls Jack Hyde. "For almost fifteen years I have dressed masculine and lived masculine. I look very masculine. Some people probably consider me very macho, you know, a tough guy. They're right. I certainly dress the part, and most of the time I act it."

Transmen and FTMs do not always rigidly adhere to stereotypes. Consequently, they challenge the prevailing paradigm by bringing into question what it means to be a man or masculine. Many are more fluid in their identifications with the signs or props of masculinity and maleness. All men, transgendered or not, use props and display signs of their maleness. Whether wearing business suits and power ties, more casual attire, or more casual clothing still, working-class, redneck, cowboys, and even drunks on the street signal their masculinity. Many social behaviors indicate how they do so. Are they macho or do they exhibit new age sensitivity? Does the person consider himself to be a virile womanizer, a liberated man, Mr. Nice Guy, an average Joe, a red-blooded Marlboro Man, or a man among men. The difference is that transmen and FTMs have additional props and most are more consciously aware of the constructedness of masculinity and manhood. Using props, however, often brands individuals as "fake" men, as does being flexible and comfortable in expressing a wide range of masculine behaviors.

The Heterosexuality Stereotype

FTMs and transmen "form stable and enduring intimate sexual relationships with biological women. These female-to-male transsexuals and their partners considered their relationships heterosexual" (Fleming, MacGowan, and Costos 1985:47–48). From childhood, transmen and FTMs are purportedly attracted only to "feminine females" (Benjamin 1964:467; Stoller 1972:48, 1975:224). But not all FTMs and transmen agree, even when married to or partnered with women. "I'd have to say my sexuality shifts— mostly I identify as bisexual—sometimes I think of myself as a gay married man—but I never think of myself as straight," observes Jack Watson.

Repeatedly the medico-psychological literature, and consequently the majority of practitioners, has insisted that transmen and FTMs are attracted only to feminine women and are "repelled by the idea of sexual relations with males" (Stoller 1973:386). But some individuals contradict the heterosexual stereotype. "What I really want is a sexual relationship with a gay man, as a gay man. One clinic told me that I could not possibly live as a gay man since gay men were primarily interested in large penises and were not sexually aroused when shown photos of female-to-male surgeries" (Sullivan 1989:69–70).

While the biases of medico-psychological practitioners toward heterosexuality is being challenged by transsexuals and some practitioners, homophobia still prevails (Bockting 1987; Coleman and Bockting 1988; Pauly n.d.). It is of note that transsexual discourses have stated that FTMs and transmen "deny that they are homosexual and avoid homosexual women, except occasionally as nonsexual acquaintances" (Stoller 1982:48). Yet some FTMs do live as lesbians before living as men (chapter 3). "I can't remember *ever* being happy about being female," a correspondent told me in a personal communication. "I can't remember being happy but for two years that I was involved in a homosexual relationship. That happiness was not in the sexual aspect, but of being the 'man' and of being with people who accepted me as I was. I *don't* consider myself gay. I only consider myself 'straight' with a woman's body structure." Steiner, too, states that "all transsexual biological females are homosexual in erotic object choice" (1985:353). In less confusing words, the erotic choices of all transmen and FTMs are said to be women.

That position has long existed within medico-psychological discourses and is part of practitioners' "incorrigible beliefs" (Devor 1989:2). De Savitsch has acknowledged that both males and females "desire to change sex," but for females the primary motivation to do so is "homosexual libido" (1958:86). Benjamin reports that transmen's and FTMs' "love objects" are feminine women and that they "deny being homosexual" (1964:467). Early in his career Stoller stated, "Female[-to-male] transsexualism strikes me as a form of homosexuality more than a distinct condition" (1973:387). Similarly, Pauly has observed that "by definition, all female[-to-male] transsexuals are homosexual, in that these biological females who psychologically reject their femaleness and assume a masculine role are interested in and at one point become involved with females as sexual partners" (1974a:502). Devor (1997) likewise insists that FTMs and transmen, regardless of personal and social identities, have homosexual relationships with women.

Equating FTMs' and transmen's relationships with women as homosexual is a biological-determinist argument. If an individual does not self-identify as a man and chooses women as sexual partners, then she would indeed have a homosexual erotic choice. When an individual self-identifies as a man, however, and chooses women as sexual partners, then his erotic choice is heterosexual. The insistence that transmen and FTMs are homosexual because they are attracted to women is a component of the body-equals-sex-equals-gender formula and demonstrates the inflexibility of that rigid equation.

Nonetheless, it is a compelling formula. Pauly, for example, also states that the "failure to discriminate between gender and the sexual aspects of this condition is a source of great confusion" (1974a:502). "In distinguishing these two conditions," he adds, "the lesbian would *never* request that her breasts or genitalia be removed surgically, any more than the heterosexual individual would permit this. Obviously, one is not going to sacrifice organs which are a source of pleasure and stimulation" (504).[12]

How then can transmen and FTMs "by definition" be homosexual? Pauly fails to realize just how enmeshed he is and does not discriminate between lesbians and FTMs/transmen or between gender identity and sexual identity when he discusses the sexual identity of FTMs/transmen.

Thus, he (along with Steiner, Stoller, Money, Devor, and others) views FTMs/transmen relationships with females as homosexual instead of heterosexual.

Elsewhere, however, Pauly has concluded that "the statement that all female-to-male transsexuals are homosexuals in their sexual preference can no longer be made" (1998:243). He refers to FTMs and transmen who have relationships with women as "heterogenderal" and those who have relationships with men as "homogenderal" (244), terms similar to what Devor refers to as "gendered sexuality," that is, the "interactions of sex and gender with sexuality" (1997:xxv–xxvi). She uses the terms *bisexual, homosexual,* and *heterosexual* "when considering persons' bodies" and *bi, gay, lesbian,* and *straight* "when considering their genders" (xxvi), a schema that makes it "possible to speak with accuracy and without contradiction about a cross-living transsexual man who is sexually attracted to female women as both homosexual and straight." Such a plan, however, does not take into consideration how a person feels and self-identifies, thus it neither speaks with accuracy nor ends confusion. The arguments are further examples of essentializing the body and imposing a worldview on others.

It would be much less confusing and far more respectful if the "experts" would listen to transpeople and attempt to move beyond the reification of bodies in order to understand their perspective. They are not "cross-living" but rather living. Those who have relationships with and are attracted to women are heterosexually identified; those who have a "homosexual preference" (Pauly 1974a:501) are attracted to and have sexual relationships with men. Some who have relationships with and are attracted to both men and women are bisexually identified. That simple scheme is based on identities rather than bodies. In the long run, sexual orientation matters only to those who are in relationships, regardless of whether the individuals identify as gay, lesbian, bi, straight, homosexual, heterosexual, or bisexual.

The Obsession with Having Penises Stereotype

According to transsexual discourses, FTMs and transmen are obsessed with ridding themselves of breasts and internal female organs and "with the idea of having a penis" (Lothstein 1983:13; cf. Steiner 1985:353). Numerous studies have documented that almost all transmen and FTMs elect to have chest reconstruction and that the majority have hysterectomies (Fleming, Costos, and MacGowan 1984:585; Fleming, MacGowan, and Costos 1985:49). Although they wish to be rid of their breasts, it is the rare individual who becomes obsessed with doing so. Likewise, the primary motivation for removing internal female organs (after testosterone has caused menses to cease) is to prevent potential disease. The majority of transmen and FTMs ignore their breasts until they are able to obtain chest surgery, and they deal with menses matter-of-factly before experiencing the effects of testosterone.

The "absence of the penis [is] loathsome" and the "ultimate goal is the attainment of a functional penis" (Krueger 1983:77; Pauly 1974b:521). As I was informed in a personal communication, "I am content with my choice to change and if I had to do it all again—I certainly would. But I don't feel whole because of my lack of 'genitals' and don't feel comfortable even thinking of initiating sex with someone." Yet Alex W. observed, "When you ask me, if I am a transsexual I have to pause—because although I take hormones, have had a mastectomy and a hysterectomy—I don't intend to have any more surgery. I'm comfortable and happy where I am. I present as a man in my life but I have no problem with having a vagina."

Only a few clinicians have recognized that all FTMs and transmen are not obsessed with attaining a penis. As early as 1964, for example, Benjamin realized that phalloplasty was "too complicated an undertaking and [FTMs and transmen] rarely insist upon it" (467). Stoller, too, noted, "Most do not insist on an *artificial* penis—*but only* because they are told by the urologists that it is not possible to make a *real-appearing* penis that can be urinated through or has erectile capacity" (1973:387, emphases added). Surgery is a possibility for some but by no means a necessity or obsession. "I'm living full-time as a man now," David Hughes has said. "I feel comfortable at the stage I'm at. Depending on finances, priorities, and the degree of medical risk I'm willing to take once, and if, I can afford these further procedures [hysterectomy and genital surgery] I will decide whether or not to have them done; they are not necessary at this point, as I see it."

Challenging Surgical Necessity

Transsexuals are not wholly male or female either before or after transition.
—Green 1994b:6

One challenge to transsexual discourses is the necessity of genital surgeries. One contributing factor of this challenge is that no significant changes have been made or accomplished in the quality, functionality, or aesthetics of genital surgeries since the 1960s, despite surgeons' claims to the contrary. Some FTMs/transmen call the results of phalloplastic surgeries "frankendicks," a term that conjures up an image of foreign parts attached to one's body, with resultant scarring and ugliness. Many feel that the term is an apt descriptor for the results of most phalloplasties.[13]

At one time, surgeons, even in the early 1990s, considered phalloplasty to be the only procedure adequate to meet the needs of FTMs and transmen. For example, Noe and Birdsell stated, "Hypertrophy [enlargement] of the clitoris by means of hormonal therapy has not been accepted as an adequate substitute for a penis" (1975:153), and a prominent genital surgeon declared during a 1991 conference that he did not do "clitoral free-ups [metoidioplasties] because, what's the point? It certainly doesn't provide an adequate penis."[14] Of course, "adequate" is, in this formulation, related to the ability to penetrate one's partner during intercourse, an activity for which most surgeons would consider metoidioplasties inadequate.

The surgeon has since changed his mind and now performs metoidioplasties because FTMs/transmen continue to request them over phalloplasties. But who should determine what is adequate, FTMs/transmen or their surgeons? In the surgeon's case the answer was the clients, even though metoidioplasties are still not adequate in his personal opinion.[15] Transmen and FTMs who are considering genital surgeries, for the most part, do choose metoidioplasty. For many, the surgery is more than adequate; for many others, genital surgery is unnecessary because their genitalia are already fully functional.

At least some FTMs and transmen dislike their genitalia and neither look at them nor touch them except as necessary for hygiene. A few hate them. The majority have felt hate for their genitals at some point in life. Many, however, have come to terms with having female genitalia. Some few have even come to the point of loving them.

It is a very rare transman or FTM who has never wished he could have a large erection or that he did not have to use props (e.g., dildoes and urinary devices). But those desires are not obsessive and no different than those other people hold deeply. Every FTM/transman measures the costs of genital surgery. Some go into phalloplastic surgery knowing the risks on a realistic basis. Too many, however, have gone into it with an attitude that they are "the exception" and nothing will go wrong (Kincaid 1995:8–11; Thompson 1995). It is likely that many who do elect phalloplasty regret having done so and may not be willing to admit their mistake, although that is only conjecture because no FTMs/transmen who were several years postphalloplasty agreed to talk with me. A rare few would do it again at all costs and risks, even after experiencing a failed phalloplasty (Kincaid 1995:11).

Some few FTMs/transmen feel they will never become "real" men unless they have phalloplastic surgery (Anonymous 1995:7; Thompson 1995).

It is they who have given medico-psychological practitioners the impression that all FTMs/transmen are obsessed with having penises, which is not the case at all. As Kory states, "No one thinks to ask 'why' someone is having surgery. But everyone questions 'why' I chose not to have it. I chose not to have surgery because of the costs both physically and financially. Mostly physically, though. What it does to your body, the scars, the lack of feeling, the lack of function. I think even if surgery could make my body over and it would feel and function as a male's body does, I wouldn't do it. I would lose what I've become, I would be someone different that I am and I like who I am."

It is this sense of being proud of what one has done in life and of having proven wrong the idea that men cannot be men without male genitalia (as well as the less than normal results of phalloplasties) that has led many transmen and FTMs to reject phalloplasty and, if opting for genital surgery, choose metoidioplasty instead.

Arousing the Dreadful

Like everyone else, FTMs and transmen are heterogeneous. Yet they are ignored or discounted because many do not conform to clinicians' homogeneous concept of what they should be. Garber (1989:146–47) lists a number of reasons for this: (1) gender identity clinics were set up to service males; (2) the majority of applicants are male; (3) most researchers are male, with their male bias intact; (4) social pressures ease transmen and FTMs' ability to live as men without surgery (it is considered natural or normal for women to want to be or live as men); and (5) a traditional latitude exists for men who express dysfunction. There are also deeper reasons, which Lothstein has posed as a series of questions:

> Why is there so much resistance to learning about female[-to-male] transsexualism? Is there something inherent in the female[-to-male] transsexual's quest that silences our curiosity? Does the female[-to-male] transsexual's psyche arouse something dreadful within each of us that says "hands off"? Have male researchers ignored the topic because they view a woman's desire to become a man as natural, and therefore a trivial phenomenon to investigate? Or have male researchers ignored this aspect of female sexuality, just as they have ignored other problems of female sexuality, because of their homocentrism? (1983:14)

The answer to Lothstein's last two questions is an emphatic yes—and quite similar to Garber's reasons—because of male researchers' homocentrism. First, because the desire to become men is viewed as natural, female-to-male transsexualism is trivialized.[16] The degree to which FTMs and transmen can physically become men is limited. Second, because researchers have focused on males, females have been neglected in all research areas. It should come as no surprise that transmen and FTMs are neglected also.

The more telling questions are Lothstein's first three. There is resistance to learning about FTMs and transmen because their quest arouses something dreadful in male researchers' psyches. Garber pinpoints the dreadful when she states, "What lies behind some of the resistance to or neglect of the female-to-male transsexuals is, I think, a sneaking feeling that it should not be so easy to 'construct' a 'man'—which is to say, a male body" (1989:147). The body part is, in fact, easy; hormones will provide all of the secondary sex characteristics. But the "ultimate/absolute insignia of maleness, the penis" (142) is supposedly not so easy to construct. Dan C. observed, "Throughout his slide presentation every time he [the surgeon] said 'penis' he changed it to 'phallus' immediately. It was clear to me that he doesn't make penises he makes phalluses. I wouldn't let him touch me. And it's not just his attitude. Did you see the scars that he leaves?"

Although often conflated, the terms *phallus* and *penis* are used distinctly here. The phallus is a symbol of maleness, in particular male power; the penis is a physical part of the male anatomy. This distinction is reflected in the language most surgeons use, which indicates that they believe themselves to be creating a phallus rather than a penis, hence they use the terms *phalloplasty* and *neophallus* in their discourses (Steiner, ed. 1985:339) and at conferences.[17] That is, surgery can only construct a poor facsimile of a penis but never a real one. David Gilbert, a surgeon, has stated, "It's never a God-given penis, but a phallus" (cited in Denny and Schaffer 1992:27). In other words, only real men can possess real penises. "In sex reassignment surgery there remains an implicit privileging of the phallus, a sense that a 'real one' can't be made, but only born. The (predominantly male) surgeons who do such reconstructive surgery have made individual advances in technique, but the culture does not yet strongly support the construction of 'real men' by this route" (Garber 1989:149).[18]

A phallus is a symbol that represents social power. As such, it "is not the equivalent of the penis" (Vance 1980:130; Grosz 1993:105). I do not believe that surgeons think of phallus as a symbol of social power but rather as not equivalent to a penis—as a "pretended or fantasmatic unity" (Reich 1992:116). Nevertheless, it is common knowledge among transmen and FTMs that surgeons do not create real penises. "I've said for years," Dan C. told me, "that surgeons can't and won't construct a 'real penis' simply because to do so would be a threat to their definition of what it is to be male. If female bodies can have penises made then what does being a man mean? What we need is an FTM to become a surgeon. Then the surgery will improve because he won't be threatened."

One reason that many transpeople do not have surgery is resistance to a system that dictates that one has to be either a man (with a penis) or a woman (with a vagina). "I've chosen not to have genital surgery," Paul T. says. "On the one hand, the cost is too much for the end result. On the other hand, I see not having a penis as a subversion of the notion that in order to be a man I must have one. I get great pleasure out of knowing other people assume I have one when I don't." There is also resistance to stereotypes of maleness and femaleness as well as to heterosexuality, a requirement to qualify for the surgery. "I live very successfully as a man," Paul T. comments. "Surgery just isn't a priority right now. I don't think it ever will be. But not having surgery doesn't keep me from being sexual. I enjoy sex with gay men as well as lesbians, anyone who identifies themselves as queer. I'm a queer bi-gendered person."

More and more, transsexuals do not invest in their genitalia as signifiers of womanliness or manliness. Perhaps an alternate explanation is that many individuals now recognize that genitals do not signify gender. "What most men don't realize is that having a penis isn't what makes them a man" suggests David S. Through networking and the sharing of discourses many transpeople are resisting the imposed order that dictates the necessity of being either a man or a woman. Those who choose not to give into that order find that their self-definition does not have to include society's "ultimate insignias" (e.g., Bornstein 1994). Of course, Stoller and others would argue that they are not real or true transsexuals. Many individuals, however, do not care how the dominant discourses attempt to construct them and the validity of their lives.

The Construction of Female Transvestism

> The authority of authoritative discourses is never absolute,
> always problematic.
> —DiGiacomo 1992:113

Although discourses attempt to homogenize the existence of FTMs and transmen, they also deny the existence of female transvestites. Dekker and van de Pol state that female transvestism has not existed since the end of the nineteenth century (1989:102–3). To explain that statement, they offer the closing gap between men and women and the cultural tolerance of women wearing men's clothing. It is not clear whether their analysis is limited to their geographic area. If that is not the case, however, their analysis is grossly inaccurate.[19] In England and the United States at least, the tradition has not ended but rather has been made invisible. In part, that is because sexologists have limited the definition of transvestism. A transvestite is a heterosexual male who dresses as a woman and is erotically aroused by doing so (Stoller 1975:143).

> I do not remember ever wanting to wear "girls" clothes. But my mother was in control and I had to wear what she bought. As I got older, I had more choice—or really more power to make decisions about what I would wear. I gradually added more and more men's clothes to my wardrobe. At the age of thirty, I remember taking my dresses, shoes, purses, etc. and depositing them in a dumpster. I wore women's slacks and very tailored blouses to work. Finally, at the age of about thirty-three or thirty-four, I began wearing men's clothes 100 percent of the time. I did not meet another woman like myself until just a few months ago. (personal communication)

Because Stoller considers transvestism in females to be extremely rare, he argues that an absence of eroticism in female individuals who dress as men is because they are really transsexuals (Stoller 1968:195, cited in Garber 1989:143–44).[20] Many female transvestites neither dress for erotic purposes nor consider themselves to be men or identify themselves as such (cf. Devor 1989:chs. 4, 6). "I daily wear men's clothing, but I only dress fully to pass less than once a month," says Jay P.

Although behavior is only a small part of some female transvestites' lives, for others it is significant. "When I tell people I feel more comfortable in men's clothing, I don't mean physical comfort (anyone who has ever properly worn a men's tie, knows it is not physically comfortable). When I wear men's clothing I feel a deep sense of satisfaction. I feel very right, emotionally. I feel free. I like what I see when I look at myself in the mirror" (Bernstein 1991:5). Stoller's definition excludes females, but it also excludes males (both heterosexual and homosexual) who cross-dress for reasons other than eroticism. Given those limitations, there are very few male transvestites. That fact leaves the majority of men who cross-dress with no definition or label for their behavior.

> In the lay vocabulary, the term *transvestism* most often means the simple act of cross-dressing; hence, laymen sometimes refer to cross-dressing homosexual males as transvestites. Nowadays, few sexologists use the term *transvestism* to mean simply cross-dressing. Sexologists, oddly enough, have never gotten around to inventing a dignified label for cross-dressing nontranssexual homosexuals, and so are sometimes reduced to re-

ferring, in their scholarly works, to "drag queens." (Steiner 1985:5, emphasis in the original)[21]

Equating the term *transvestite* with cross-dressing is helpful, but it still focuses on males to the exclusion of females. The danger of limited definitions is that they can create confusion for women who dress as men (and vice versa). Following an appearance on the *Geraldo Show* in September 1989, for example, I received the following communication:

> Recently, I saw a talk show where they were talking about having changed their sex. This isn't what I want but I don't know where else to turn. I feel so confused. When I get home from work I like to change into men's clothes. Sometimes its just jeans and t-shirt. But other times I wear jockey shorts, t-shirt, suit and tie, everything else men wear. I bind my breasts and stuff rolled up socks in my shorts. When I feel like I really look like a man I go out. I don't try to pick up anybody, male or female. I just like to go out that way. Is something wrong with me? Am I sick? Am I a transsexual?

I replied that her behavior did not mean she was a transsexual but rather that she was a cross-dresser. "I can't tell you how relieved I was to read your letter," she replied. "I've heard about and read about men who wore women's clothes but I've never heard of women wearing men's clothes." The writer is just one of many who have been confused by the lack of a definition for their behavior or confused by ambiguous or restrictive definitions.

Another danger of limited definitions of transvestism is found in Garber (1989; see also Garber 1992), who cites Stoller as a recognized authority on transvestite and transsexual issues. In using such an authority Garber and others are doing just what feminists protested about during the beginning of the women's movement: Men are speaking for women's experiences and claiming to know what women were or should be. Until Bolin (1988), Newton (1972), and Stone (1991) there was no academic writing about the experiences of transvestites and transsexuals other than that by "authorities" such as Stoller and Lothstein.[22]

Garber sees "these apparently marginal and aberrant cases, that of the transvestite and the transsexual" as viable for both defining and problematizing the concept of "male subjectivity" (1989:143), but I disagree. Although male transvestites do retain a male identity, I suspect that most male-to-female transsexuals do not. Furthermore, although male transvestites retain a male identity, it is not, as Stoller purports, an eroticized identity focused on the retention of penises. Based on my research, it seems that Stoller's so-called mechanisms of transvestism are phallocratic posturings of eroticism that may reflect the experiences of a few male transvestites. They are by no means the experience of the majority, nor are they the experiences of female transvestites. Furthermore, transmen and FTMs have their own ways of defining male subjectivity and what it means to be female-bodied men.

Dangerous Actors

Meaning and experience cannot be read literally and directly
out of discourse.
—DiGiacomo 1992:113

In order to understand the fear invoked by the existence of fearful others, we must ask, as Smith-Rosenberg suggests (taking Mary Douglas's lead), "Who is the dangerous actor? Who is endangered? What is the dangerous act?" (1989:105). For this discussion, the dangerous actors are female-bodied transpeople (as well as all male-bodied transpeople) who do not become one or the other but instead choose a middle ground. The endangered are men in particular, but it seems that some women feel endangered also, especially those who invest in the maintenance of sex and gender structures (biological determinists). The dangerous act is that of living as the other gender with little or no surgical intervention. That action may be seen as endangering because observers have no control over how the sexed body is signified as a gendered being. They can be seemingly tricked by outward signs of gender. Pagliassotti states that fear clearly: "Although genitalia may be hidden beneath clothing, they are the 'true' signifiers of sex, which can be uncovered by inspection, whereas the clothes in contrast, may be 'false' signifiers of sex" (1993:480). Thus the dangerous actor is capable of revealing the arbitrary relationship between the signifier and the signified and reconstructing the notion of sex and gender as bodies that are naturally gendered and sexed (cf. Butler 1990:123). The dangerous act is especially dangerous to discourses (both transsexual and mainstream) that maintain the status quo of sex and gender differences. To live as men (or women) with partial or entirely female (or male) bodies may mean that ultimately there is no, or little, difference. The act is also dangerous because it resists and subverts dominant ideologies. The individual has "declared . . . *self*hood and [a] *will*fulness against the determination of biology" (Smith-Rosenberg 1989:105, emphasis in the original).

Critics view transsexuals and transvestites as representatives of "a challenge to traditional notions of maleness and femaleness" (Irvine 1990:270) as well as making "the referent ('man' or 'woman') knowable" (Garber 1989:156). Although both views may be a possibility, they remain an improbability. On the one side, biological determinists—and on the other side, perpetuators of a mental illness model (also biological determinists)—are really the same. Both seek to cure and would rather eradicate than accept (cf. Irvine 1990:257).

What both sides need to understand is that although a wrong body discourse may lead to a cure for some, it also constructs gender diversity as pathology and not everyone wants to be cured. For many, "There is something about being both male and female, about having an entry into both worlds. Contrary to some psychiatric tenets, half and halfs are not suffering from a confusion of sexual identity, or even from a confusion of gender. What we are suffering from is an absolute despot duality that says we are able to be only one or the other. It claims that human nature is limited and cannot evolve into something better. But I, like other queer people, am two in one body, both male and female" (Anzaldúa 1987:19).

For individuals who conceive of themselves as men with vaginas or as female-bodied men, or even as transsexuals or transgendered, it is normalcy not pathology that leads them to reject the surgeon's knife. The same holds true for individuals who have sex reassignment surgery.

In order to move beyond the dominant discourses we must ask why critics keep turning to "medical discourses for specificity and distinction, [only] to find, instead a blurring of categories and boundaries?" (Garber 1989:152). Perhaps it is because they have neglected to consult the individuals about whom the discourses are ostensibly written. But the discourses are not really about transsexuals and transvestites. They are about the beliefs of doctors, clinicians, and society concerning what it is to be male or female, transvestite and/or transsexual, neither/nor as well as both/and.

CHAPTER 9

Queering the Binaries: Transsituated Identities, Bodies, and Sexualities

How can you be rigidly "oriented" toward something that is
amorphous, shifting, fluid, tricky, elusive?
—Scott 1997:66

"If I identify as an FTM, and if I have sex with a gay man who identifies as a woman, are we a straight couple?" asks Jack Hyde. For most people the answer to that question would be yes. But such a response would be superficial and limited to bodily configurations (i.e., a female-bodied person paired with a male-bodied person) and leave out the dynamics of trans-subjectivity. The "ontological premise" (Mageo 1995:284) of such a response is based on biological determinism. Transpeople and people with nonheterosexual identities queer the Western binaries of body-equals-sex-equals-gender-equals-identity as well as the binary of heterosexual and homosexual.

Jack's query was meant to bring into question these very binarisms. I have known Jack for more than a decade and have seen him shift from stone butch to FTM transsexual to transgender to amorphous shape-shifter to something else. Although he prefers to be referred to with male pronouns, he is also comfortable with female ones. In the final analysis, Jack is what Jack chooses to be, whenever and however he chooses.

If, as Steele asserts, "human sexuality is constructed" (1996:167), then construction sites that are left out of the picture or constructed as nonexistent are those of transbodies, transsexualities, and transidentities. This chapter will explore further the terrain of queering the binaries within transsituated identities, bodies, and sexualities. By "queering the binaries," I mean that they are made peculiar, seem bizarre, and spoil the effectiveness of categories.

Traditionally, both the homogeneous portrait and the etiological constructs were a moral discourse that proscribed and, too frequently still proscribes, how transpeople were and are to identify (including their personal histories) and how they are supposed to feel (past and present) and behave (past, present, and future).[1] Although nineteenth-century sexologists were concerned more with "aberrant" females than with males, once the "transsexual" category was established their vision became almost myopic, to the near-exclusion of female-bodied people.[2]

The Etiological Construction of FTMs and Transmen

Transsexuals make a big scrap heap out of everybody's tidy life. If they can file us some place they are happy, but when they can't they are tormented.
—Vern, cited in Martin 1992:104

Beginning with the first literature on transsexuals, specific characteristics, behaviors, identities, and sexualities have been attributed to them. All individuals were to have fit within these attributions, which became diagnostic criteria and were considered the etiological factors in the diagnosis of "true" transsexualism.[3] FTMs and transmen, if included at all, classically were described as having masculine behaviors and interests by age three or four. They were said to possess no femininity, be physically active and aggressive, and play only with boys' toys. They were described as inventing a male name by the age of seven or eight and openly stating a desire to be a boy and then a man. By adolescence they were insisting on being treated as, and dressing as, boys. They hated the onset of puberty, especially the development of breasts and menses. By adulthood they were passing as and being accepted as men and were employed only in masculine occupations. Furthermore, as children they were not considered beautiful or feminine by their parents. The mother was distant and depressed, and the father was masculine but unsupportive of the mother's depression. He did not encourage the child's femininity, whereas both parents encouraged the child's masculinity. FTMs and transmen were said to be attracted only to feminine, nonhomosexual females (Stoller 1972:48, 1973:386, 1975:223–27; see also Benjamin 1964, 1969; Ehrhardt, Grisanti, and McCauley 1979; Lothstein 1983; Money and Brennan 1968; Pauly 1974a, 1974b).

Clear distinctions were made between lesbians, masculine women, and FTMs and transmen (Ehrhardt, Grisanti, and McCauley 1979; Lothstein 1983; Money and Brennan 1968; Pauly 1974a, 1974b; Stoller 1972, 1973). Lesbians desired other lesbians, masculine women desired heterosexual men, and transmen/FTMs desired heterosexual women. FTMs/transmen avoided being touched or touching their own genitalia, whereas masculine women and lesbians did not (Pauly 1969:68, 76, 82).[4] Finally, transmen/FTMs wanted to be husbands and fathers but lesbians and masculine women did not (Lothstein 1983:27).

Regardless of their expressed desires, transgendered people in general—transsexuals specifically—were denied sexuality, and, by implication, so were their partners (cf. Whittle 1996:207). Medico-psychological practitioners insisted that "true transsexuals" had low libidos, were asexual or autoerotic, or were only able to engage in sexual relationships (homosexual or heterosexual) by using intense fantasies of themselves as women (if MTFs/transwomen) or as men (if FTMs/transmen).[5] They were also said to feel disgust and abhorrence for their sex organs (Benjamin 1977[1966]:27, 36).

Although many practitioners still maintain that is the case, by the late 1970s some, not all, were becoming aware that transpeople are sexual beings. Feinbloom, for example, recognized that MTFs not only identified as heterosexuals but also as bisexuals and as lesbians (1976:31). Stone, too, noted with some irony that "Benjamin's subjects did not talk about any erotic sense of their own bodies. Consequently nobody else who came to the clinics did either" (1991:291).[6] Benjamin's book 1977[1966] became the bible of transbehavioral characteristics. All subsequent published works by practitioners perpetuated the stereotype of transsexuals as nonsexual or as disgusted by sex and genitalia.

Some, if not most, transsexuals have been complicit in denying their sexuality. Most intentionally presented themselves to practitioners as if they fulfilled all the stereotypes in order to gain the services the clinics provided (Bolin 1988:64–65; see also Walworth 1997). As early as 1975, Stoller was aware of that complicity and noted, "Those of us faced with the task of diagnosing transsexualism have an additional burden these days, for most patients requesting 'sex change' are in complete command of the literature and know the answers before the questions are asked" (248). By the 1980s most practitioners assumed that all transsexuals "distort their autobiographies" and "tend to be less than honest about their personal histories" (Lothstein 1983:46, 160). Nonetheless, they continue to use the same diagnostic criteria.

Although only a few gender identity clinics still exist, some clinics and numerous private practitioners continue to withhold hormones and deny surgeries if a transperson identifies as gay or lesbian (pre- and post-transition); is incapable or unwilling to pass as "normal" and nontransgendered; refuses to behave or dress in stereotypical ways; and does not want complete sex reassignment or states they want some surgical procedures but not all (Denny 1996:40).[7]

Transsubjectivities

What is oppressive in our society is the linking of biological sex
(female or male) to gender identity (woman or man).
—MacGowan 1992:318

As a "dynamic map of power" the moral discourses both constitute and erase, deploy and paralyze transsituated identities, bodies, and sexualities (Butler 1993:117). Based on limited case studies, practitioners, as gatekeepers, determined what constituted a "true transsexual." Transsubjectivities were defined and subject to control by moral discourses. Gatekeepers elevated and regulated transidentities (cf. Butler 1993:117), forcing those who did not and could not take those positions to seek elsewhere. "My pretransition 'presentation' was pretty feminine," observes Arthur Freeheart. "My life-style, as full-time parent, was pretty 'female.' All the gender professionals I've dealt with have said they never met an FTM like me. So they were rather reluctant to take me seriously or think that I had much of a chance of being perceived as male. My struggle to get hormonal and surgical alterations was made much more difficult by that." Despite his difficulties with clinicians, Arthur now successfully lives as a man.

Both FTMs/transmen and MTFs/transwomen were treated similarly. At another clinic, Margaux was told that she would "have trouble passing" and was rejected as a candidate for hormones but the clinicians would help her accept herself as a homosexual. When she protested that she was not a homosexual she was told, "We're not here to negotiate! You've heard our terms. Take them or leave them" (cited in Denny 1992a:15). Identities framed within a medicalized border effectively negated individual identity and erased those whose histories, identities, bodies, and sexualities did not fit within the criterial boundaries of "true transsexual."

Furthermore, identity as a transperson was to be paralyzed and erased, left in an operating room, whereupon, following recovery, a "new man" or "new woman" was to emerge. "That treatment [hormones and surgeries] is supposed to make us feel normal. We are not supposed to want attention as transsexuals; we are supposed to want to fit in as 'normal' men. We are supposed to pretend we never spent fifteen, twenty, thirty, forty plus years in female bodies, pretend that the vestigial female parts some of us never lose were never there. In short, in order to be a good—or successful—transsexual person, one is not supposed to be a transsexual person at all" (Green 1996:7). Consequently, a "true" transidentity was constituted and deployed as legitimate only if the individual either denied they had ever been a transsexual or had ever identified as such—one had to become normal (i.e., heterosexual and identify solely as a male/man or a female/woman).

Although normal should be in the eye of the beholder, frequently it is a moral command: "Normal does not mean what people do, on the average, but what they ought to do" (Money 1986:4). Medico-psychological practitioners and the literature they generated were (and still are to a large extent) moral discourses with "ethical prescriptions" that tell transsexuals how they should behave in order to receive the diagnosis of transsexual (Mageo 1995:285).

What the clinicians fail to realize is that "identifications are multiple and contestatory" (Butler 1993:99). Butler discusses the power positions that disallow non-normal (i.e., nonheterosexual) identities and identifications. From a legal standpoint (and possibly from her philosophical perspective) such positions are illegitimate. In everyday life, however, the non-normal occurs with great frequency. Although those in positions of power continually try to erase subject-positions outside of what is viewed as culturally legitimate (and consequently normal and viable), people who live those subject-positions continue to attempt to articulate them. As they find their tongues, they subvert the concept of identity and the binary construction of bodies, sexes, genders, and sexualities.

Identities Subversive

I'm sort of fluid, and it varies with who I'm with.
—Vern, cited in Martin 1992:105

Although the moral discourses perpetuated by the medico-psychological practitioners have attempted to prevent the articulation of transidentities outside their prescribed borders, transpeople have persisted. Unable to articulate or "expunge the censured dimension of the sel[ves] from 'their' behavior[s]" (Mageo 1995:291) or from the realities of their lives, transpeople have begun to develop other discourses. "For the record," says Del La Grace Volcano, "I see myself as FTM. 'Inter' rather than 'trans' sexual. Though this hardly matters in terms of how I am treated. I see myself as BOTH (male and female) rather than NEITHER (male nor female). In my case, the two add up to something non-numerical. I am simply gender-variant."

Transidentity in some cases is "an identity distinct from male and female—a combination of the two *plus* everything excluded by them" (Roscoe 1995:449, emphasis in the original). Transgender and transsexual are genders that exist outside the binary of two. That has become more evident since more and more individuals are retaining the labels, and subsequently the identities, of transpeople, however they may define themselves. Grace (1996:60) has said, "I call myself a 'hermaphrodyke' for now, which I like to think of as my own custom gender blend. . . . I see myself as BOTH male and female; 'either/or' rather than 'neither/nor.'" And, as I have observed to someone asking about how I define myself,

> I don't know that I've ever really felt like a man. I'm not even sure I, as a transperson can feel that way. I [did] not have most, if any, of the experiences that boys growing into manhood have. I am most comfortable and really only able to present to the world as a man. I am not comfortable, although I'm probably capable of, presenting as androgynous. It was, and still is, impossible for me to present as a woman. I do not identify as a man. I identify as an "other," as a transman. What I've come to realize over the years is that regardless of what others think of me, whether I take hormones or not, I am what I am. For appearances sake, I am a man. But I'm not an ordinary man. Never could be and never will be.

What we both have expressed is the awareness that we are not like other men. Many transpeople acknowledge that their histories, identities, bodies, and sexualities are different from nontransgendered men and women. Their partners also recognize the difference.

> I don't find all FTMs attractive. There are those still stuck in a state of arrested penis envy—you know, "If I just had a penis, I'd be a real man and all my problems would be over." Those guys are defining themselves and their masculinity from the outside in—they're letting the outside world be their judges. What I find incredibly attractive and sexy are those FTMs who have defined themselves from the inside out. They've integrated into their personalities everything about themselves that "fits" them and the hell with what *you* think. To me, these guys are the essence of masculinity. (Bonnie C.)
>
> I'm attracted to the yin/yangness—polarity is sexy to me. TSmen have an otherness, a differentness, that I like. (Amy H.)

Transsituated identities disrupt the binary notions of male and female as opposites.

> I certainly don't fit the "man trapped in a woman's body" or any other stereotyped idea of what a "real transsexual" is like. I'd be just as bored with being a manly man all the time as I was being a girly girl. Truthfully

I look much better in hot pink sheer tops now than I did as a girly girl. (Joshua Goldberg)

I don't force myself to identify with one or the other but explore both my male and my female sides. It is okay to feel/be male with a feminine side. I think that what makes me/us so special is that we are aware of both sides of our persona and we can express them. (Chris K.)

Disruption occurs because an individual is capable of articulating an identity founded upon both/and as well as neither/nor and either/or.

Bodies Subversive

Gender *per se* is not the problem.
—MacGowan 1992:318

For convenience sake, most transpeople present to the world as men or women. Although passing as nontransgendered is almost always a reflection of identity, it is also safer than presenting as gender-ambiguous or androgynous. After all, "fitting in is less work than dealing with the fallout from not fitting in" (Vern, cited in Martin 1992:109). Consequently, passing also includes being erased as transgendered. "For transsexual men who self-identify solidly and nonproblematically as men, and especially if they don't self-identify as FTMs or as trans," C. Jacob Hale observes, "I would guess that there's no sense of erasure in 'passing' as a non-ts man, indeed that they would not think of it as 'passing' at all but rather just showing the world who they really are. That's not me, though."

However much they may pass, transpeople, whether they identify as trans or not, are always aware of their transness—an awareness situated in their bodies.[8] "I cannot say that I was a man trapped in a female body. I can only say that I was a male spirit alive in a female body, and I chose to bring that body in line with my spirit, and to live the rest of my life as a man" (Green 1996:18). Transpeople, especially those who take hormones and have had surgeries, are aware that their bodies are or have been transsexed or reconstructed. As I have written to a correspondent,

At one point, I recall thinking seriously about buying what was then a popular slogan t-shirt for pregnant women. It read, "under construction" with an arrow pointing downward. I was entering the first-stage of a three- to four-stage groin-flap phalloplasty. My body, at least my genitalia, at that time, was under construction. Prior to that surgery I had a bilateral mastectomy to remove my breasts. I had my chest reconstructed into a more male-appearing one.

Surgeries allowed me to reconstruct my body, just as bodybuilding allows me to construct my body. Surgeries allowed removal of parts or the addition of parts. Bodybuilding is a similar removal and addition. Removal of fat, addition of muscle. The point is my body has been constructed to better suit my self-image as a man.

According to Butler, "Thinking the body constructed demands a rethinking of the meaning of construction itself" (1993:xi). Technology, whether surgical or hormonal, has enabled transpeople "to exert control over the body" (Boddy 1995:135) and to reconstruct them, albeit within the parameters maintained by medico-psychological practitioners. "I think FTMs who do hormones and, perhaps, surgical alterations end up with inter-sexed bodies," Arthur Freeheart has said, "whether they want to or not. But if you SAY you want an intersexed body, it's next to impossible to get professional support and services."

Many, if not all, practitioners will refuse to perform surgeries on anyone who does not declare a desire for all the procedures. In practice, many transpeople, especially FTMs and transmen, do not return for all of the surgeries deemed necessary for complete sex reassignment. "The phalloplasty was not successful," Jack Watson reports, "and I did not proceed past the first stage. This left me with a pedicle flap penis that has no sensation and is non-erectile, that is, it is a nonfunctioning penis (although it does function as a pants-filler). Over the years I've thought about having it removed, but it has become a part of me." Or people stop short of having surgeries at all. "I'm a guy without a dick," Mitch G. says. "I have a vagina. That's my reality. I don't think anyone could truly relate to me as a woman even seeing me naked anyway. I don't look like a woman and I don't act like a woman."

The body is the site on which individuals "erect a reliable sense of self" (Boddy 1995:135). Those who choose nonsurgical or limited surgery routes use their sense of self, their experiences, and their bodies to determine what is normal rather than the senses of self, the experiences, and the bodies of nontransgendered people (cf. Green 1996:12).

Nontransgendered people can and do have transsituated perspectives when it comes to the bodies of their partners.

My partner has a dick. He isn't "missing" anything—he has a complete, wonderful, sexy body. (Bonnie C.)

I am very comfortable with his body. Sometimes I forget that male bodies can look any other way. (Amy C.)

Prior to his having surgery I had no problem with him having breasts.

After surgery I realized that I had a veil in my mind, it acted as a filter. After surgery the filter was no longer necessary. His chest was now in reality what it had always been in my head. (Kristen K.)

Many transpeople and many of their partners reconstruct transbodies as both normal and different. To acknowledge transbodies as normal is a disruption of the binary body-equals-sex.[9] What is disrupting is the pairing of opposite-sexed parts in one body. A normal transbody may well have both a penis and breasts. Another normal transbody will bear the marks from chest surgery, and a penis may not be present but an enlarged clitoris (probably renamed) may be.[10] A woman, that is, can be other than female-bodied and a man can be other than male-bodied. "I feel that I have a great deal of choice in how I express my gender and that I am blessed rather than cursed," observes Del La Grace Volcano.

Another disruption occurs in the binary of feminine and masculine. "I can't identify with the culturally normative notions of male or female," says Justin M. "But I id[entify] as male, because to me there is a big difference between being considered female with a strong masculine side and being considered male with a strong feminine side. I am not a butch woman. I am a feminine gay man." Contrary to the medico-psychological practitioners (and many others within mainstream Western society), these bodies (and experiences and identities) are not wrong. They are different (cf. Green 1997:18).[11]

Subversive Sexual Desires

> The body's structure, physiology, and functioning do not directly or simply determine the configuration or meaning of sexuality.
> —Vance 1989:7–8

Because transsituated identities and bodies are different, sexual desires likewise defy the binary of heterosexual and homosexual and play havoc with the concept of bisexual. These "categories and terms always assume a nontransgendered paradigm—nontrangendered people's subjectivities and embodiments are always the reference points for these categories" (Hale 1997b:39). By attempting to fit everyone into a nontransgendered paradigm, medico-psychological practitioners have attempted to desexualize transpeople.

Within the narratives made available through the medico-psychological literature (and, for that matter, through published autobiographies), both MTF and FTM transsexuals are disgusted by and hate their genitalia, and, by implication, sexual acts of any kind are considered equally disgusting and abhorrent. Some theorists go beyond making implications and state emphatically that "disgusted by their genitals, transsexuals masturbate rarely and indulge less in sexual relations with others" (Stoller 1975:173; see also Pauly 1974:501).[12] As Arthur Freeheart says, "Sexuality is a subject that many gender professionals have problems with. It seems that having a sex life and/or being able to take pleasure in your own sexual feelings 'presurgery' is either seen as a 'cure' for gender discomfort or proof that you must not have enough body hate and body repulsion to be transsexual."

In fact, most clinicians have been dumbfounded by learning of transpeople using genitalia for sexual reproduction. Regarding an FTM/transman, Lothstein stated incredulously, "What was remarkable was that Barbara was willing to allow herself to be penetrated, to enact the role of a woman and have sex with a man" (1983:103).[13] Many would be even more astounded by those who derive pleasure from genitalia, including vaginal penetration.

> I am one of those who "enjoy my cunt" but still see myself as male. I do not identify as a lesbian or a dyke. I am a sexual being and will be sexual with the organs I have. (Rich)

> I'll use the equipment I've got. To me, that's a sign of strength, of my manhood. (Mark Craig)

In most of the literature, FTMs/transmen are allowed sexuality, albeit a very limited one in which a heterosexual paradigm prevails. They supposedly are attracted only to "feminine, heterosexual women with no homosexual drives visible or present in history, women who desire pregnancy and motherhood, and who like male bodies" (Stoller 1975:224; see also Pauly 1969:72).

> After I fell in love with Jack I was confused for about a week. Then I decided I am a dyke in love with an FTM. I didn't fall in love with a gender, but with a person. (Kristen K.)

> Het[erosexual], bi[sexual], lesbian don't work. Nothing mainstream does. I'm an "other" lover. (Bonnie C.)

Just as medico-psychological practitioners assume that FTMs/transmen are attracted only to heterosexual, feminine women, they also assume that those women also identify as heterosexual.[14] It is possible that like FTMs/transmen themselves, their partners are complicit in perpetuating such beliefs.

Nonetheless, although it has recognized that transmen and FTMs have partners, most of the literature has denied them actual physical sexuality.

Stoller asserts that FTMs/transmen are "cut off" from sexual pleasure because masturbation makes the individual aware "of the femaleness of the genitals, no matter how powerful the fantasies of being a male." Relations with women are also viewed as undesirable because only an abnormal (i.e., a lesbian) would want to touch a transman's/FTM's genitals. A heterosexual ("normal") woman would not want to do so and "would not be permitted to do so anyway" (Stoller 1973:387). Pauly, too, maintains, "Because they do not wish to be exposed as females, they avoid genital contact themselves. Their satisfaction comes in being accepted as men, and even after prolonged, intimate contact, their female partners are not aware of their *true* identities" (1969:86, emphasis added; see also Stoller 1972:48).[15]

"When I was being seen as a butch dyke I was stone in that the only contact my partners had with my genitalia was through the transference of pleasure my dildo could convey," says Spencer Bergstedt. "However, once I came out as male and my then-partner acknowledged that she saw me as male, it became much easier for me to allow myself the pleasure of relating to my genitalia." Counter to Stoller's claim that FTMs/transmen "make every effort to keep [their female bodies] secret" (1973:387), Kristen K. reports, "I go down on both cocks. I can suck his dick [dildo] off or I can suck off what medically would be his clit, but I see both of them as cocks."

According to the literature, both FTMs/transmen and MTFs/transwomen are reported to deny any homosexuality and to avoid contact with homosexuals because if homosexuals desire transsexuals they are announcing a preference for same-sexed (and concomitantly same-gendered) bodies. Such desire is viewed as a threat to the transsexuals' body image (Benjamin 1977[1966]:34; Stoller 1975:224). "With my current partner, the changes in my body due to the T[estosterone]—facial and body hair, chest surgery, etc.—have been instrumental to me in feeling that she sees me as a man rather than as the butch dyke she used to know," Bergstedt notes. "The fact that my dick has grown (and for me, I use the terms dick, cock, neo-phallus—I don't call it a clit—but that's my choice—others choose differently) is more like a bonus."

Many FTMs and transmen before identifying as a transperson have (or have had) relationships with lesbian women. Some of these relationships survive the identity transition from butch dyke to transman/FTM. The female partners may or may not shift their identity from lesbian to straight or bisexual or queer woman.[16]

> I think of myself as more or less a dyke. But the word lesbian now seems too confining. Mostly I just think of myself as queer. Whatever I am, I ain't straight. (Amy H.)

I have been a queer/lesbian. I'm viewed as heterosexual when I go out in the world, but I have always identified as queer. (Allie H.)

Not only do transmen and FTMs have relationships with lesbian-iden-tified women but they also do so with men. Most clinicians remained un-aware of this, however, until the late 1980s. For example, Stoller declares that FTMs/transmen are "repelled by the idea of sexual relations with males" (1973:386), and Feinbloom hesitantly states, "I am unaware of any female to male transsexuals who consider the possibility of male homo-sexuality" (1976:31).

I look for men who I describe as fluid in their sexual orientation. The men I've had the most fun with are the men for whom their identity, their orientation, is not an issue. (Harrison, cited in Nataf 1996:33)

If a guy wants to be with me because he likes my looks *and* my parts, then why should it bother me? I also don't think that it makes a guy "ungay" because he likes being with one of us. Attraction is on many levels with genitals being only one of those. (Mitch G.)

Men, whether they identify as straight, gay, or bisexual, are attracted to FTMs/transmen and have sexual relations with them.[17]

I met a handsome man who I wanted to get to know. Then I was told that he is not just a man but an FTM man. He is still the same attractive and quality person I met. (Gabriel M.)

The hot, sexy wetness when my FTM partner is turned on makes my knees weak (and other things strong)! I also love to get fucked once in awhile, but I'm not too fussy about what device is used. Feels the same either way. (Erik K.)

Transpeople also have sexual relationships with other transpeople.

I am a transman (FTM) in a relationship with another transman. I am an FTM who has not, as yet, had surgery. [My lover] sees past what I see in the mirror every day. We utilize every body part, nothing is off limits. We are two men exploring all the possibilities that we can with each other. (Anderson 1997:23)

What is it when a transfag and a transdyke get together and make magic together with their bodies and hearts? It's beauty and delight and peace-fulness and excitement and. . . . Whatever else it is, it isn't lesbian or gay or bisexual or heterosexual, because all of those miss the crucial fact that his transsexuality and queerness, her transsexuality and queerness, are a major part of what gets them together in the first place and keeps it fun and exciting and hot and lets it pass into beauty. (C. Jacob Hale)

Contrary to Califia's view (1997:217), such relationships are not strategies for avoiding the problems inherent in having relationships with nontranspeople, nor do they make passing more problematic. They are one of the multiple ways in which transpeople have relationships.

> With a heterosexual man I can be their best nightmare fantasy in the shape of a boy hustler. With a heterosexual woman I can be a pretty hetero male; or if I perceive her as a fag hag, I can be a faggot with bi tendencies. With a lesbian top femme I can be a high heel worshipping boy bottom or a third sex butch, a lesbian man. With a gay man I can be a cock worshipping catamite or a fisting top. With gender ambiguous bi men and women and sexually ambiguous transgendered people maybe I can just be myself. (Nataf 1996:32)

These strategies or constructions are "queer gender play," within which the people involved commit to what Hale refers to as a "recoding":

> Genitals, sex toys, voices, body shapes, and much more, are recoded in ways fairly commonly understood within these worlds, and specific recodings, even ones unusual within these worlds, are fairly easily communicated between two sex partners. This kind of recoding only works when the recoding of a specific element of gender categorization is done in concert with recodings of other specific elements of gender categorization in such a way as to produce an internally consistent whole, understood and allowed—not disrupted—by both partners.
>
>   As descriptive truth, then, this view works by creating a culture of two (or more) in which the elements of the dominant cultural gender categorizations are not ignored but reorganized. (1995:16)

Transsexualities are grounded within a paradigm that uses transsituated language to express multiple ways of being identified, of being embodied, and of being sexual.

Transsituated Strategic Discourse

We can't be whole, balanced people if we are living a lie.
—Green 1994b:8

Transpeople's acknowledgment of identities, bodies, and sexualities as different rather than wrong is the creation of strategic discourse. Those take what was defined as wrong, whether bodies, identities, or sexual desires, and reframe them as different based on experience. The reframing is a subversion of the dominant paradigm and its discourses. Part of the reframing occurs in the renaming of body parts, or in framing them with mental veils, or in having body parts reconstructed to match mental images.

My use of the term *reconstructed* is deliberate. Transpeople both construct and reconstruct their bodies, identities, and sexualities. Through medical interventions body parts are added on (e.g., breast implants and some genitoplastic procedures) and subtracted or relocated/repositioned (e.g., vaginoplasties [vaginal reconstructions], chest constructions, and other genitoplastic procedures). But long before medical interventions may occur most transpeople have constructed and reconstructed their bodies in many different ways. For some, the construction is a process of disassociation and disconnection. That construction has been viewed by medico-psychological practitioners as a mentally disordered process labeled *gender dysphoria,* although more accurate terms would be *body dysphoria* or *body-part dysphoria.* These constructions and reconstructions, at least the stated desire for them, are made the chief criteria for diagnosis as a transsexual. Most medico-psychological practitioners still view transpeople as needing, and being obsessed with, surgical interventions.

"The Problem—No Penis"

The problem as stated in the subheading—and the attitudes the statement reveals—infuriates many FTMs and transmen.[18] For them, not having a penis is not a problem because what they do have, no matter how configured, are fully functional genitalia that give them and their partners great pleasure. The problem is the attitude that without surgically constructed penises they are not real men or even able to be categorized as such. The prevailing attitude (and what constitutes a further problem) is the reduction of maleness to specific genitalia (Rubin 1996:175). "One of the things that was really hard for me," recalls C. Jacob Hale, "was that I knew I didn't fit classical definitions of 'transsexual' and I didn't think I had much interest in genital surgery. What helped me a lot was to stop asking 'What am I?' and to start asking instead, 'What changes do I need to make to be a happier person?' For me, that included testosterone and elective breast removal/chest reconstruction."

Transmen and FTMs (as well as the transwomen and MTFs who also see the surgical imperative as a problem) realize that reconstructing their bodies is not what makes them a whole person. For them, all things carry equal value: body, identity (spiritual, as well as personal and social), and sexuality. That is the reconstruction—reassociation and reconnection with the body—whereby a transperson becomes a whole person.

Medico-psychological literature is inevitably presented with practitioners' subjective perspective but is presented as objective, leaving false impressions of what transpeople were or could be or want to be. So long as medico-psychological practitioners control the discourses about transsubjectivity, and as long as transsexuals remain complicit, the binaries remain seemingly intact. Once transpeople begin articulating their own transsubjectivities, however, new discourse, and thus the expansion of binaries, can begin.

Transsituated discourses are produced by transpeople whose identities, bodies, and sexual desires fall outside of the dominant discourses and even outside of the available lesbian and gay discourses. Available discourses are inadequate because they "cannot communicate about our gendered sexual desires and practices" (Hale 1996:118n8). "Maybe it's so far beyond our words that we don't know how to talk about it," Hale says. "Maybe male and female provide the parameters or limits or constraints, embedded as male and female are in our bodies and subjectivities. But maybe the core is that our distance from male and female, painful and alienating though our distance can be at times, lets us get at something more bound up in being human, lets us touch the purely human places in one another in ways specific to our transness."

Transsituated discourses reverse ontological premises. While such pre-mises try through moral discourse to "condemn alternative experience to obscurity" (Mageo 1996:291), transsituated discourses begin the process of reordering the order of things (Foucault 1970). By articulating their experiences and identities, by affirming their bodies as their own and as viable, and by revealing their sexualities, transpeople and their partners disallow themselves "to be distorted," "consigned to silence," or prejudi-cially interpreted. "It's not the act or the partner, it's the identity," says Mike Hernandez. "For instance, sex involving a penis penetrating a vagina is not determinate of orientation. If it's a straight man and woman and that's how they identify, it's het[erosexual] sex. If the penis happens to be a dildo and the parties happen to be dykes, it's lesbian sex. If it's a gay man and a transfag, it's gay sex. If it's a fag and a dyke, it's queer sex."

Everyone has an identity and a body and—to paraphrase Erchak (1992:55)—anyone is sexy. The possibilities open in unexpected and mul-tiple ways. For many within the mainstream of society, the reordering of things and the expression of that reordering in transsituated discourses are threatening and subversive. Nonetheless, transsituated identities, bod-ies, and sexual desires exist and will continue to queer the binaries.

CHAPTER 10

Making the Invisible Visible

Theory cannot ignore the burden of invisibility and enforced silence
female transgendered persons face.
—Wieringa and Blackwood 1999:25

We are invisible because we are presumed not to exist.
—Green 1994b:8

Since the 1960s, particularly since 1995, female-bodied transpeople have
become somewhat more visible. One indication is the publication of books
focused on FTMs and transmen: Cameron's (1996) book of photographs;
three British autobiographies (Hewitt 1996; Rees 1996; Thompson 1995);
two biographies, one on Billy Tipton (Middlebrook 1998) and the other
on Brandon Teena (Jones 1996); a sociological study (Devor 1997); and
even a novel whose main character is a FTM/transman (Tremain 1992).
In addition, there is a volume edited by More and Whittle (1999) and also
Rubin (1999).[1]

The publication of these books would have been unfathomable in the
1960s. Before 1991 only one autobiography existed on the topic (Martino
1977), in addition to two biographies (Hodgkinson 1989; Sullivan 1990a)
and one psychological study (Lothstein 1983). A paradigm shift has occurred, however (Denny 1995, 1997; see also Boswell 1998). The power
and self-determination of the transgendered community has increased as
the authority of medico-psychological practitioners has become more
questionable and their ability to control lives has waned.

The forces that have resulted in the shift are difficult, if not impossible,
to sort out. Nonetheless, one of primary ones must be the increase in networking among transpeople. Networking has resulted in increasing numbers of transmen and FTMs coming out rather than living in isolation.

Because they have begun to come out, support groups, Internet mailing lists, bulletin boards, and chat rooms have formed that connect people all over the world. Newsletters are being published, and educational and political organizations are beginning to coalesce and become increasingly active. Many FTMs and transmen, both individually and collectively, are speaking out about issues that affect them and challenging the prevailing paradigms.

Challenging the Mental Illness Model of Transness

Surgery is not what transsexualism is about.
—Green 1994b:6

In some arenas, however, no paradigm shift is recognizable. There are still practitioners, for example, who refuse to acknowledge, or are even cognizant of, the fact that their power over transsexual lives is waning. A few still consider transpeople to be mentally ill and unstable and in desperate need of intercession that will cure them of their gender disorders. Those who continue to search for a cause in order to cure them do so because they desire to prevent transgendered individuals from occurring (cf. Rubin 1989:304). Fortunately—and increasingly—such people are in the minority, although some still prevail.

During the 1997 meetings of the Harry Benjamin International Gender Dysphoria Association (HBIGDA) in Vancouver, B.C., Stephen Levine, chair of the revisions committee, while discussing the revisions of the standards of care (SOC), repeatedly referred to "suffering" and "afflicted" transsexuals. (Surprisingly, but perhaps merely reflecting FTMs' and transmen's invisibility, after eight drafts the SOC still treats female-bodied transpeople as if they are mirror images of male-bodied transpeople.) Mike Hernandez finally responded by stating, "As a non-suffering FTM, I would like to know who the FTMs were that were consulted for the SOC?" Levine replied that none had been involved. When Hernandez pointed out that representatives from two national organizations (FTM International and the FTM Conference and Education Project) were present and "would be happy to act as consultants," Levine acquiesced and subsequently sent a copy of the revisions to Jamison Green, then the president of FTM International and a recognized leader of FTM communities.

Green sent copies of the revision draft to eight other FTM and transmen, including myself. In the cover letter, dated November 15, 1997, to the committee Levine had stated, "There were several suggestions [concerning a prior draft] that I did not take basically because I did not agree with them," an attitude that did not bode well for suggestions the group might make. Although through no fault of Green's the committee was given only two weeks to reply, it did have a number of concerns: the attitude of the revisions committee chair (Levine); the language of pathology; the trans-sexual-centric nature of the revisions, especially the assumption that all transpeople want genital surgeries; the lack of insight about FTMs and transmen; and, closely related to that point, the lack of distinction between female-bodied and male-bodied transpeople.

The language of pathology is disturbing in several ways. There is an underlying assumption that transpeople are incapable of making informed decisions. Coupled with that, it is condescending to assume that therapists, doctors, and surgeons know what is best for transpeople. For example, draft eight of the SOC states, "The surgeon should be knowledgeable about more than one of the surgical techniques for genital reconstruction so that *the surgeon will be able to choose the ideal technique* for the individual patient's anatomy and medical history" (26, emphasis added). The language of pathology is also revealed in specific terminology: "patients," "gender identity disorders," "gender problem," and "gender dysphoria." For the former, the committee suggested that *patients* be replaced by *clients,* a term of empowerment; instead of the latter terms the committee suggested the unpathological *gender issues* or *gender concerns.*

In a section on "Development of the Nomenclature," the revised SOC includes "transgender" as a term that "arose to denote any person with any type of *gender problem"* (11, emphasis added). In other words, the revision committee now recognized the word *transgender* as a term but misconstrued its meaning and pathologized it as well. There is no acknowledgment that the term arose out of the transcommunity. Furthermore, as Jamison Green stated in his summary of the ad hoc committee's comments, transgender "was adopted as a political term in the mid-1990s to broaden the categories. . . . In addition, for some people, the term transgender also is equated with transcending gender, and is not related to the notion of changing physical bodies or social roles." The most pathologizing is, of course, the insistence that transgendered identities constitute a mental disorder.

The eighth draft of the SOC is no different than past versions that have a surgical focus. The assumption is that all transpeople want genital surgeries. That idea becomes especially blatant when viewed from an FTM/transman's perspective that ties into the observation that the SOC lacks insight into the differences between male-bodied and female-bodied transpeople. The SOC completely disregards the variety of surgical procedures that are available to FTMs and transmen. There is only minor acknowledgment of the necessity for procedures to remove female reproductive organs and for metoidioplasty (also spelled "metaoidioplasty"). That is a significant elision because metoidioplasty (or "clitorial free-up") is the least invasive and least expensive genital surgery for FTMs and transmen.[2] The clitoris is released from its suspensory ligaments, but there is more to the procedure than common phraseology would suggest. Nonetheless, the SOC makes no mention of metoidioplasty as an alternative to invasive and expensive phalloplastic surgeries.

The SOC also advocates a minimum of twelve months of therapy before a transperson can be referred for genital surgery, which, remarkably, includes breast surgery. To be inclusive of FTMs and transmen the SOC should recognize that breasts are not genitalia and that the surgery for their removal is, more accurately, chest reconstruction. Breasts are markers of femaleness, and, depending on size, they are often difficult to hide by binding. They can also impede the safety of FTMs and transmen and put them at risk for violence and other discriminatory acts.

The "real life experience" (RLT), a requirement that an individual live for a minimum of a year in the gender role consistent with their identity, is yet another indication of the SOC's bias. What the drafters of the SOC fail to realize is that the majority of FTMs and transmen have lived as, or been taken as, men for many years before seeing a therapist or seeking medical technologies. Contrary to most MTFs and transwomen, the majority of FTMs and transmen do not need time to make a gender transition. Many have never participated in the female role, and some have done so only minimally. Whatever suffering that may have been experienced has resulted from living a lie by presenting a social identity incongruent with their personal identities. Most only need to adjust to having their social identities recognized by others and thus being in harmony with personal identities.

The ad hoc committee's recommendations were ignored when the ninth draft of the revisions was released to the HBIGDA membership for review. The only change was in the inclusion of metoidioplasty. Furthermore, eligibility requirements were made more stringent. The SOC reads more like requirements than the guidelines they are intended to be. Fortunately, because of the networks that FTMs and transmen have formed, the majority are able to avoid working with providers who use the SOC as a mandate. As a result, they challenge and subvert the transsexual discourses and the medico-psychological practitioners who stand behind them.

Ending Invisibility

I was completely unfamiliar with terms such as "transgendered,"
"transsexual," etc. AND, I thought I was the only one.

—Bobby Gene 1992:49, emphasis in the original

Although their attempt to influence reforms in the SOC revisions was for
naught, transmen and FTMs have taken other significant steps to overcome invisibility. The first concerns the activism of the transcommunity
as a whole. An issue of *Transgender Tapestry*, for example, lists 283 organizations worldwide devoted to transgendered individuals, including ones
in the United States, Canada, Europe, Japan, Australia, New Zealand,
Turkey, Pakistan, Nigeria, and South Africa. Many, but not all, of these
organizations are active in making changes for the betterment of transpeople.

> The transgendered community is viewed . . . as a reflection of the expand-
> ing concerns of the individuals involved who wanted a voice in treatment,
> in defining themselves and in offering activities, conferences, support
> groups and other events to further their interests and needs as a grow-
> ing community. The social construction of identities has become the
> property of a community with a political agenda. . . . Ideally, the interests
> of no single group are privileged and the political focus can be kept on
> common concerns rather than differences. This realignment illustrates
> the shifting identities as part of a strategy for empowerment and extends
> the national level to the local level. (Bolin 1994:465, 471).

Transmen and FTMs have been and are an active part of that community-
building.

One agenda and a strategy for empowerment is reclaiming history. Lou
Sullivan, an FTM who died in 1991, was active in reclaiming the lives of
female-bodied men. He wrote a biography of Jack Garland (née Elvira Virginia Mugarreta, 1869–1936) based on newspaper accounts of Garland's
life (Sullivan 1990a). He also collected references from books, numerous
clippings from California and Wisconsin newspapers (states in which Sullivan lived), and the rare volumes on females who lived as men for all or part
of their lives.[3] It did not matter whether they were described as transvestites,
female husbands, or mannish lesbians. The earliest is dated 1870 and concerns a female who committed suicide dressed in men's clothing ("Suicide
of a Woman"). There are no details of that person's life, but other clippings
Sullivan collected do describe the lives of several individuals after their discovery, for example, Delia Hudson/Frank Dubois, Cora Anderson/Ralph

Kerwineo, James Barry, and Murray Hall. He discussed them as well as many others in a book (Sullivan 1990b) that was, for many transmen and FTMs, the first publication to make them aware of their history.

Transpeople have also begun to object to people who are like themselves yet are considered women and lesbians. In 1993, for example, Candice Brown and Ken Morris began a campaign in Portland, Oregon, to have Alan Hart (née Alberta Hart) recognized as a man. To that end, they formed the Ad Hoc Committee of Transsexuals to Recognize Alan Hart and petitioned Right to Privacy (RTP), a political group, not to name its annual fund-raiser after Hart. In October 1995 committee members, wearing buttons proclaiming HIS NAME WAS ALAN HART, passed out four hundred fliers to those who attended the benefit.

RTP failed to respond to the campaign, but the committee pressed on. In December they requested that transpeople send faxes, e-mail, and letters to RTP's Portland office with the same message as was printed on the buttons. Then, in January 1996 committee members met with representatives of RTP, and Brown and Morris were invited to the RTP board meeting in February. The following month RTP dropped Hart's name and agreed to use that of someone more appropriate for a gay and lesbian organization (chapter 5).

Many FTMs and transmen are also publishing in local and national media and undertaking a great deal of public speaking on behalf of the transcommunity. Most presentations focus on explicating and dispelling myths and generalizations about female-bodied transpeople. It is necessary to demythologize FTMs and transmen and cease dealing in generalities because many, if not most, do not pursue complete sex changes. By doing so they create "intermediate bodies, somewhere between male and female" (Rubin 1992:476).

Yet the majority do not have intermediate gender identities. That idea may result from those who claim trans-status to be a part of their identities. To do so is not to claim an intermediate identity, but it is an acknowledgment of pride in self and origin. Furthermore, the concept of intermediate bodies arises from the concept of the permanence of the body (biological determinism). FTMs and transmen refuse complete sex changes because, as Green has said, "We are aware of the limitations of surgery and aware of our masculinity in a deeper, more spiritual way" (1994a:52). Regardless of how they construct their lives, bodies, genders, and sexual desires, not all female-bodied people identify as women. There is no pretense; they are masculine-identified people in varying degrees, from butch dykes to men.

Another strategy for empowerment is education as manifested in conferences and other networking venues such as the Internet. In August 1995, for example, the first FTM Conference of the Americas was held in San Francisco. When it was being planned, Jamison Green and I felt we would be lucky if a hundred FTMs and transmen attended. Much to our surprise, nearly 320 did so—people in all stages of transition and from all ethnic, racial, and social backgrounds. The beginnings of community and a newfound sense of pride arose from that conference. There have been two more such events since the first and also two others called "True Spirit" that were for anyone who was assigned as a female at birth but identifies as other than female. In addition there have been two FTM/transmen retreats, and many Internet lists, boards, and Web sites have begun. One is specifically for FTMs/transmen who identify as gay or bisexual men; another is solely for discussions about sex and sexual desire and practices; yet another is for those who identify as "just men." Others are broader and cover more general topics.

The most significant result of the conferences and Internet sites is that many FTMs and transmen have learned to put away the shame learned from stigmatization and to claim pride in their identities, no matter how manifested. These actions will result in increased visibility.

FTMs and transmen offer an uncommon perspective on the constructions of sex, gender, masculinity, femininity, maleness, and femaleness. It is unique because they are socialized to be females; their identities, however, no matter how bodies are constructed, are aligned with signs that are culturally symbolic of masculinity and maleness. For many nontransgendered people, those identities are not intelligible. As a result, FTMs and transmen are too frequently stigmatized as pathological beings that have defective gender identities. They have been rendered invisible because of being born with female bodies and thus discounted or ignored as people who have agency and have chosen to live in a variety of ways labeled masculine, man, and male. Anthropological, historical, and transsexual discourses have not discussed them, in part due to the early transsexual discourses and medico-psychological practitioners' insistence that they blend in and become normal. But FTMs and transmen are challenging the dominant discourses and prevailing paradigm by expressing pride in their unique individuality—in being female-bodied yet masculine men in identity and social expression.

Further Excerpts from a Journey

It is one thing to be erased from discourse, and yet another to be present as an abiding falsehood.

—Butler 1991:20

Earlier I outlined the ways in which transsexual discourses and the medico-psychological practitioners provided an etiology for FTMs and transmen. I had some attributes and was devoid of others: I was masculine in both my behaviors and my interests. I was not remotely feminine, nor was I considered so by others. I wasn't considered pretty or beautiful either. I was physically active, but I was not aggressive nor did I play with boys' toys. The former, had I possessed it, my stepfather would have beaten out of me. He did not allow us to play with toys of any kind.

I secretly had a male name for myself long before I was seven. I called myself Jimmy because it sounded somewhat like my given name of Jeannie. I never stated a desire to be a boy, nor did I insist that I would be a man when I was older. To do so would have resulted in severe beatings. Furthermore, I didn't "desire to be" but rather *I was* a boy, if only in my mind.

During adolescence I did not insist on being treated as a boy, although I did dress as one as much as my family would allow. I was not permitted to wear "boys' clothes" to school until my senior year, when girls were allowed to wear pants. When I lived with my mother she was neither distant nor depressed beyond life's usual ups and downs. We, in fact, had a close relationship. Neither of my stepfathers encouraged my masculinity. One tried desperately to make me feminine. I hated puberty, however, and the development of breasts and menses. The latter prompted a suicide attempt at age thirteen.

By adulthood I was being seen as a man by others, but I was not passing as a man, I simply *was* one. In the early years I was seldom employed in male occupations, and since 1979 I haven't been employed at all. I've gone to school and gotten a Ph.D. and been a stay-at-home parent and a house husband. Finally, as I said at the beginning of the book, I am equally attracted to both men and women.

I know few FTMs and/or transmen who fit neatly within these parameters. The fact that many medico-psychological practitioners and the transsexual discourses continue to perpetuate a false etiology is detrimental to the lives of many of us. Had I not known and recognized my truth I might have let not fitting the etiology deter me as it has countless others. It is time to discard these outdated modes of thinking about transmen and FTMs and begin to recognize the multiple ways of identifying oneself as a human being.

Epilogue

Another symbol of identity is the name a person bears.
—Aceves 1974: 126

Seattle: March 1998

We are slowly gathering in the basement of a local restaurant. The room is provided to us as part of the owner's support of the queer community. The walls are painted a stark white, the lighting is tolerable but not overly bright. There are two tables forming a vee, with a number of black padded chairs making an irregular circle in the center of the room. Off to one side is a loveseat with cushions that sink deeply into its framework. The space is not much to look at, but it's free and the attendees are always welcoming.

The space has been used since October 1996 for the twice-monthly meetings of the Spectrum FTM Support Group and the Discussion Group for anyone who was assigned female at birth but has masculine gender expression (we keep trying to come up with an acronym that will encompass this statement but so far to no avail). Both groups were founded by Spencer Bergstedt, Billy Lane, and myself because we perceived the need for a space and times in which the atmosphere was not only sex-positive but also where the focus was not on surgery as the final outcome of our lives.

It is a regularly scheduled support group, but the agenda is being set aside. Earlier in the week, I'd asked Spencer if we could set up a meeting to talk about the names we'd chosen for ourselves. He suggested we have the discussion in lieu of the regular meeting. He sent out a notice telling

everyone on the e-mail list that we were going to talk about names. I sent
another post saying I would read the prologue to my book. People are late
as usual. We start at 7 P.M. We're not sharp about it—depends on whose
around when it's time. We're a pretty laid-back group. Most of us have been
either meeting here or attending Spectrum from the very beginning.

We are a diverse collection of people. Some of us are very masculine
without macho posturings, whereas others of us are more feminine. In
spite of some of our male appearances, none of us act very typical. Our
hairstyles range from buzz cuts to past shoulder length; our clothing styles
go from punk to polo shirts and slacks. Most of us are in one way or another queer-identified. The majority of us are members of the Seattle
Leather Community. Several of us are out as FTMs or transmen. No one
would take us for an average group of men.

In addition to Spencer and me, there is Danny B., Skye Walker, Justin,
and Jackal plus somebody I don't know and don't recognize but whom
Spencer and a couple others seem to know. Yet they seemed perplexed
by her/his presence. About ten minutes after seven Aidan Key and Gauge
McLeod come in together and are followed shortly by Rafe McCoullough.
Eventually there would be thirteen of us.

Spencer reminds everyone what we're doing tonight. He suggests I start.
I say I want to wait because I don't want to have to start over. We talk about
a lot of different things, and eventually Billy and Dan M. come in. Spencer and I agree to start. I say a few words about the book. Only one person doesn't know what it's about. I explain that I start the book with a
prologue on our given names, and I want to end on the names we choose.
I read and at the same time worry about what people think about what
I'm reading. I finish and say again that I want to talk about how and why
we choose the names we have.

Skye suggests that I start, which I do even though I feel like I've told my
naming many times already. "In the old days," I say jokingly, "before there
were support groups like this, a lot of what you heard said you should pick
a name with the same initials. Supposedly it made the change process
easier. So, I sort of followed that, but I changed my last name." I explain
how because of living with stepfathers and my grandparents I had to use
different last names as I was growing up, and I decided I'd had enough
of that and picked my father's name. I had a list of three names I liked
and rejected two of them and chose the most masculine one because I
wanted a name that there was no mistaking for female.

In turn as we go around the room each person talks about their name.
Spencer, Billy, and Rena's first names happened by default. Spencer's was
given to him when an old girlfriend asked if she could call him that. Billy

had been nicknamed by childhood peers. And Rena's had been shortened so there was no confusion between him and his aunt, after whom "she" had been named. Danny, Dan M., Gauge, and I had all picked our last names because of our heritage. Danny also picked his first name because it's what his family would have named him. Rafe, Aidan, Skye, and Justin picked their first names because they liked the sound of them. Jackal's name came from a dream. Spencer, Billy, Skye, and Jackal's names were chosen or given to them while they were still trying to live as women. Kate says she would probably pick Joe or Joseph as a male name, and Rena says he's used the name Rex on occasion.

Surprisingly, with one exception everyone mentions their birth names without hesitation. In fact, we joke about how feminine they were and how foreign they felt to us. Our birth names were Anne, Jennifer, Julie, Joanne, Jeannie, Paula, Pamela, Bonnie, and Beverly (an English translation of the Czechoslovakian "Bjelica"), Robin, Rowena, Ginger, and Marianne. Billy suggests that we'd been given these names because intuitively our parents knew we were not like other girls yet hoped that giving us very feminine names would squelch our masculine tendencies. We all have a hearty laugh about the possibilities. Our laughter is simultaneously an acknowledgment of our given names and a recognition of the empowering nature of renaming.

As with all groups, the focus on the specific topic begins to fade and we talk about other things as the meeting comes to an end. As we say our slow good-byes and begin to drift our separate ways for the evening, I muse on the changes I've seen over the years and the growing kinship of my community. One thing I have learned in my own journey and by observing those of others is that there is but one truth: There are multiple truths. We, as transmen and FTMs, are living our truths.

Doing Fieldwork with a Nonsituated Population

My interest in female gender diversity rather than gender itself developed from what I came to find out through graduate work in anthropology was fieldwork, which I had begun to conduct inadvertently. I had begun in 1983 with a support group for transpeople in Seattle, Washington, which I initially attended because I wanted to meet and be with others like myself. Like most researchers, my initial focus was on males who either identified as transvestites or as MTFs. Nonetheless, because my fieldwork involved contact with both male-bodied and female-bodied individuals it was not long before I realized there still were few support resources for female-to-male transsexuals and no support resources for female transvestites, nor was there much literature about them.

Beginning in 1990 I began my research concerning female-to-male transpeople and since then have made numerous contacts throughout the world. The transcommunity can only be loosely described as a community (Cromwell 1995c) in that there is no single locale where individuals live, work, or socialize. Gathering data is also a loosely organized endeavor. Even though transpeople do not live together in socially isolated enclaves, many do gather for support groups, social events, and national conferences. I have attended support groups in San Francisco and Seattle and gone to conferences in a number of cities. Furthermore, I have corresponded via mail and e-mail with individuals who reside in countries throughout the world, including Finland, South Africa, Great Britain, Germany, France, Australia, New Zealand, Japan, Canada, Mexico, and Brazil as well as the United States. Support groups, however, have been the primary gateway for contacting individuals because that is where transpeople meet. Data for this book were gathered through these social contexts as well as through personal contacts.

Support Groups

The word *group* is used here in two senses: as an organized event or meeting and as "an entity that consists of interacting people who are aware of being bound together in terms of mutually linked interests" (Deutsch 1968:265; cited in Brown and Levinson 1979:298; cf. Isaacs 1975:34–36).

I have worked with four distinct groups. The first was composed of two to four co-facilitators (two to three transsexuals, including myself and a transvestite), first-time attendees, regulars, old-timers, and occasionally significant others as well as other supportive and interested persons (i.e., persons not directly connected to a member of the group). This composition of facilitators and attendees is considered an open group, and it meets weekly. Facilitators use the terms *first-time attender, regulars,* and *old-timers* to describe various members' statuses based on attendance within the group context rather then where individuals were or are on the continuum of being transgendered.

The second group was a peer support group for FTMs and transmen that met two times a month and was facilitated by three female-bodied transpeople, including myself. Because the group was only open to FTMs, it constituted a closed group. Given the awareness that partners and significant others who have need for support as well, periodic and informal social gatherings are arranged to meet that need. The second group and its subsidiary meetings were and are sponsored by the Ingersoll Gender Center in Seattle.

The third and fourth groups are also peer groups. Although separated, there is considerable overlap in membership. One is a support group for any person who identifies as FTM or transman, regardless of whether they have begun taking steps toward living as men. The other group, Spectrum, is a discussion group for anyone born or assigned as female but who has a masculine identity. Both groups are sponsored by the FTM Conference and Education Project (FTMCEP). FTMCEP was founded by Spencer Bergstedt, Billy Lane, Sky Renfro, Mike Hernandez, and myself among others in July 1996.

For the open group, the typical pattern of attendance was from first contact to weekly attendance for the first three to six months, to once or twice a month for the next six months to a year, to a visit once or twice a year. A regular would become an old-timer after six months or longer. The attendance pattern for the closed Ingersoll-sponsored FTM group was somewhat different in that most attended for a briefer time, generally only three to six months with occasional rare visits thereafter. Many personal contacts are often maintained indefinitely over the years, however.

The attendance pattern for the FTMCEP groups is different than for the Ingersoll-sponsored groups. More than half of those who attend have been meeting since the groups' inceptions. A few have dropped out completely, and others drop in regularly but do not attend every meeting. A third of the regulars think of each other as friends and family and consider the groups as their primary social network.

For many, a support or discussion group is the first situation in which they have been public about gender issues. Security and confidentiality are priorities. Some in the Ingersoll open group used pseudonyms to protect their identities and were evasive when questioned about their outside lives. Regardless of what group a person attended, first-time attendees reported hearing about the support group in a number of ways: through crisis lines, therapists or physicians, gay newspapers, national transpublications, "the grapevine," and more recently via the Internet. Occasionally, individuals reported having learned about a group through a friend who was attending or who had attended it.

The Ingersoll groups met at the same location year-round, including holidays. The facilitators believed that "consistency [was] vital because sometimes we don't see people for years at a time; but when they do return, we are there for them" (Van Cleve n.d.:1). I discuss Ingersoll's open support group in the past tense because I am no longer involved with it. It has existed since the 1970s, the longest continuous period for such a group to endure in the United States. The second Ingersoll-sponsored group, that devoted to FTMs and transmen, has met sporadically since 1985 and continues to be active.

The open group was divided into three sections: discussion among the group; a check-in period during which everyone was given an opportunity to speak without interruption; and an informal session in which individuals could get together for conversations with others or meet with a facilitator.

The content of discussions and check-in varied, but some subjects were repeated frequently, even weekly. Commonly repeated topics included how to tell family and friends about one's trans-issues; which public restroom to use when "dressed"; first-time cross-dressing experiences; getting caught while being dressed; being stopped for a traffic violation; and purging (e.g., vowing to never dress again and throwing away all feminine apparel and accoutrements). Unlike male-bodied transpeople, FTMs and transmen do not purge, in part because it is legitimate for female-bodied people (trans or otherwise) to wear so-called men's clothing. Consequently, they do not have the feelings of disgust and guilt that many male-bodied individuals feel following episodes of cross-dressing or a compelling need to purge themselves of those feelings. Few female-bodied transpeople consider wearing men's clothing cross-dressing, but most call or refer to wearing women's clothing as "drag."

Both the Ingersoll FTM group and the FTMCEP support group have a different format in that a variety of discussion topics are set up in advance: the social ramifications of transition; external and internalized transphobia and homophobia; body issues and image; sex, sexuality, and dating; coming out and dealing with family, friends, co-workers, and employers; masculinity and femininity; binding, padding, and the effects from (and risks of) taking testosterone; whether to have surgeries and which to have; how to embrace the past; anger management; spirituality; and building community. The FTMCEP group also has a monthly open discussion group. In both groups, however, topic discussions are regularly set aside when an attendee has needs outside the scheduled topic.

The Spectrum group is somewhat different in that its members select one or more topics to discuss at each meeting. Those who suggest the topics then facilitate the meeting. The following are examples of topics:

1. Coming out (or not) to a friend or relative: Aidan spoke about traveling out-of-state to visit his sister. He was making the trip specifically to come out to her but was uncertain about telling her. Although he wanted to do so, he was uncertain about how to go about it as well as the outcome. Concerning the latter, he was afraid she might reject him because she was a born-again Christian. They had always been close, and he tentatively thought it would all be okay.

Aidan was seeking advice on how to tell a loved one and also expressing very real fears of rejection. It is common for transpeople to be disowned by family members as well as friends, either temporarily or permanently. There are a multitude of reasons for wanting to come out to family and friends. One of the primary ones concerns the need for honesty.

2. Negotiating new environments: Les talked about using the men's restroom for the first time. "I was so nervous. But I remember everything you guys talked about and just walked in. It was pretty busy, but I did a quick scan and headed for the nearest empty stall. I closed the door and started taking care of business. At first, even though I knew I shouldn't, I worried that my feet pointing toward the door would expose me. Then this guy came into the stall next to me and sat down. I finished up, went to the sink, washed my hands really quickly, and left without looking around."

It is also common for transmen and FTMs to be anxious about using public facilities. There are several reasons, the foremost of which is that men's restrooms and locker rooms are, initially, unknown territory for most of us. When young we are warned about the sometimes-real dangers of male-only spaces. Although it may be unwarranted, men have a reputation of being immodest, and transmen and FTMs often feel that they will be required to expose themselves.

Sharing stories elicits attention; knowing nods, other gestures, and comments are made to acknowledge similar experiences and feelings. Green has described his feelings after attending his first support group: "After all these years of knowing the truth and trying to avoid it, I was then starting to face a reality that was both exhilarating and terrifying. The men at this meeting were living proof that I could make this transition. And the risks of social and economic loss, the health risks of hormonal effects, and the surgical risks of possible mutilation or even death, while daunting, did not seem so dangerous as a life unfulfilled" (1994b:2). Support groups fulfill several needs among members: They relieve feelings of alienation and isolation by providing a "sense of belongingness" (Isaacs 1975:34); provide role models; teach acceptance; validate transition processes; and confirm identities. Weeks (1980–81) makes similar observations about homosexual subcultures.

Methodology

With rare exceptions (Bolin 1988; Newton 1972), previous studies concerning transpeople have been confined to clinical settings. The difficulty with such studies is that they are conducted in "highly structured and artificial settings which is very little like real life" (Denny 1993a:169). Consequently, the resulting literature is significantly less rooted in everyday experience.

By contrast, my research is conducted through personal surveys and personal narratives in combination with participant observation, both inside and outside support groups and during conferences. Before the interviews and the formal questionnaire, however, and based on observations of people I met at the support group, I designed an anonymous survey to assess female-bodied transpeople's conformity to the homogeneous picture that transsexual discourses had constructed of them. My first hypothesis was that what I observed during support group meetings corresponded with what female-bodied transpeople did on a daily basis. That was confirmed by the anonymous survey results. Respondents did not conform to the transsexual discourses and clinicians' claims about identities, sexual orientations, amounts of surgery, and desire for genital surgery.

Armed with the information garnered from the anonymous survey, I set about interviewing people. Since 1990 I have been interviewing, "hanging out" with, and talking to FTMs and transmen. Open-ended, informal interviews were conducted individually as well as within small groups that range from three to twenty individuals. In addition to telephone interviews, individual and group interviews occurred in private or public locations such as restaurants, hotel rooms and lobbies, individuals' homes, and, on one occasion, in a law office.

Open-ended interviews were conducted through questions around central issues that included identity, sexuality, and embodiment. The interviews ranged in length from fifteen minutes (via long-distance telephone conversations) to two hours (in large groups), but the average was one hour. Furthermore, I socialize with as many individuals as possible on a daily basis during conferences and after support group meetings as well as in other social venues. I am thus able to know them and assess their responses.

In 1991 I began attending conferences held by an umbrella organization, the International Foundation for Gender Education (IFGE). The conferences were held in Denver (1991), Houston (1992), Philadelphia (1993), Portland (1994), Atlanta (1995), Minneapolis (1996), and Long Beach (1997). Between 1991 and 1996 I also participated in four conferences in Atlanta sponsored by the Southern Comfort organization. In 1993 I attended another conference, the Be All Weekend, sponsored by a different organization in Chicago. I also attended, or was a presenter at, each of the FTM Conferences of the Americas (in San Francisco in 1995, Seattle in 1996, and Boston in 1997) as well as the first True Spirit conference in 1997 in Laurel, Maryland. A number of people from more than one of these events have continued to maintain contact with me. Through these means I have conducted several interviews with thirty-two former participants over a number of years. There are primarily three sets of data: informal interviews, formal interviews, and responses to a formal questionnaire. In addition, I have spoken with more than two hundred FTMs and transmen and heard their stories. Therefore, a continuing source of data is ongoing research.

Overview of the Anonymous Survey Results

A total of 105 surveys were returned out of 400 distributed throughout the United States. Two states returned the most surveys: twenty-five were from California and twenty-three came from Washington. Twelve had British postmarks, and one was postmarked from British Columbia. The age of the respondents ranged from eighteen to sixty-eight, with an average age of 35.4. Ethnic and racial identity varied; one person did not reply. The majority of people identified as white/Caucasian ($n = 76$). The remainder identified as Asian ($n = 4$), Latino/Hispanic ($n = 7$), Native American/white ($n = 5$), Native American ($n = 3$), and African American ($n = 2$). One each identified as Asian/white, Pacific Islander/white, African American/Native American, East European Jew, Italian/American, and Jewish. Education levels ranged from the ninth grade to a postgraduate degree, with an average of 15.9 years of schooling; two people did not reply.

Annual household incomes ranged from under $5,000 to $90,000, with an average of $29,000; two people did not indicate their incomes.

All respondents were employed, with the exception of nineteen individuals (student, $n = 11$; disabled, $n = 2$; and unemployed, $n = 6$). People worked in service occupations (bus driver, chef/cook, custodian, firefighter/police officer, mail carrier, or postal clerk [$n = 33$]); as professionals (attorney, psychologist, biologist, professor, nurse, or teacher [$n = 13$]); in technical fields (computer programmer, laboratory technician, engineer, and systems analyst [$n = 14$]); and as skilled and unskilled labor (as a carpenter, pressman, and welder or in odd jobs or shipping and receiving [$n = 10$]). There were also five artists. One person did not reply. Marital and partner status was 58 percent single, including eight individuals who indicated they were divorced.

Respondents were not asked the sex/gender of their partners because at the time the survey was distributed I had only heard of one FTM/transman who had been in a relationship with a man, therefore I erroneously assumed that most relationships would be with females. Even so, I asked about people's sexual identity. Participants were predominantly heterosexual ($n = 59$), however twenty identified as bisexual, thirteen as gay, five as asexual, and four as lesbians; four did not reply.

Formal Interviewee Demographics

Interviewees covered the gamut of transgendered behaviors and life-styles, from occasional transvestism to transsexuals as well as variations between the two. Yet all identified as men. Ethnic and racial diversity was also varied and included white (eighteen), white/Native American (three), Latino (three), African American/Native American (three), Asian American (one), white/Hawaiian (one), and Native American/Latino (one).

Social divisions ranged from lower to upper middle class, and incomes ranged from $9,000 to $80,000 a year. Occupational statuses also varied and included lawyer, paralegal assistant, substance abuse counselor, computer programmer, prison guard, systems analyst, construction worker, cable installer, postal clerk, postal carrier, waiter, technical writer, small business manager, laboratory technician, artist, salesperson, teacher, and social sciences graduate student. Just over half (seventeen) of the interviewees were married or in long-term relationships with either women or men. Sexual orientation also varied; individuals identified as heterosexual, gay, bisexual, or queer. Ages ranged from twenty-three to sixty-eight.

In addition, twenty individuals (eight of whom had been formally interviewed previously) participated via the Internet. Each was asked to supplement the data collected over the Internet with an extensive questionnaire transmitted via electronic mail.

Questionnaire Demographics

Questionnaire participants also covered the gamut of transbehaviors and life-styles, from occasional transvestism to transsexuals as well as variations in between. Ethnic and racial diversity included white ($n = 12$) and one each of the following: African American/Native American, African/European/Native American, Asian/American, Eurasian/white, Hispanic, white/Latino, white/Latino/Native American, and white/Native American. Social class background ranged from self-identified "white trash" to upper class (lower to lower middle, $n = 7$; middle, $n = 7$; and upper middle to upper, $n = 6$). Current social classes included lower to lower middle ($n = 6$); middle ($n = 11$); and one each upper middle and upper class. There was one "no response." Overall there was a decrease in social class, however the lowest echelon rose in status. Average annual income was $26,000, with a range of $4,300 to $60,000. Levels of education ranged from high school/GED to Ph.D.s, with an average of 16.8 years of formal schooling. Occupational statuses included artist, attorney, bridge tender, chemical technician, computer programmer ($n = 2$), corporate training specialist, electrical engineer, electronic bulletin board manager, laboratory assistant, law professor, library clerk, medical biller/bookkeeper, peace officer, shipping manager, systems manager ($n = 2$), and three graduate students. Ten people were married or in long-term relationships with either men ($n = 3$) or women ($n = 7$). Sexual orientation included bisexual ($n = 6$), gay ($n = 2$), heterosexual ($n = 4$), lesbian ($n = 1$), queer ($n = 3$), undefined ($n = 1$), and no response ($n = 3$). Gender role presentation was predominately male ($n = 15$), with four androgynous and one female. Ages ranged from twenty-six to fifty, with an average of thirty-three.

Notes

Excerpts from a Journey

1. Both Denny (1997) and Wilchins (1997) give the single *s* spelling as the popular way of rendering a term that has been forced upon transpeople. Whether that spelling is preferred by the majority is questionable because most communication by transpeople (at least on the Internet) employs acronyms rather than complete words. I agree with Denny that people have a right to define themselves, even in such seemingly minor things as the spelling of words that are relevant to them. Nonetheless, I retain the conventional spelling.

2. The article appeared in *Look Magazine* (Berg 1970). Over the years I have tried to find that specific issue, but the pages had been torn from the library copies I did locate. I assume the piece found its way into the hands of transpeople starved for any information they could find. My appreciation to Dallas Denny for providing the article and also for establishing the Transgender Archives in Atlanta, Georgia.

Chapter 1: Making the Visible Invisible

1. My questions are in response to similar questions posed by Wieringa and Blackwood (1999). My appreciation to Evelyn Blackwood for letting me review a prepublication copy. The definitions of terms are found in chapter 2

2. I am the pseudonymous Simon in Devor (1997).

3. Griggs found that being a transsexual person reassured some but not all of those she approached for her research. She, too, found that the fact she was trans was the only reason some agreed to meet with her (1998:xi).

4. Jacobs and I (1992) have defined "gender variance" as I have here for gender diversity. Following publication of this definition, we recognized that the meaning could be misconstrued as deviance in its most negative connotations. We believe that "gender diversity" more accurately expresses the different cultural expressions of gender. Although American society does not recognize more than two genders, many individuals fall within and without the categories of transvestite, transsexual, and transgender. Thus I use *gender diversity* (along with numerous emic terms) as an encompassing term to facilitate discussion of such individuals.

5. It became clear to me at the Feminist Anthropologists business meeting held during the 1997 American Anthropology Association meetings in Washington, D.C., that many feminists do not recognize that issues involving transpeople are relevant beyond discussions of sexuality. An informal survey was conducted during the meetings to determine what topics feminist anthropologists felt the association should address. I listed "gender especially transgendered issues" and sexuality. When the quickly tabulated report was distributed, transgender was subsumed under sexuality. Although it is true we have sexualities, the primary concern should be gender and the multiple ways in which one can construct gender and gender identities.

6. Studies include Johnson (1997) on Southern Philippines male transgendered people, Kulick (1998) on Brazilian transgendered male prostitutes, Prieur (1998) on male transvestites in Mexico City, and Robertson (1998) on the Japanese Takarazuka.

7. Phallocentric, androcentric, and heterosexist arguments all take males as the center. Specifically, phallocentrism centers maleness as located in male genitalia, particularly the penis. Phallocentric positions argue that those who lack penises are less than males. Androcentric arguments focus on males and ignore the contributions of females both contemporarily and historically as well as cross-culturally. Homocentric biases take homosexuality as a central position such that when an individual's behavior is the only manifestation of gender-variance it is automatically assumed the individual also has a homosexual orientation. Denny has cogently stated that homocentrism is looking "through gay-colored spectacles" (1993b:11). Transcentrism see things from a transgendered perspective. Biological-determinist or essentialist arguments give primacy to the body as "the definer of public, social behavior" (Vicinus 1992:467). Biological-determinist or essentialist arguments are discussed more fully in chapter 3.

Chapter 2: Transsexual Discourses and Languages of Identification

1. David O. Cauldwell is credited with coining the term *transsexual* in 1949 (275–80). Hirschfeld (1991) used the term as early as 1910, however. Regardless of its coinage, it did not come into general use until the 1950s following Christine Jorgensen's return to the United States after her "sex change" surgery in 1953. Cauldwell, in a commentary on Jorgensen, did not use the term *transsexual*. He stated unequivocally that only hermaphrodites ("true" and "pseudo") can change their sexes (1953:494–503). Thus it is ironic that Cauldwell's case of "psychopathia transexualis" involved a female-bodied individual who was not a hermaphrodite.

2. Jon Meyer, a psychiatrist, prefers the latter usage (1974:276). He is, however, adamantly opposed to transpeople receiving body-altering surgeries and was one of the people behind the closing of the Johns Hopkins Gender Identity Clinic in 1979.

3. Although Hirschfeld is credited with coining the term *transvestite,* according to the *Oxford English Dictionary* the first use of "transvest" was in 1652 in *Camus' National Paradox*, translated by J. Wright: "Has often did shee please her fancy with

the imagination of *transvesting* herself, and by the help of a Man's disguise deceiving the eyes of those that watched her deportments?" If, as Friedli asserts, "the word transvestite originally meant a woman who wore men's clothes"(1991:4), then it is more than ironic that the term is now considered exclusively applicable to male-bodied people. The etymology of the term lends credence to her claim.

4. Devin Hathaway explained his coinage of this term in a personal communication (March 12, 1998): "Some people may reject the labels 'girl' and 'woman' and also not rush to embrace the default choices, 'boy,' 'man,' 'butch,' etc." That is especially true for "folks who have not transitioned yet and/or do not pass all the time." After transition some people may "begin to self-identify as men (with the twist that they are men with unusual sexual anatomy or history)." The term is meant to be "open on the point of self-identity."

5. Many of these individuals define themselves as *bi-gendered*, signifying their belief that they are both male/men/masculine and female/women/feminine and also rejecting the terms *transvestite* and *cross-dresser*.

6. Transpeople refer to the community in at least three ways: "gender community," "transgendered community," and "transcommunity" (which I use throughout).

7. Examples of these terms can be found in Benjamin (1969; 1977[1966]); Pauly (1974a,b); Steiner, ed. (1985); and Stoller (1975).

8. By subjectivity I mean the sense of self, conscious and also unconscious, and how individuals understand themselves as persons. Transsubjectivity is the sense of self and understanding of the self as a transperson.

9. My appreciation to Carolyn Allen for re-posing this dilemma and to Sue-Ellen Jacobs, Evelyn Blackwood, Jeff Dickemann, Rena Davis Phoenix, and Spencer Bergstedt for many discussions concerning the differences between butches, mannish lesbians, mannish women, and female-bodied transpeople. See Burana, Roxxie, and Due (1994); Kennedy and Davis (1993); Nestle, ed. (1992); and Newton (1993).

10. Most of these studies operate from several premises: (1) all lesbians and FTMs/transmen have masculine gender identities (based on masculinity/femininity measurements); (2) both lesbians' and transmen/FTMs' sexualities (desire and behavior) are abnormal; (3) these identities and sexualities are defective and as a result (4) both FTMs/transmen and lesbians are maladjusted; and (5) an etiology must be determined to explain these defective identities and abnormal sexualities.

11. My sincere appreciation to Jackal, Spencer Bergstedt, Rena Davis Phoenix, Jamison Green, Max Fuhrmann, Stephen Whittle, C. Jacob Hale, Gary Bowen, and Mike Hernandez for their comments and suggestions on terminology.

12. A hysterectomy and a bilateral salpingo-oophorectomy are the surgical methods of removing all female reproductive organs: the uterus, ovaries, and fallopian tubes.

13. Bowen points out in a personal communication (1998) that this terminology is not inclusive of intersexed people. It is not my intent to be exclusive; however, as Bowen also notes, intersexed people are not diagnosed as transsexuals according to the *Diagnostic and Statistical Manual of Mental Disorders* (American Psychiatric Association 1987). I agree that intersexed people have unresolved

needs and issues because of being excluded from the diagnostic category. To my knowledge, no intersexed people have been a part of my research, and thus I feel unqualified to specifically include them.

Chapter 3: Bodies, Sexes, Genders, and Sexualities

1. Blacking's recognition of the historicity of the body predates Gallagher and Laqueur by a decade: "Each body in history is also an event in the history of the body" (1977:2).

2. Scheper-Hughes and Lock (1987) note that Douglas (1982[1970]) discussed the body from two perspectives, physical and social, and that O'Neill has viewed the body as physical, communicative, world, social, politic, consumer, and medical. They state that this proliferation of bodies had them "stumped for a bit," and although they found O'Neill's work "provocative and insightful" they limit their discussion to a "tripartite domain."

3. Butler argues that we should be suspicious about the naming of sex parts: "That the penis, vagina, breasts, and so forth, are *named* sexual parts is both a restriction of the erogenous body to those parts and a fragmentation of the body as a whole. Indeed, the 'unity' imposed upon the body by the category of sex is a 'disunity,' a fragmentation and compartmentalization, and a reduction of erotogeneity" (1990:114, emphasis in the original).

4. For an excellent historical accounting of sex as constructed through the bodies of hermaphrodites, see Epstein (1990). See also Kessler (1990, 1998) for a discussion of the medicalization of intersexed bodies in the United States. For discussions of sex as a social construction, see Epstein and Straub (1991). For discussions of the body, sex, sexuality, and gender as social construction, see Butler (1990; 1993). For discussions concerning the suppression and constraints on gender ambiguities, see Scott (1991) and Jacobs and Cromwell (1992).

5. Namaste (1994:4) critiques Butler's position by noting that drag performances are context-sensitive: "Given the overwhelming gendered nature of such a setting [gay bars], it is problematic to merely cite drag practice as an exposition of the constructed nature of all gender."

6. See Gilman (1989) and Epstein (1990) for discussions of hermaphrodites and the intersexed as monsters.

7. An example of homosexuality and transsexuality being equated as nearly the same can be illustrated by Stoller, a psychiatrist, who has observed, "I believe homosexuality can be roughly quantified according to the intensity of transsexual wishes. For males, those with the least transsexual desire are the most masculine. . . . Those who are most feminine (which indicates powerful transsexual wishes) . . . have no heterosexual needs to speak of. They need most of all a person of the same anatomic sex because their psychologic sex (gender identity) contains so many elements of the attitudes and role of the opposite sex" (1973:282). Embedded within Stoller's statement is the heterosexual imperative. Too, he discusses only male-bodied individuals, another indication of female-bodied transpeople being marginalized.

8. I first heard about being "seen" from Ilya Pearlman during a Spectrum meeting in 1997 (a description of Spectrum appears in the appendix). My appreciation to him for providing a more accurate descriptor of transexperiences.

9. Lazreg, among others, has critiqued feminist academics for reducing "women to one dimension of their lives (such as reproduction and housework)" (1990:331). Thus, the phrase "one-dimensional women" seems appropriate in this regard.

10. Transmen and FTMs are met with these verbal sanctions when beginning the coming-out process, particularly those who were once a part of (or tried to be a part of) lesbian communities. Halberstam has noted that FTMs and transmen are seen as "traitors to a 'women's' movement who cross over and become the enemy" (1998:287). The more separatist and radical feminist lesbian communities are the most adamant in rejecting FTMs and transmen.

11. Namaste astutely points out that many of these theorists are not only "complicit with hegemonic definitions" but also "heavily influenced by psychoanalytic theory," which misinterprets transpeople's experiences and disallows their voices to be heard (1994:8–10). She asserts, and I agree, that these theorists' claims about gender, performance, and transgender constitute the "most tragic misreading of all" (1994:11).

Chapter 4: Visible Yet Invisible

1. See Cromwell (1995c) for a shorter version of this chapter. My appreciation to Sue-Ellen Jacobs for a careful reading of and comments on an earlier draft. I am also indebted to Bonnie Cromwell for helping me articulate some of this material more clearly. Parts of this chapter and chapters 5 and 6 are included in Cromwell (1996).

2. Many anthropologists and Native Americans consider "berdache" to be an inappropriate term. Following the lead of the contributors to Jacobs, Thomas, and Lang, eds. (1996), I indicate this inappropriateness by enclosing "berdache" and its derivatives in quotation marks.

3. Murray (1994) rightly criticizes Fulton and Anderson for their position, but he is incorrect in equating *transsexualism* as a sex or sexuality term. It has less to do with sex than with gender. The misunderstanding arises from equating sex with gender, and many individuals prefer terms prefixed by *trans* (e.g., *transgender, transman,* and *transwoman*) as a move away from the sexed connotations inherent in the word *transsexual.*

4. Gooren states that "information on female-to-male transsexualism in other cultures is not available" (1997:n.p.). Preceding that statement he cites the hijras, the Omani xanith, and Native American "berdache" as examples of male-to-female transsexualism. Although I believe he wrongly equates these cultural examples as transsexualism itself, I also fault him for not recognizing the similarities found cross-culturally among females. The omission provides an example of why I believe it important to make female gender diversity visible.

5. Feinberg (1996) contributes to FTM/transmen's history, however that topic is not the book's main focus. Furthermore, Feinberg takes some cases out of their cultural and historical context.

6. Blackwood (1984a:41) cites Levy as providing a brief reference to Tahitian females who lived as men but reports that such had not existed for some time. The citation does not indicate whether Levy provides a term for the female counterpart of the *mahu.*

7. I have found only one reference to the gender-transformed among the Chukchi. It refers only to the shamanistic aspects and notes that under the "Russifying" Soviet period "transformed men and women were doubly reviled [and that] in the 1920s and 1930s they were prosecuted both as shamans and sexual deviants" (Balzer 1996:175). Balzer conjectures that with increased interest in spirituality it is possible that transformed shamans may reemerge.

8. Blackwood (1984a:113–15) lists the following non-Native American groups as having "cross-gender" statuses for females: Balinese, Buginese-Makassarese, Chukchee, Cubeo, Fanti, Koryak, Mehinaku, Nyakyusa, Philippine, and Tahitian.

9. Contemporary academic writers also make this mistake. For examples, see Roscoe's (1988, 1991) interpretation of We´Wha, a Zuni *llamana*, and Williams (1992[1986]) on Native American "berdaches" as "gay" ancestors.

10. Feinberg uses both male and female markers in reference to her/himself.

Chapter 5: Transvestite Opportunists, Passing Women, and Female-Bodied Men

1. A version of this chapter appears in More and Whittle (1999).

2. A book from an FTM/transman perspective would be required to cover the gamut of female-bodied people who transgressed their historical categories. At least one transman has undertaken such a project.

3. Dekker and van de Pol (1989) make a distinction between "soldiers" and "land army."

4. A play, *The Women Pirates: Ann Bonney and Mary Read,* has been written about the exploits of Read and Bonny (Gooch 1978).

5. From a transperspective it is possible to see Velazquez as a female-bodied man. The dress was equivalent to contemporary FTMs' and transmen's tricks of the trade, which include (but are not limited to) chest bindings, crotch padding, and stage makeup to create beard lines. Further, Velazquez was recorded as saying she had wished she were a man. Although that statement is no doubt common among many females, most do not go to the extent that Velazquez did (and that FTMs and transmen do). Even so, I have included Velazquez among the transvestic opportunists because her cross-dressing was episodic rather than constant. When opportunity forced her hand she used femaleness and femininity to advantage rather than keep her female body a secret.

6. Vicinus notes that How is a "notable exception" to females who married women because she was neither punished nor persecuted when brought to authorities' attention (1992:477). It is possible that How was not persecuted or punished because How's wife had died by the time the blackmailer was confronted and there was no reason to prosecute anyone but the blackmailer.

7. Hudson as Frank Dubois was arrested and charged with assault and battery in March of 1883 without being discovered to be female, according to *Milwaukee Sentinel* (March 8, 1883, 5).

8. I am using masculine pronouns exclusively for de Erauso, a step I believe is warranted, because, as the translators of his memoir note, he "almost invariably used masculine endings to describe" himself (de Erauso 1996[1829]:xlvi).

9. Although aware that females also wanted to "change their sex," de Savitsch

clearly equates that possibility with males (1958:86). Early in his book he states that he will be concerned only with males (as these are problematic), yet he provides several examples concerning female "homosexuals" who either live as or state a desire to be men. He also defines "change of sex" operations as concerning only males who become women and states that such operations are only "plastic" because uteruses and ovaries cannot be created or transplanted: "When we refer to the change of sex operation, we mean here the surgical procedure by which the external appearance of the male genitalia is changed to that of a woman" (53). De Savitsch mentions no possibility of such operations for female-bodied people, therefore it is improbable that he would recognize de Raylan as an FTM/transman who fashioned his own male genital apparatus. It is likely that females are relegated to "homosexuals" or "male wannabes" because it is impossible to create or transplant testes, vas deferens, and spermatic chords. Consequently, females can never become men. In an appendix, Dr. Charles Wolf, a surgeon, notes that there are females who want to become men and that undergoing hysterectomy, salpingo-oophorectomy, and vaginectomy are enough to render them as legal males. Phalloplasty, however, is fraught with problems and should be avoided (117). De Savitsch never uses the term *transsexual* or its derivatives.

10. Hall (1993:24) puts the amount at $12 a month, whereas Wheelwright (1990:140) gives it as $70.

Chapter 6: He Becomes She

1. For a similar argument see Garber (1992), especially 67–71.

2. Parts of the following section have appeared as Cromwell 1989, 1993b, 1994, 1995a, and 1995b.

3. Even though Middlebrook declares in her preface that she consulted FTMs/transmen (xiv), it is clear that she has no understanding of their issues. In her initial research I was contacted by her research assistant, Mary Ellen Foley, and asked a number of questions about being trans as well as whether I thought Tipton was also. I answered the latter question in the affirmative, and contact by Foley and Middlebrook ended. When later asked why she had not contacted FTMs/transmen, Middlebrook stated that she had tried to contact me but had been informed that I wanted no part of the project (Leonard, personal communication, June 1998), which was not the case. Elsewhere, however, Middlebrook has stated, "I will say very candidly that somebody else could make a very good case for Billy as a transgendered person. His masculinity is pretty thoroughgoing" (Holt 1998:D1).

4. It is ironic that many lesbians would have rejected Tipton while he was alive yet claim him as a part of their history after his death. They certainly would have ignored or excluded him (as well as others such as Jack Garland) as a part of women's and lesbian culture while he lived. It is unlikely, for example, that he would have been invited to the Michigan Women's Music Festival. In 1991 male-to-female transpeople were excluded from participating in that event. Beginning in 1992, however, transgendered activists held protests and staffed information tables outside the gate of the festival, and since 1995 MTFs have been allowed to attend if they are post-surgical. For a more detailed accounting of these actions see Wilchins (1997).

5. For other examples of this linguistic and social phenomenon, see popular media accounts concerning the death of Billy Tipton (Boss 1989; Chin 1989; "Estate of an Adoptive Father Sued" 1989). *Time Magazine* ("A Secret Song" 1989) did not make a linguistic switch and retained masculine markers in its brief report. The linguistic and social phenomenon of retaining feminine pronouns in popular media accounts when the discussion concerns pre-operated male-to-female transsexuals is also of note ("When the Bough Breaks" 1992).

Chapter 7: "They Are a Part of My History"

1. C. Jacob Hale has said that he could relate more to male "berdaches" because they usually did not engage in warfare and most often performed domestic chores that are more like his own life choices than the war and hunting activities of female gender transformers (1998, personal communication). Although I had never considered that possibility as a reason for FTMs/transmen not relating to these categories, I assume there are others, too, who might feel a similar affinity.

2. My appreciation to Anne Bolin for this formulation.

3. Transphobia is manifested by skepticism about the existence of transpeople or a dislike or hatred of, and occasionally hostility toward, them (Denny 1993). Some transpeople manifest transphobia by expressing dislike, hatred, and hostility toward other transpeople—most frequently those who are out.

Chapter 8: Fearful Others

1. Although this quotation does not in itself marginalize FTMs and transmen, I use it as an example of the paucity of literature on the topic. As I will argue later on in this chapter, it is because there is so little data on FTMs/transmen that the dominant discourses are capable of marginalizing them.

2. A version of this chapter appears in Denny (1998). At the time the article was published I had not received permission to quote people by name. Many are now out as transpeople, and their names, initials, or chosen pseudonyms are used in place of the age and occupation designations previously used.

3. Irvine (1990:270) makes a similar argument but without the additional conceptualization of fearful other. The concept of gender borderlands is taken from Anzaldúa.

4. See Chauncey (1989) for an excellent discussion of the history of homosexuality and Rosario (1994) for a cogent explication of the confusion in the early literature between homosexuality and what came to be labeled as transsexuality.

5. There are significant differences between male-to-female transsexuals and female-bodied transpeople regarding the "corrective" benefits of surgical sex reassignment. There is, in fact, a significant difference in attitude toward transsexualism as a disorder. For example, following a transgender speakout in Seattle on April 29, 1992, where a male-to-female transsexual repeatedly used the term *affliction* to describe her transsexualism, one FTM/transman consultant said, "I resent people using words like 'afflicted.' I'm not afflicted." Also see chapters 9 and 10 of this volume.

6. In a juxtaposition, Shapiro (1991), a transsexual discourse, follows Stone (1991), a transdiscourse. Many consider Stone to be the founder of trans theory because she was the first out transperson to publish at the academic level and in doing so to challenge transsexual discourses.

7. Rather than "men with vaginas" some practitioners use the term *penisless men* (e.g., Steiner, ed. 1985:356). In a Freudian sense (men have penises, women do not) that seems like an underhanded way of labeling female-bodied transpeople who do not have surgery as females rather than men.

8. John Taylor is a pseudonym I used in 1983 before coming out as a transperson. The original article was written for a journal published by Quakers. At the time I felt it was imperative to protect my identity because I was uncertain about how my spiritual community would respond to the fact that I am trans. I am fortunate, however, in that the community has never shunned me but rather welcomed me.

9. These latter two considerations may, in themselves, be artifacts of FTMs and transmen being male-identified as well as being unwilling to jump through hoops for results that will be less than satisfactory.

10. My appreciation to Jacob Hale for our discussions concerning the discrepancies in numbers.

11. Steiner's claim of homogeneity for FTMs/transmen is curious in that her edited collection contains few references to FTMs and only one small section takes up FTMs as subjects separate from MTFs/transwomen.

12. Pauly presumes that all women derive pleasure and stimulation from their breasts. He is unaware that a few lesbians have their breasts removed because they do not like them.

13. This is in no way intended to denigrate those who choose phalloplastic surgeries but rather an explanation of why a number of individuals elect not to have particular procedures.

14. One example of how, even within the transcommunity, FTMs and transmen are invisible is demonstrated by an experience I had at this conference. After settling into my room, I went to register for the meeting and was asked, "Is it under Jason or your 'femme' name?" "I don't have a femme name," I replied. "I gave it up years ago." The registrar's mouth dropped open when I told her I was an FTM.

15. This surgeon is not alone in his attitude. Surgeons who perform genital surgeries are invested in creating penises for penetration. Gail Lebovic, Dr. Donald Laub's associate, has stated, "I don't really understand why they have this surgery [metoidioplasty]. I mean, if you're going to have a penis. . . ." (cited in Bloom 1994:44). Laub stated this attitude more overtly: "Men want penises. But the metoidioplasty mimics nature, and that's appealing. . . . Sexual and urinary functioning is intact and they can go on having sex however they have it. Like lesbians do." Some FTMs and transmen have interpreted that statement as implying—at least to many surgeons—that those who do not have phalloplasty are really lesbians.

16. Both Garber (1989) and Irvine (1990) discuss this point.

17. One surgical technique that male-to-female transsexuals have is referred to as penile inversion. If the attitude was the same, then it would be "phallo-inversion."

18. I know of only one female surgeon, Gail Lebovic, who performs genital

surgery in the United States. There are, however, a number of female surgeons who do chest reconstructions and hysterectomies.

19. As opposed to Dekker and van de Pol, the San Francisco Lesbian and Gay History Project states that "the tradition of passing women, begun in the nineteenth century, lives on today, a small but important part of lesbian and women's history" (1989:194).

20. When Stoller (1965:194) discusses an individual who expresses a disinterest in having a penis or the surgery to create one, he places all masculine referents in quotation marks, signifying that the individual's identity as a man is invalid. "He" is really a "she." This devaluing of and judgment upon the individual's self-identity is both phallocentric and Freudian; the absence of a penis or the absence of a desire for one equals female.

21. How ironic that the word *queens* is considered undignified for scholarly works—and how revealing it is that Steiner bemoans that no sexologist has invented a label more suitable to medico-psychological practitioners' tastes.

22. It is significant that Bolin's *In Search of Eve* (1988) is regarded by many MTFs/transwomen as an accurate and honest interpretation of their lives and the process they must undergo with respect to medico-psychological practitioners. Even more significant, and likely because it is so highly regarded, the book is virtually ignored by the medico-psychological establishment. I have seen only one book review concerning her work in any of their publications, and that review denigrated the value of Bolin's work because data had been collected on only 16 individuals versus the 150 in the reviewer's study. It was also denounced because of its criticism of the controlling nature of medico-psychological practitioners and its social cultural perspective "rather than a psychological or empirical research standpoint" (Mate-Kole 1992:209–10). The same reviewer also felt the book would be of great "assistance to the student or avid reader in sociology/anthropology than to the clinician or psychology/psychiatry student."

As Denny (1993a:169–70) pointed out in a letter of response (which the journal initially rejected), the reviewer had put things "precisely backwards: It is the clinician who has the most to gain by reading" Bolin's book. The fact that a clinician has seen 150 clients does not invalidate Bolin's study when one considers the amount of time spent with individuals in each study. The reviewer also fails to recognize the artificial environment in which patients are seen and "the imbalance of power between clinicians and patients."

A point can be made concerning the control of discourses and how they are validated and made legitimate. I am aware of only one review of Bolin's book, and it appeared in 1992—four years after publication. By way of contrast, the work of Lothstein, a psychoanalyst who is considered an authority, was reviewed in 1984—a year after publication.

Chapter 9: Queering the Binaries

1. The etiological factors sound suspiciously like those postulated for lesbianism over the course of the history of homosexuality. For example, Stoller states that all types of masculinity in females (including butch lesbians, masculine women, and FTM/transmen) are caused by a mother who is distant during the child's infancy

and childhood; the mother does not encourage the child's femininity; and the father, if present, encourages the child's "masculine" behaviors and activities (Stoller 1973:391; see also Pauly 1974a:497–98).

2. For example, Benjamin (1977[1966]) has one chapter of thirteen pages; Stoller (1975) includes one chapter with twenty-one pages; and Green and Money (1969) have three chapters (sixty-four pages) devoted exclusively to FTMs/transmen. It would not be until Lothstein (1983) that an entire volume would be purportedly about that topic. An additional fourteen years would pass before another would appear (Devor 1997).

3. MTFs/transwomen classically were described as devoid of masculine behavior and interests. They are thought to have had feminine behaviors since early childhood and to be pretty children. They are commonly dressed in girls' clothing by an important family member (usually the mother). They talk of wanting to be a girl. They are smothered by their mothers, whose husbands are passive and barely present. Their physical body is a source of great discomfort, and they want surgery to turn them into women (Stoller 1975:74).

Clear distinctions were made between effeminate homosexuals, transvestites, and transsexuals. Homosexuals were said to wear female clothing as parody or to attract other homosexual men; transvestites are believed to be erotically excited by women's clothes; and MTFs only wear such clothing as an expression of their identity. Homosexuals and transvestites are comfortable in male roles, MTFs are not. Transvestites are employed in masculine endeavors; their behaviors, mannerisms, and other gender cues are masculine when cross-dressing is not involved. MTFs/transwomen are employed in female occupations and are feminine in attire; they also have feminine behaviors and mannerisms. Homosexuals and transvestites develop masculine identities, MTFs/transwomen do not. Homosexuals and transvestites alternate between masculinity and femininity, MTFs/transwomen do not. Homosexuals and transvestites are effeminate, MTFs/transwomen are feminine. Homosexuals desire other homosexuals as partners, transvestites may be bisexual but are usually heterosexuals married to women. MTFs/transwomen desire only masculine, heterosexual males as partners. Homosexuals and transvestites like and want their own penises, MTFs/transwomen do not (Stoller 1975:130–47).

4. Clearly, Pauly (and presumably others as well) did not know about stone butches.

5. Although a few practitioners still deny transpeople sexuality (cf. Denny 1996:40), attitudes began to change during the late 1970s and early 1980s. The shift appears to have occurred when practitioners began to realize that some transsexuals changed their sexual preference (Bullough and Bullough 1998:21).

6. The majority of practitioners and most of the early research on transsexuals took place within gender identity clinics (Lothstein 1983:83).

7. The first gender identity clinic was established at Johns Hopkins University in 1965–66 (Bullough and Bullough 1998:20; Denny 1992b:10). During the late 1960s and early 1970s, more clinics were started at university medical schools (e.g., the University of Minnesota, University of California at Los Angeles, University of Virginia at Charlottesville, and University of Washington, and at Vanderbilt, Stanford, Case Western Reserve, and Duke Universities). Eventually, there were at least forty

clinics in the United States and Canada (Denny 1992b:10). Although many trans-people went for treatment, most clinics were research-oriented and considered transsexualism and treatments related to it experimental. Most were staffed by medico-psychological practitioners who were seldom trained in sexuality but were interested in research (Denny 1992b:11–12). Clinics began closing following the closure of the Johns Hopkins Clinic in 1979. Those which survived (there were fewer than twelve in the late 1990s) are no longer affiliated with universities (19).

8. This is the case no matter what. How else can one explain the existence of an Internet list closed to non-FTM/transmen and to transmen/FTMs who iden-tify as transgendered? Members of this exclusive list are female-to-male transsexuals who do not want nontranspeople to know they are transsexuals yet feel the need to talk with others who have the same or similar experiences and the same desire to be closeted. While lurking I have observed individuals deny that they were ever female, even to the point of denying that their families treated them like girls. I have also seen statements such as "I was transsexual, now I'm just a man" and "I had a female body, now I have male body." Those who post to the list insist that being trans was or is unimportant. As such it is hard to fathom why they join other Internet lists as well as bulletin boards and chat rooms. What is ironic about their presence in these venues is their insistence that they must cease being trans and go into the world as "just men," which they seem incapable of doing.

9. Whittle (1996:205) argues that transpeople not only challenge the crossing of morphological boundaries but also challenge the notion that boundaries ever really existed.

10. See Hale (1997a) for a discussion of the renaming of body parts.

11. Cameron's book of photographs (1996) is testimony to the increasing vis-ibility of transpeople (especially transmen/FTMs).

12. I have never heard an FTM or a transman express disgust or repulsion for their genitalia. I have heard mild expressions such as "didn't like" or "don't like" and that they "don't belong" or "aren't mine." These are hardly expressions of revulsion or disgust, however.

13. This example also serves another purpose in that it illustrates how adamantly some clinicians were in maintaining sex and gender paradigms as well as reifying the body. Lothstein (as did many others) refused to use his clients' preferred names or pronouns. He (as do others) also strongly maintains that transsexuals or any-one who presented themselves to a clinic as such suffered from a "disorder of the self-system involving an early childhood developmental arrest, disturbances in ego functions, and stemming primarily from borderline personality and narcissistic disorders" (1983:10).

14. Stoller asserts (1972:48n2) that FTMs/transmen's partners had prior failed heterosexual relationships and none of the partners enjoyed penetrative sex. He also claims that nonlesbians would reject FTMs/transmen, whose bodies are fe-male. FTMs/transmen would be able to find lovers only among lesbians but would be rejected by them as well (Stoller 1973:386). Unfortunately, too many FTMs and transmen believe that to be the case.

15. Pauly's (and others) framework reifies the body such that the true identity is, of course, the body.

16. The word *queer* is used as an encompassing term for anyone who does not identify as heterosexual. Many avoid the term and use lengthy expressions such as "lesbian, gay, bisexual, transgendered, and friends" (LGBTF) (cf. Queen and Schimel 1997:19).

17. Specialized terms have arisen for nontranspeople who are attracted to and have sexual relations with transpeople: *trannytrollop, t-bird, transhag, transfaghag,* and *trannyhawk.* The latter term has a negative connotation and refers to men who fetishize and prey upon MTFs/transwomen.

18. "The Problem—No Penis" was a slide presented by Donald Laub, a plastic surgeon, during the First FTM Conference of the Americas, August 1995, San Francisco (see also Rubin 1996 and Hale 1997a).

Chapter 10: Making the Invisible Visible

1. Rubin (1999) is a sociological study, and More and Whittle (1999) is an edited anthology by transpeople who identify in a variety of ways, half of which are as FTMs/transmen.

2. In a personal communication in 1998 Blackwood pointed out that in addition to being "exceedingly masculinist" this terminology "suggests that the clitoris is a confined or restricted penis," which as a "parallel construction for male bodies would mean that the penis is an overblown clitoris."

3. Sullivan left his materials to the San Francisco Gay and Lesbian History Archives. I am indebted to him for collecting these materials and to Susan Stryker and Will Walker for providing access to them.

Bibliography

Abramson, Allen. 1987. "Beyond the Samoa Controversy in Anthropology: A History of Sexuality in the Eastern Interior of Fiji." In *The Cultural Construction of Sexuality*, ed. Pat Caplan, 193–216. London: Routledge.

Aceves, Joseph B. 1974. *Identity, Survival, and Change: Exploring Social/Cultural Anthropology*. Morristown: General Learning Press.

Adriani, N., and Albert C. Kruyt. 1950. *De Bare'e-sprekende Toradjas van Midden-Celebes (de Oost-Toradjas)* [The Bare'e-speaking Toradja of Central Celebes (the East Toradjas)]. Vol. 1, 2d ed. Trans. Henni K. Moulton. Amsterdam: Noord-Hallandsche Uitgevers Maatschappij.

Allen, Paula Gunn. 1981. "Beloved Women: Lesbians in American Indian Cultures." *Conditions* 7: 67–87.

———. 1992 [1986]. *The Sacred Hoop: Recovering the Feminine in American Indian Traditions*. Boston: Beacon Press.

American Psychiatric Association. 1987. *Diagnostic and Statistical Manual of Mental Disorders*. 3d ed. Washington: American Psychiatric Association.

Anderson, Kathryn, and Dana C. Jack. 1991. "Learning to Listen: Interview Techniques and Analyses." In *Women's Words: The Feminist Practice of Oral History*, ed. Sherna Berger Gluck and Daphne Patai, 11–26. New York: Routledge.

Anderson, Maxwell. 1997. "Man Loving Man." *Boy's Own* 24: 23.

Angelino, Henry, and Charles L. Shedd. 1955. "A Note on Berdache." *American Anthropologist* 57: 121–26.

Anonymous. 1995. "The X-Files: Trapped in the Wrong Body." *FTM Newsletter*, no. 32 (Oct.): 11–12.

Anzaldúa, Gloria. 1987. *Borderlands: La Frontera—The New Mestiza*. San Francisco: Aunt Lute Books.

Ardener, Shirley. 1987. "A Note on Gender Iconography: The Vagina." In *The Cultural Construction of Sexuality*, ed. Pat Caplan, 113–42. London: Routledge.

Balzer, Marjorie Mandelstam. 1996. "Sacred Genders in Siberia: Shamans, Bear Festivals, and Androgyny." In *Gender Reversals and Gender Cultures: Anthropological and Historical Perspectives*, ed. Sabrina Ramet, 164–82. London: Routledge.

Basden, G. T. 1921. *Among the Ibos of Nigeria*. London: Seeley, Service.

Benjamin, Harry. 1964. "Clinical Aspects of Transsexualism in the Male and Female." *American Journal of Psychotherapy* 18: 458–69.

————. 1969. "Introduction." In *Transsexualism and Sex Reassignment*, ed. Richard Green and John Money, 1–11. Baltimore: Johns Hopkins University Press.

————. 1977 [1966]. *The Transsexual Phenomenon*. New York: Warner Books.

Benjamin, Jessica. 1988. *The Bonds of Love: Psychoanalysis, Feminism, and the Problem of Domination*. New York: Pantheon.

Berg, R. H. 1970. "The Transsexuals: Male or Female?" *Look Magazine*, Jan. 27, 28–31.

Bernstein, Sandy. 1991. "A Crossdresser's Closet: A Different Kind of 'Coming Out'." *FTM Newsletter*, no. 16 (July): 5.

Birke, Lynda I. A. 1982. "From Sin to Sickness: Hormonal Theories of Lesbianism." In *Biological Woman: The Convenient Myth*, ed. Ruth Hubbard, Mary Sue Henifin, and Barbara Fried, 71–90. Cambridge: Schenkman Publishing.

Blacking, John. 1977. "Towards an Anthropology of the Body." In *The Anthropology of the Body*, ed. John Blacking, 1–28. London: Academic Press.

Blackwood, Evelyn. 1984a. "Cross-Cultural Dimensions of Lesbian Relations." Master's thesis, San Francisco State University.

————. 1984b. "Sexuality and Gender in Certain Native American Tribes: The Case of Cross-Gender Females." *Signs* 10(1): 27–42.

————. 1985. "Breaking the Mirror: The Construction of Lesbianism and the Anthropological Discourse on Homosexuality." *Journal of Homosexuality* 11(3–4): 1–17.

————1997. Comments on "Queer Challenges: Lesbian/Gay/Bisexual/Transgender Issues in Anthropology." Presented at the annual meeting of the American Anthropology Association, Nov. 19–23, Washington, D.C.

————. 1999. *"Tomboi's* in West Sumatra: Constructing Masculinity and Erotic Desire." In *Female Desires: Same-Sex Relations and Transgender Practices across Cultures*, ed. Evelyn Blackwood and Saskia Wieringa, 181–205. New York: Columbia University Press.

Blackwood, Evelyn, and Saskia Wieringa. 1999. "Sapphic Shadows: Challenging the Silence in the Study of Sexuality." In *Female Desires: Same-Sex Relations and Transgender Practices across Cultures*, ed. Evelyn Blackwood and Saskia Wieringa, 39–63. New York: Columbia University Press.

Blanchard, Ray. 1985. "Research Methods for the Typological Study of Gender Disorders in Males." In *Gender Dysphoria: Development, Research, Management*, ed. Betty Steiner, 227–57. New York: Plenum Press.

Blanchard, Ray, and Kurt Freund. 1983. "Measuring Masculine Gender Identity in Females." *Journal of Consulting and Clinical Psychology* 51(2): 205–14.

Bloom, Amy. 1994. "The Body Lies." *New Yorker*, July 18, 38–49.

Bobby Gene. 1992. "The Self-Discovery Process." *TV-TS Tapestry Journal*, no. 63, 49–51.

Bockting, Walter. 1987. "Homosexual and Bisexual Identity Development in Female-to-Male Transsexuals." Presented at the conference on "Homosexuality beyond Disease," Dec. 10–12, Amsterdam.

————. 1997. "Transgender Coming Out: Implications for the Clinical Management of Gender Dysphoria." In *Gender Blending*, ed. Bonnie Bullough, Vern Bullough, and James Elias, 48–53. Amherst: Prometheus Books.

Boddy, Janice. 1995. "The Body Nearer the Self." *American Anthropologist* 97(1): 134–37.

Bogoras, Waldemar. 1975 [1904–8]. "The Chuckchee." In *Memoirs of the American Museum of Natural History* 11(2), ed. Franz Boaz, and in *Publications of the Jesup North Pacific Expedition* 7: 448–57. New York: G. E. Stechert.

Bohan, Janis S. 1993. "Regarding Gender: Essentialism, Constructionism, and Feminist Psychology." *Psychology of Women Quarterly* 17(1): 5–21.

Bolin, Anne. 1988. *In Search of Eve: Transsexual Rites of Passage*. South Hadley: Bergin and Garvey.

———. 1994. "Transcending and Transgendering: Male-to-Female Transsexuals, Dichotomy, and Diversity." In *Third Sex, Third Gender: Beyond Sexual Dimorphism in Culture and History*, ed. Gilbert Herdt, 447–85. Chicago: University of Chicago Press.

Bornstein, Kate. 1994. *Gender Outlaw: On Men, Women, and the Rest of Us*. New York: Routledge.

Boss, Kit. 1989. "No Rest in Peace." *Seattle Times*, March 19, L1, L6.

Boswell, Holly. 1998. "The Transgender Paradigm Shift toward Free Expression." In *Current Concepts in Transgender Identity*, ed. Dallas Denny, 55–61. New York: Garland.

Bradley, Susan J., Ray Blanchard, Susan Coates, Richard Green, Stephen B. Levine, Heino Meyer-Bahlburg, Ira Pauly, and Kenneth Zucker. 1991. "Interim Report of the DSM-IV Subcommittee on Gender Identity Disorders." *Archives of Sexual Behavior* 20(4): 333–43.

Brown, Candice, and Kendall Morris. 1995. "The Alan Hart Story: A Typical Transsexual Tale." Unpublished ms., Portland.

Brown, Judith. 1983. "Comment on Callender and Kochems." *Current Anthropology* 24(4): 457–58.

Brown, Penelope, and Stephen Levinson. 1979. "Social Structure, Groups and Interaction." In *Social Markers in Speech*, ed. Klaus Scherer and Howard Giles, 291–341. New York: Cambridge University Press.

Bullough, Bonnie, and Vern L. Bullough. 1998. "Transsexualism: Historical Perspectives, 1952 to Present." In *Current Concepts in Transgender Identity*, ed. Dallas Denny, 15–34. New York: Garland.

Bullough, Vern L. 1975. "Transsexualism in History." *Archives of Sexual Behavior* 4(5): 561–71.

———. 1976. *Sexual Variance in Society and History*. Chicago: University of Chicago Press.

Bullough, Vern L., and Bonnie Bullough. 1993. *Cross Dressing, Sex, and Gender*. Philadelphia: University of Pennsylvania Press.

Burana, Lily, Roxxie, and Linnea Due. 1994. *Dagger: On Butch Women*. San Francisco: Cleis Press.

Butler, Judith. 1990. *Gender Trouble: Feminism and the Subversion of Identity*. New York: Routledge.

———. 1991. "Imitation and Gender Insubordination." In *Inside/Out: Lesbian Theories, Gay Theories*, ed. Diana Fuss, 13–31. New York: Routledge.

———. 1993. *Bodies That Matter: On the Discursive Limits of "Sex."* New York: Routledge.

Cahn, Susan K. 1993. "From the 'Muscle Moll' to the 'Butch' Ballplayer: Mannishness, Lesbianism, and Homophobia in U.S. Women's Sport." *Feminist Studies* 19(2): 343–68.

Califia, Pat. 1997. *Sex Changes: The Politics of Transgenderism.* San Francisco: Cleis Press.

Callender, Charles, and Lee M. Kochems. 1983. "The North American 'Berdache.'" *Current Anthropology* 24(4): 443–56.

Cameron, Loren. 1996. *Body Alchemy: Transsexual Portraits.* San Francisco: Cleis Press.

Caplan, Pat. 1993. "Learning Gender: Fieldwork in a Tanzanian Coastal Village, 1965–85." In *Gendered Fields: Women, Men and Ethnography*, ed. Diane Bell, Pat Caplan, and Wazir Jahan Karim, 168–81. London: Routledge.

Castendyk, Stephanie. 1992. "A Psychoanalytic Account for Lesbian." *Feminist Review*, no. 42 (Autumn): 67–81.

Cauldwell, David O. 1949. "Psychopathia Transexualis." *Sexology Magazine*, Dec., 275–80.

———. 1953. "Man Becomes Woman." *Sexology Magazine*, March, 494–503.

Charke, Charlotte. 1827 [1755]. *A Narrative of the Life of Mrs. Charlotte Charke, Written by Herself.* London: n.p.

Chauncey, George. 1989. "From Sexual Inversion to Homosexuality: Medicine and the Changing Conceptualization of Female Deviance." In *Passion and Power: Sexuality in History*, ed. Kathy Peiss, Christina Simmons, and Robert Padgug, 87–117. Philadelphia: Temple University Press.

Chin, Paula. 1989. "Death Discloses Billy Tipton's Strange Secret: He Was a She." *People Weekly*, Feb. 30, n.p.

Christensen, James B. 1952. *Double Descent among the Fanti.* New Haven: Human Relations Area Files.

Christina, Greta. 1997. "Loaded Words." In *PoMoSexuals: Challenging Assumptions about Gender and Sexuality*, ed. Carole Queen and Lawrence Schimel, 29–38. San Francisco: Cleis Press.

Clover, Carol J. 1986. "Maiden Warriors and Other Sons." *Journal of English and Germanic Philology* 85(1): 35–49.

Cole, Collier M., and Walter J. Meyer III. 1998. "Transgender Behavior and the DSM IV." In *Current Concepts in Transgender Identity*, ed. Dallas Denny, 227–36. New York: Garland.

Coleman, Eli, and Walter Bockting. 1988. "Heterosexual prior to Sex Reassignment—Homosexual Afterwards: A Case Study of a Female-to-Male Transsexual." *Journal of Psychology and Human Sexuality* 1(2): 69–82.

Cole, Sandra S. 1998. "The Female Experience of the Femme." In *Current Concepts in Transgender Identity*, ed. Dallas Denny, 373–90. New York: Garland.

Collins, Patricia Hill. 1991. "Learning from the Outsider Within: The Sociological Significance of Black Feminist Thought." In *Beyond Methodology: Feminist Scholarship as Lived Research*, ed. Mary Margaret Fonow and Judith A. Cook, 35–59. Bloomington: Indiana University Press.

Cordova, Jeanne. 1992. "Butches, Lies, and Feminism." In *The Persistent Desire: A Femme-Butch Reader*, ed. Joan Nestle, 272–92. Boston: Alyson Publications.

Cromwell, Jason. 1987. "Transsexualism and Concepts of Gender." Unpublished ms., Seattle.

————. 1989. "What about Billy's Life as a Man?" [letter to the editor]. *Seattle Gay News*, Aug. 18, n.p.

————. 1995a. "Default Assumptions; or, The Billy Tipton Phenomenon." *Cross-Talk: The Transgender News and Information Monthly* 67: 15–16, 23.

————. 1995b. "Talking about without Talking about: The Use of Protective Language among Transvestites and Transsexuals." In *Beyond the Lavender Lexicon: Authenticity, Imagination and Appropriation in Lesbian and Gay Languages*, ed. William Leap, 267–95. Amsterdam: Gordon and Breach.

————. 1995c. "Traditions of Female Gender Diversity and Sexualities." Presented at the International Congress on Gender, Cross-Dressing, and Sex Issues, Feb. 25, Van Nuys, Calif.

————. 1996. "Traditions of Gender Diversity and Sexualities: A Female-to-Male Transgendered Perspective." In *Two-Spirit People: Native American Gender Identity, Sexuality, and Spirituality*, ed. Sue-Ellen Jacobs, Wesley Thomas, and Sabine Lang, 119–42. Urbana: University of Illinois Press.

————. 1998. "Fearful Others: Medico-Psychological Constructions of Female-to-Male Transgenderism." In *Current Concepts in Transgender Identity,"* ed. Dallas Denny, 117–44. New York: Garland.

————. 1999. "Passing Women and Female-bodied Men: (Re)Claiming FTM History." In *Reclaiming Genders: Transsexual Grammars at the Fin de Siècle*, ed. Kate More and Stephen Whittle, 34–61. London: Cassell.

Davidson, Arnold I. 1990 [1987]. "Sex and the Emergence of Sexuality." In *Forms of Desire: Sexual Orientation and Social Constructionist Controversy*, ed. Edward Stein, 88–132. New York: Garland.

Dekker, Rudolf M., and Lotte C. van de Pol. 1989. *The Tradition of Female Transvestism in Early Modern Europe*. New York: Macmillan.

D'Emilio, John. 1983. *Sexual Politics, Sexual Communities: The Making of a Homosexual Minority in the United States, 1940–76*. Chicago: University of Chicago Press.

Denny, Dallas. 1992a. "On the Front Lines in the Gender Wars." *Chrysalis Quarterly* 1(3): 13–16.

————. 1992b. "The Politics of Diagnosis and a Diagnosis of Politics: University-Affiliated Gender Clinics and How They Failed to Meet the Needs of Trans-Sexual People." *Chrysalis Quarterly* 1(3): 9–20.

————. 1993a. Letter to the Editor. *Archives of Sexual Behavior* 22(2): 169–71.

————. 1993b. "You're Strange, and We're Wonderful: The Relationship between the Gay/Lesbian and Transgender Communities." Unpublished ms., Atlanta.

————. 1995. "The Paradigm Shift Is Here!" *AEGIS News* 1(4): 1.

————. 1996. "In Search of the 'True' Transsexual." *Chrysalis: The Journal of Transgressive Gender Identities* 2(3): 39–44.

————. 1997. "Transgender: Some Historical, Cross-Cultural, and Modern-Day Models and Methods of Coping and Treatment." In *Gender Blending*, ed. Bonnie Bullough, Vern Bullough, and James Elias, 33–47. Amherst: Prometheus Press.

Denny, Dallas, ed. 1998. *Current Concepts in Transgender Identity*. New York: Garland.

Denny, Dallas, and Margaux Schaffer. 1992. "An Interview with David Gilbert, M.D." *Chrysalis Quarterly* 1(4): 23–28.

De Lauretis, Teresa. 1990. "Eccentric Subjects: Feminist Theory and Historical Consciousness." *Feminist Studies* 16(1): 115–50.

De Savitsch, Eugene. 1958. *Homosexuality, Transvestism, and Change of Sex.* Springfield: Charles C Thomas.

Devereux, George. 1937. "Institutionalized Homosexuality of the Mohave Indians." *Human Biology* 9(4): 498–527.

———. 1976 [ca. 1850–95]. "The Case of Sahaykwisa." In *Gay American History: Lesbians and Gay Men in the U.S.A.,* ed. Jonathan Katz, 304–5. New York: Thomas Y. Crowell.

Deutsch, Morton. 1968. "Group Behavior." In *International Encyclopedia of the Social Sciences,* ed. David Sills. Vol. 6. New York: Macmillan.

Devor, Holly. 1989. *Gender Blending: Confronting the Limits of Duality.* Bloomington: Indiana University Press.

———. 1997. *FTM: Female-to-Male Transsexuals in Society.* Bloomington: Indiana University Press.

Dickemann, Mildred. 1997. "The Balkan Sworn Virgin: A Traditional European Transperson." In *Gender Blending,* ed. Bonnie Bullough, Vern Bullough, and James Elias, 248–55. Amherst: Prometheus Press.

DiGiacomo, Susan M. 1992. "Metaphor as Illness: Postmodern Dilemmas in the Representation of Body, Mind and Disorder." *Medical Anthropology* 14(1): 109–37.

Dimen, Muriel. 1989. "Politically Correct? Politically Incorrect?" In *Pleasure and Danger: Exploring Female Sexuality,* ed. Carole S. Vance, 138–48. London: Pandora.

"Disguised as a Man." 1883. *Milwaukee Sentinel,* Oct. 30, 5.

Docter, Richard. 1988. *Transvestites and Transsexuals: Toward a Theory of Cross-Gender Behavior.* New York: Plenum Press.

Douglas, Mary. 1982 [1970]. *Natural Symbols: Explorations in Cosmology.* New York: Pantheon Books.

Drorbaugh, Elizabeth. 1993. "Sliding Scales: Notes on Stormé DeLarverié and the Jewel Box Revue, the Cross-Dressed Woman on the Contemporary Stage, and the Invert." In *Crossing the Stage: Controversies on Cross-Dressing,* ed. Lesley Ferris, 120–43. London: Routledge.

"The Dual Personage." 1883. *Milwaukee Sentinel,* Nov. 2, 8.

Duberman, Martin B. 1986. *About Time: Exploring the Gay Past.* New York: Gay Presses of New York.

Durova, Nadezhda. 1988. *The Cavalry Maid: The Memoirs of a Woman Soldier of 1812.* Trans. John Mersereau and David Lapeza. Ann Arbor: Ardis.

Dushoff, Ira M. 1973. "Economic, Psychologic and Social Rehabilitation of Male and Female Transsexuals." In *Proceedings of the Second Interdisciplinary Symposium on Gender Dysphoria Syndrome,* ed. Donald Laub and Patrick Gandy, 197–203. Stanford: Stanford University Press.

Echols, Alice. 1989. "The Taming of the Id: Feminist Sexual Politics, 1968–83." In *Pleasure and Danger: Exploring Female Sexuality,* ed. Carole S. Vance, 50–72. London: Pandora.

Edmunds, Sarah Emma E. 1865. *Nurse and Spy in the Union Army: Comprising the Adventures and Experiences of a Woman in Hospitals, Camps and Battle-Fields.* Hartford: W. S. Williams.

Edwards, Tim. 1990. "Beyond Sex and Gender: Masculinity, Homosexuality, and Social Theory." In *Men, Masculinity, and Social Theory,* ed. Jeff Hearn and David Morgan, 110–23. London: Unwin Hyman.

Ehrhardt, Anke A., Gudrun Grisanti, and Elizabeth McCauley. 1979. "Female-to-Male Transsexuals Compared to Lesbians: Behavioral Patterns of Childhood and Adolescent Development." *Archives of Sexual Behavior* 8(6): 481–90.

Ellis, Havelock. 1937. *Studies in the Psychology of Sex.* Vol. 2. New York: Random House.

———. 1938. *Psychology of Sex: A Manual for Students.* New York: Emerson Books.

Epstein, Julia. 1990. "Either/Or—Neither/Both: Sexual Ambiguity and the Ideology of Gender." *Genders* 7 (March): 99–142.

Epstein, Julia, and Kristina Straub. 1991. "Introduction: The Guarded Body." In *Body Guards: The Cultural Politics of Gender Ambiguity,* ed. Julia Epstein and Kristina Straub, 1–28. New York: Routledge.

Erauso, Catalina de. 1996 [1829]. *Lieutenant Nun: Memoir of a Basque Transvestite in the New World.* Trans. Michele Stepto and Gabriel Stepto. Boston: Beacon Press.

Erchak, Gerald M. 1992. *The Anthropology of Self and Behavior.* New Brunswick: Rutgers University Press.

"Estate of an Adoptive Father Is Sued—'He' Was a Woman." 1989. *Seattle Post Intelligencer,* May 19, B1.

Faderman, Lillian. 1991. *Odd Girls and Twilight Lovers: A History of Lesbian Life in Twentieth-Century America.* New York: Columbia University Press.

Fausto-Sterling, Ann. 1993. "The Five Sexes: Why Male and Female Are Not Enough." *The Sciences,* March–April, 20–25.

Feinberg, Leslie. 1992. *Transgender Liberation: A Movement Whose Time Has Come.* New York: World View Forum.

———. 1996. *Transgender Warriors: Making History from Joan of Arc to RuPaul.* Boston: Beacon Press.

Feinbloom, Deborah. 1977. *Transvestites and Transsexuals: Mixed Views.* New York: Delta Books.

Findlay, Deborah. 1995. "Discovering Sex: Medical Science, Feminism, and Intersexuality." *Canadian Review of Sociology and Anthropology* 32(1): 26–52.

Finque, Susan. 1989. *T.S./Crossing.* Performed on Jan. 12–14, Seattle.

Fleming, Michael, Daniel Costos, and Brad MacGowan. 1984. "Ego Development in Female-to-Male Transsexual Couples." *Archives of Sexual Behavior* 13(6): 581–94.

Fleming, Michael, Brad MacGowan, and Patricia Salt. 1984. "Female-to-Male Transsexualism and Sex Roles: Self and Spouse Ratings on the PAQ." *Archives of Sexual Behavior* 13(1): 51–57.

Fleming, Michael, Brad MacGowan, and Daniel Costos. 1985. "The Dyadic Adjustment of Female-to-Male Transsexuals." *Archives of Sexual Behavior* 14(1): 47–55.

Fonow, Mary Margaret, and Judith A. Cook. 1991. "Back to the Future: A Look at the Second Wave of Feminist Epistemology and Methodology." In *Beyond Methodology: Feminist Scholarship as Lived Research,* ed. Mary Margaret Fonow and Judith A. Cook, 1–15. Bloomington: Indiana University Press.

Forgey, Donald G. 1975. "The Institution of Berdache among the North American Plains Indians." *Journal of Sex Research* 11(1): 1–15.

Foucault, Michel. 1970. *The Order of Things: An Archaeology of the Human Sciences.* New York: Vintage Books.

————. 1980a. *The History of Sexuality.* Vol. 1: *An Introduction.* Trans. Robert Hurley. New York: Vintage Books.

————. 1980b. "Introduction." In *Herculine Barbin: Being the Recently Discovered Memoirs of a Nineteenth-Century French Hermaphrodite.* Trans. Richard McDougall. New York: Pantheon Books.

"Found at Last." 1883. *Milwaukee Sentinel,* Nov. 4, 2.

Fraser, Antonia. 1985. *The Weaker Vessel.* New York: Vintage Books.

Freid, Barbara. 1982. "Boys Will Be Boys Will Be Boys: The Language of Sex and Gender." In *Biological Woman: The Convenient Myth,* ed. Ruth Hubbard, M. S. Henifin, and Barbara Fried, 47–69. Cambridge: Schenkman.

Freund, Kurt. 1985. "Cross-Gender Identity in a Broader Context." In *Gender Dysphoria: Development, Research, Management,* ed. Betty Steiner. 259–324. New York: Plenum Press.

Friedli, Lynne. 1987. "'Passing Women': A Study of Gender Boundaries in the Eighteenth Century." In *Sexual Underworlds of the Enlightenment,* ed. G. S. Rousseau and Roy Porter, 234–60. Manchester: Manchester University Press.

————. 1991. "In Male Disguise." *Connexions* 37: 4–5, 30.

Fulton, Robert, and Steven W. Anderson. 1992. "The Amerindian 'Man-Woman': Gender, Liminality, and Cultural Continuity." *Current Anthropology* 33(5): 603–10.

Fuss, Diana. 1989. *Essentially Speaking.* New York: Routledge.

Gallagher, Catherine, and Thomas Laqueur, eds. 1987. "Introduction." In *The Making of the Human Body: Sexuality and Society in the Nineteenth Century,* vii–xv. Berkeley: University of California Press.

Gandavo, Pedro de Magalhaes. 1922 [1576]. *The Histories of Brazil.* Vol. 2, 89–232. Trans. John Stetson. New York: The Cortes Society.

Garber, Marjorie. 1989. "Spare Parts: The Surgical Construction of Gender." *Differences: A Journal of Feminist Cultural Studies* 1(3): 137–59.

————. 1992. *Vested Interests: Cross-Dressing and Cultural Anxiety.* New York: Routledge.

"Gertie's 'Husband'!" 1883. *Milwaukee Sentinel,* Nov. 28, 3.

Gifford, Edward W. 1976 [1933]. "Female Transvestites." In *Gay American History: Lesbians and Gay Men in the U.S.A.,* ed. Jonathan Katz, 325. New York: Thomas Y. Crowell.

Gilbert, O. P. 1932. *Women in Men's Guise.* London: Bodley Head.

Gilbert, Sandra M., and Susan Gubar. 1988. *No Man's Land: The Place of the Woman Writer in the Twentieth Century.* Vol. 2: *Sexchanges.* New Haven: Yale University Press.

Gilman, Sander. 1989. *Sexuality: Representing the Sexual in Medicine.* New York: John Wiley.

Gilmore, David D. 1990. *Manhood in the Making: Cultural Concepts of Masculinity.* New Haven: Yale University Press.

Gilmore, Leigh. 1994. *Autobiographics: A Feminist Theory of Women's Self-Representation.* Ithaca: Cornell University Press.

"Girl-Man Is Free Again." 1914. *Milwaukee Journal,* May 7, 10.

"Girl-Man Says That Real Man Is a Hunter of Women." 1914. *Milwaukee Journal,* May 13, 7.

"Girl Masquerader Refuses to Talk." 1914. *Milwaukee Sentinel,* May 4, 1.

Glazer, Nathan, and Daniel P. Moynihan. 1975. "Introduction." In *Ethnicity: Theory and Experience,* ed. Nathan Glazer and Daniel Moynihan, 1–26. Cambridge: Harvard University Press.

Goffman, Erving. 1963. *Stigma: Notes on the Management of Spoiled Identity.* Englewood Cliffs: Prentice-Hall.

Goldman, Irving. 1963. *The Cubeo: Indians of the Northwest Amazon.* Urbana: University of Illinois Press.

Gomes, Edwin H. 1911. *Seventeen Years among the Sea Dyaks of Borneo: A Record of Intimate Association with the Natives of the Bornean Jungles.* London: Seeley.

Gooch, Steve. 1978. *The Women Pirates: Ann Bonney and Mary Read.* London: Pluto Plays.

Gooren, Louis. 1997. "Transsexualism, Introduction and General Aspects of Treatment." http://www.xs4all.nl/~txtbreed/gooren/html (March 1998).

Gossett, Hattie, and Carolyn Johnson. 1980. "Jazz Women." *Heresies,* no. 10, 65–69.

Gould, Stephen Jay. 1981. *The Mismeasure of Man.* New York: W. W. Norton.

Grace, Della. 1996. "Regular Guys, Irregular Attitudes." *Dazed and Confused* 25 (Oct.): 56–61.

Grahn, Judy. 1984. *Another Mother Tongue: Gay Words, Gay Worlds.* Boston: Beacon.

Greed, Clara. 1990. "The Professional and the Personal: A Study of Women Quantity Surveyors." In *Feminist Praxis: Research, Theory and Epistemology in Feminist Sociology,* ed. Liz Stanley, 145–55. London: Routledge.

Green, James. 1994a. "All Transsexuals Are Not Alike." *TV/TS Tapestry Journal,* no. 68, 51–52.

———. 1994b. "Inside the TS Closet." Unpublished ms., Emeryville, Calif.

———. 1997. "Look! No, Don't! The Visibility Dilemma for Transsexual Men." Presented at the Second International Congress on Sex and Gender Issues, June 21, King of Prussia, Pa.

Green, Richard, and John Money, eds. 1969. *Transsexualism and Sex Reassignment.* Baltimore: Johns Hopkins University Press.

Grémaux, René. 1989. "Mannish Women of the Balkan Mountains: Preliminary Notes on the 'Sworn Virgins' in Male Disguise, with Special Reference to Their Sexuality and Gender-Identity." In *From Sappho to De Sade: Moments in the History of Sexuality,* ed. Jan Bremmer, 143–72. London: Routledge.

———. 1994. "Woman becomes Man in the Balkans." In *Third Sex, Third Gender: Beyond Sexual Dimorphism in Culture and Society,* ed. Gilbert Herdt, 241–81. New York: Zone Books.

Griggs, Claudine. 1998. *S/HE: Changing Sex and Changing Clothes.* Oxford: Berg.

Grosz, Elizabeth. 1993. "Lesbian Fetishism?" In *Fetishism as Cultural Discourse,* ed. Emily Apter and William Dietz, 101–15. Ithaca: Cornell University Press.

Gumperz, John. 1982. *Discourse Strategies.* New York: Cambridge University Press.

Gutheil, Emil A. 1954. "The Psychologic Background of Transsexualism and Transvestism." *American Journal of Psychotherapy* 8: 231–39.

Haddon, Alfred C., and Laura E. Start. 1936. *Iban Sea Dyak Fabrics and Their Patterns: A Descriptive Catalogue of the Iban Fabrics in the Museum of Archaeology and Ethnology, Cambridge.* New York: Cambridge University Press.

Halberstam, Judith. 1998. "Transgender Butch: Butch/FTM Border Wars and the Masculine Continuum." *GLQ: A Journal of Lesbian and Gay Studies* 4(2): 287–310.

Hale, C. Jacob. 1995. "Transgendered Strategies for Refusing Gender." Presented at the Society for Women in Philosophy, Pacific Division, May 20, Los Angeles.

———. 1996. "Are Lesbians Women?" *Hypatia* 11(2): 94–121.

———. 1997a. "Leatherdyke Boys and Their Daddies: How to Have Sex without Women or Men." *Social Text* 15(3–4): 225–38.

———. 1997b. "Lesbians Talk Transgender" [book review]. *Transsexual News Telegraph* 7 (Spring): 38–40.

———. 1998. "Consuming the Living, Dis(re)membering the Dead in the Butch/FTM Borderlands." *GLQ: A Journal of Lesbian and Gay Studies* 4(2): 311–48.

Hall, Richard. 1993. *Patriots in Disguise: Women Warriors of the Civil War.* New York: Paragon House.

Halperin, David M. 1990. *One Hundred Years of Homosexuality and Other Essays on Greek Love.* New York: Routledge.

Haraway, Donna J. 1991. *Simians, Cyborgs and Women: The Reinvention of Nature.* London: Free Association Books.

Harrison, David. 1997. "The Personals." In *PoMoSexuals: Challenging Assumptions about Gender and Sexuality,* ed. Carol Queen and Lawrence Schimel, 129–37. San Francisco: Cleis Press.

Hart, Alan. 1936. *The Undaunted.* New York: W. W. Norton.

Haug, Frigga, ed. 1992. *Female Sexualization: A Collective Work of Memory.* Trans. Erica Carter. London: Verso.

Hausman, Bernice L. 1995. *Changing Sex: Transsexualism, Technology, and the Idea of Gender.* Durham: Duke University Press.

Heidenreich, Linda. 1997. "A Historical Perspective of Christine Jorgensen and the Development of an Identity." In *Gender Blending,* ed. Bonnie Bullough, Vern Bullough, and James Elias, 268–76. Amherst: Prometheus Books.

Hemmings, Clare. 1996. "From Lesbian Nation to Transgender Liberation: A Bisexual Feminist Perspective." *Journal of Gay, Lesbian, and Bisexual History* 1(1): 37–59.

Herrmann, Anne. 1991. "Passing Women, Performing Men." In *The Female Body: Figures, Styles, Speculations,* ed. Laurence Goldstein, 179–89. Ann Arbor: University of Michigan Press.

Herdt, Gilbert. 1981. *Guardians of the Flutes: Idioms of Masculinity.* Berkeley: University of California Press.

———. 1991. "Representations of Homosexuality: An Essay on Cultural Ontology and Historical Comparison, Part 1." *Journal of the History of Sexuality* 1(3): 481–504.

Hewitt, John P. 1989. *Dilemmas of the American Self.* Philadelphia: Temple University Press.

Hewitt, Paul, with Jane Warren. 1996. *A Self-Made Man: The Diary of a Man in a Woman's Body.* London: Headline Books.

Higham, Eileen. 1984. Review of *Female-to-Male Transsexualism: Historical, Clinical, and Theoretical Issues* by Leslie M. Lothstein. *SIECUS Report* (May): 17–18.

Hill, W. W. 1935. "The Status of the Hermaphrodite and Transvestite in Navaho Culture." *American Anthropologist* 37(n.s.): 273–79.

————. 1938. "Note on the Pima Berdache." *American Anthropologist* 40(n.s.): 338–40.

Hirschfeld, Magnus. 1966 [1938]. *Sexual Anomalies and Perversions*. London: Encyclopedic Press.

————. 1991. *Transvestites: The Erotic Drive to Cross Dress*. Trans. Michael A. Lombardi-Nash. Buffalo: Prometheus Books.

Hofstader, Douglas R. 1982. "Metamagical Themas: 'Default Assumptions' and Their Effects on Writing and Thinking." *Scientific American* 247(5): 18, 22, 26, 30, 36.

Hodgkinson, Liz. 1989. *Michael, née Laura*. London: Columbus Books.

Holly. 1991. "The Transgender Alternative." *TV/TS Tapestry Journal*, no. 59, 31–33.

Holt, Patricia. 1998. "Unraveling the Secret Life of a Man Who Was a Woman." *San Francisco Chronicle*, June 23, D1.

Horan, James D. 1952 *Desperate Women*. New York: G. P. Putnam.

Husain, Shahrukh. 1996. *Handsome Heroines: Women as Men in Folklore*. New York: Doubleday.

Irvine, Janice. 1990. *Disorders of Desire: Sex and Gender in Modern American Sexology*. Philadelphia: Temple University Press.

Isaacs, Harold R. 1975. "Basic Group Identity: The Idols of the Tribe." In *Ethnicity: Theory and Experience*, ed. Nathan Glazer and Daniel Moynihan, 29–52. Cambridge: Harvard University Press.

Jacobs, Sue-Ellen. 1968. "Berdache: A Brief Review of the Literature." *Colorado Anthropologist* 1(2): 25–40.

Jacobs, Sue-Ellen, and Jason Cromwell. 1992. "Visions and Revisions of Reality: Reflections on Sex, Sexuality, Gender, and Gender Variance." *Journal of Homosexuality* 23(4): 43–69.

Jacobs, Sue-Ellen, Wesley Thomas, and Sabine Lang, eds. 1996. *Two-Spirit People: Native American Gender Identity, Sexuality, and Spirituality*. Urbana: University of Illinois Press.

Johnson, Mark. 1997. *Beauty and Power: Transgendering and Cultural Transformation in the Southern Philippines*. Oxford: Berg.

Jones, Aphrodite. 1996. *All She Wanted*. New York: Pocket Books.

Julie G. 1991. "Comments." *Rose City Gender Center Newsletter*, May, 2–4.

Kahler, Frederic. 1993. "'The Ballad of Little Jo': Maggie Greenwald's Feminism and a Rich Conscious." *Seattle Gay News*, Sept. 10, 17, 20.

Karlen, Arno. 1971. *Sexuality and Homosexuality: A New View*. New York: W. W. Norton.

Katz, Jonathan, ed. 1976. *Gay American History: Lesbians and Gay Men in the U.S.A.* New York: Thomas Y. Crowell.

————. 1983. *Gay/Lesbian Almanac*. New York: Carroll and Graf.

Kennedy, Elizabeth Lapovsky, and Madeline D. Davis. 1994. *Boots of Leather, Slippers of Gold: The History of a Lesbian Community*. New York: Penguin.

Kennedy, Hubert C. 1981. "The 'Third Sex' Theory of Karl Heinrich Ulrichs." *Journal of Homosexuality* 6(1–2): 103–11.

Kessler, Suzanne J. 1990. "The Medical Construction of Gender: Case Management of Intersexed Infants." *Signs* 16(11): 3–26.

————. 1998. *Lessons from the Intersexed*. New Brunswick: Rutgers University Press.

Kessler, Suzanne, and Wendy McKenna. 1985. *Gender: An Ethnomethodological Approach.* Chicago: University of Chicago Press.

Kincaid, Martin. 1995. "A Guided Tour through Phalloplasty." *FTM Newsletter,* no. 31 (July): 8–11.

Knorr, Norman J., Sanford R. Wolf, and Eugene Meyer. 1968. "The Transsexual's Request for Surgery." *Journal of Nervous and Mental Disease* 147(5): 517–24.

Kochems, Lee. 1993. Comments on papers presented at "Revisiting the 'North American Berdache,' Empirically and Theoretically." 92d annual meeting of the American Anthropological Association, Nov. 17–21, Washington, D.C., and Wenner-Gren Conference, Nov. 17, Washington, D.C.

Konigsberg, Eric. 1995. "Death of a Deceiver." *Playboy,* Jan., 92–94, 193–99.

Krafft-Ebing, Richard von. 1978 [1887]. *Psychopathia Sexualis.* Trans. Franklin S. Klaf. New York: Stein and Day.

Krueger, David W. 1983. "Diagnosis and Management of Gender Dysphoria." In *Phenomenology and Treatment of Psychosexual Disorders,* ed. William E. Fann, Ismet Karacen, Alex D. Pokorny, and Robert L. Williams, 73–85. New York: SP Medical and Scientific Books.

Kubie, Lawrence S., and James B. Mackie. 1968. "Critical Issues Raised by Operations for Gender Transmutation." *Journal of Nervous and Mental Disease* 147(5): 431–43.

Kulick, Don. 1998. *Travesti: Sex, Gender, and Culture among Brazilian Transgendered Prostitutes.* Chicago: University of Chicago Press.

Lamphere, Louise. 1987. "Feminism and Anthropology: The Struggle to Reshape Our Thinking about Gender." In *The Impact of Feminist Research in the Academy,* ed. Christie Farnham, 11–33. Bloomington: Indiana University Press.

Lang, Sabine. 1991a. "Women and Not-Women: Female Gender Variance among North American Indians." Presented at the annual meeting of the American Anthropological Association, Nov. 21–23, Chicago.

———. 1991b. "Female Gender Variance among North American Indians: A Cross-Cultural Perspective." Unpublished ms., Hamburg.

———. 1994. "Manly Females, Womanly Males, Two-Spirited People: Gender Variance and the Creation of Gay Identities among Contemporary North American Indians." Presented at "The 'North American Berdache' Revisited, Empirically and Theoretically," Wenner-Green Conference, Nov. 17, Washington, D.C.

———. 1996. "There Is More Than Just Women and Men: Gender Variance in North American Indian Cultures." In *Gender Reversals and Gender Cultures: Anthropological and Historical Perspectives,* ed. Sabrina Ramet, 183–96. London: Routledge.

Lazreg, Marnia. 1990. "Feminism and Difference: The Perils of Writing as a Woman on Women in Algeria." In *Conflicts in Feminism,* ed. Marianne Hirsch and Evelyn Fox Keller, 326–48. New York: Routledge.

Lee, Linda. 1993. "Women Posing as Men Pursued Better Opportunities." *Seattle Post Intelligencer,* Sept. 10, 11.

Levine, Donald N. 1966. "The Concept of Masculinity in Ethiopian Culture." *International Journal of Social Psychiatry* 12: 17–23.

Levine, Steven, Heino Meyer-Bahlburg, Ira Pauly, and Kenneth Zucker. 1991. "Interim Report of the DSM-IV Subcommittee on Gender Identity Disorder." *Archives of Sexual Behavior* 20(4): 333–43.

Lewin, Ellen. 1991. "Writing Lesbian and Gay Culture: What the Natives Have to Say for Themselves." *American Ethnologist* 18(4): 786–92.

Lewis, Oscar. 1941. "Manly-Hearted Women among the North Piegan." *American Anthropologist* 43(n.s.): 173–87.

Lingis, Alphonso. 1994. *Foreign Bodies*. New York: Routledge.

"Lived as a Man, Dies as a Woman." 1901. *San Francisco Daily Call*, Jan. 18, 11.

Lock, Margaret. 1993. "Cultivating the Body: Anthropology and Epistemologies of Bodily Practice and Knowledge." *Annual Review of Anthropology* 22: 133–55.

Lorraine, Tamsin E. 1990. *Gender, Identity, and the Production of Meaning*. Boulder: Westview Press.

Lothstein, Leslie. 1983. *Female-to-Male Transsexualism: Historical, Clinical, and Theoretical Issues*. Boston: Routledge and Kegan Paul.

Low, Hugh. 1848. *Sarawak: Its Inhabitants and Productions*. London: Richard Bentley.

Lynn, Merissa Sherrill. 1984. "Definitions Follow-Up." *TV/TS Tapestry Journal*, no. 44, 60–61.

———. 1988. "Definitions of Terms Commonly Used in the Transvestite-Transsexual Community." *TV/TS Tapestry Journal*, no. 51, 19–31.

Lyons, Terrie. 1986. "Gender Identity and Internalized Object Relations: A Comparison of Female-to-Male Transsexuals, Lesbians and Heterosexual Women." Ph.D. diss., Wright Institute Graduate School.

MacGowan, Lyndall. 1992. "Re-collecting History, Renaming Lives: Femme Stigma and the Feminist Seventies and Eighties." In *The Persistent Desire: A Femme-Butch Reader*, ed. Joan Nestle, 299–328. Boston: Alyson Publications.

Magee, Maggie, and Diana C. Miller. 1992. "'She Foreswore Her Womanhood': Psychoanalytic Views of Female Homosexuality." *Clinical Social Work Journal* 20(1): 67–87.

Mageo, Jeannette. 1995. "The Reconfiguring Self." *American Anthropologist* 97(2): 282–96.

"Man Displays His Conquests." 1914. *Milwaukee Journal*, May 15, 10.

"Man-Girl in a Legal Tangle." 1914. *Milwaukee Journal*, May 14, 8.

"Man-Woman Writes for the *Journal.*" 1914. *Milwaukee Journal*, May 12, 5.

Marshall, Donald S. 1971. "Sexual Behavior on Mangaia." In *Human Sexual Behavior: Variations in the Ethnographic Spectrum*, ed. Donald S. Marshall and Robert C. Suggs, 103–62. New York: Basic Books.

Martin, Chris. 1992. "World's Greatest Cocksucker: Transsexual Interviews." *Fiction International* 22: 101–22.

Martino, Mario, with harriett. 1977. *Emergence: A Transsexual Autobiography*. New York: Signet.

Mate-Kole, Charles. 1992. Review of *In Search of Eve: Transsexual Rites of Passage* by Anne Bolin. *Archives of Sexual Behavior* 21(2): 207–10.

McCauley, Elizabeth, and Anke Ehrhardt. 1978. "Role Expectations and Definitions: A Comparison of Female Transsexuals and Lesbians." *Journal of Homosexuality* 3(2): 137–47.

McIntosh, Mary. 1981. "The Homosexual Role, with Postscript: 'The Homosexual

Role Revisited.'" In *The Making of the Modern Homosexual*, ed. Kenneth Plummer, 30–49. Totowa: Barnes and Noble.

Medicine, Beatrice. 1997. "Changing Native American Roles in an Urban Context" and "Changing Native American Sex Roles in an Urban Context." In *Two-Spirit People: Native American Gender Identity, Sexuality, and Spirituality*, ed. Sue-Ellen Jacobs, Wesley Thomas, and Sabine Lang, 145–55. Urbana: University of Illinois Press.

Medlicott, Alexander. 1966. "Introduction." In *The Female Marine; or, Adventures of Miss Lucy Brewer*, vii–xxix. New York: Da Capo Press.

Meek, C. K. 1937. *Law and Authority in a Nigerian Tribe: A Study in Indirect Rule*. New York: Oxford University Press.

Merriam, Alan P. 1971. "Aspects of Sexual Behavior among the Bala (Basongye)." In *Human Sexual Behavior: Variations in the Ethnographic Spectrum*, ed. Donald S. Marshall and Robert C. Suggs, 71–102. New York: Basic Books.

Messing, Simon D. 1957. "The Highland-Plateau Amhara of Ethiopia." Ph.D. diss., University of Pennsylvania.

Meyer, Jon K. 1974. "Psychiatric Considerations in the Sexual Reassignment of Non-Intersex Individuals." *Clinics in Plastic Surgery* 1(2): 275–83.

Middlebrook, Diane Wood. 1998. *Suits Me: The Double Life of Billy Tipton*. Boston: Houghton Mifflin.

Miller, Jay. 1982. "People, Berdaches, and Left-Handed Bears: Human Variation in Native America." *Journal of Anthropological Research* 38: 274–87.

Miller, Patricia Y., and Martha R. Fowlkes. 1980. "Social and Behavioral Constructions of Female Sexuality." *Signs* 5(4): 783–800.

Millot, Catherine. 1990. *Horsexe: Essay on Transsexuality*. Brooklyn: Autonomedia.

"Milwaukee 'Man' Clerk Proves Girl." 1914. *Milwaukee Sentinel*, May 3, 1–2.

Minh-ha, Trinh T. 1991. *When the Moon Waxes Red*. New York: Routledge.

Minkowitz, Donna. 1994. "Love Hurts." *Village Voice*, April 19, 24–30.

Moerman, Michael. 1988. *Talking Culture: Ethnography and Conversational Analysis*. Philadelphia: University of Pennsylvania Press.

Money, John. 1986. *Lovemaps: Clinical Concepts of Sexual/Erotic Health and Pathology, Paraphilia, and Gender Transposition in Childhood, Adolescence, and Maturity*. New York: Irvington.

——. 1990. "Foreword." In *Neither Man nor Woman: The Hijras of India*, ed. Serena Nanda, xi–xiv. Belmont: Wadsworth.

Money, John, and John Brennan. 1968. "Sexual Dimorphism in the Psychology of Female Transsexuals." *Journal of Nervous and Mental Disease* 147(5): 487–99.

Money, John, and Anke A. Ehrhardt. 1972. *Man and Woman, Boy and Girl: Differentiation and Dimorphism of Gender Identity from Conception to Maturity*. Baltimore: Johns Hopkins University Press.

More, Kate, and Stephen Whittle, eds. 1999. *Reclaiming Genders: Transsexual Grammars at the Fin de Siècle*. London: Cassell.

Murray, Stephen O. 1994. "Subordinating Native American Cosmologies to the Empire of Gender." *Current Anthropologist* 35(1): 59–61.

"The Mysterious Husband." 1883. *Milwaukee Sentinel*, Nov. 1, 8.

Namaste, Ki. 1994. "'Tragic Misreadings': Queer Theory's Erasure of Transgender Subjectivity." Presented at the Sixth North American Lesbian, Gay, and Bisexual Studies Conference, Nov. 17–20, Iowa City.

Nanda, Serena. 1990. *Neither Man nor Woman: The* Hijras *of India.* Belmont: Wadsworth.

Nataf, Zachary L. 1996. *Lesbians Talk Transgender.* London: Scarlett Press.

Nestle, Joan. 1989. "The Fem Question." In *Pleasure and Danger: Exploring Female Sexuality,* ed. Carole S. Vance, 232–41. London: Pandora.

———, ed. 1992. *The Persistent Desire: A Butch-Femme Reader.* Boston: Alyson Publications.

Newton, Esther. 1972. *Mother Camp: Female Impersonators in America.* Englewood Cliffs: Prentice-Hall.

———. 1984. "The Mythic Mannish Lesbian: Radclyffe Hall and the New Woman." *Signs* 9(4): 557–75.

———. 1993. *Cherry Grove, Fire Island: Sixty Years in America's First Gay and Lesbian Town.* Boston: Beacon Press.

Newton, Esther, and Shirley Walton. 1989. "The Misunderstanding: Toward a More Precise Sexual Vocabulary." In *Pleasure and Danger: Exploring Female Sexuality,* ed. Carole S. Vance, 242–50. London: Pandora.

Nicholson, Linda. 1994. "Interpreting Gender." *Signs* 20(1): 79–105.

Noe, Joel, and Dale Birdsell. 1975. "A Surgical Program for Female to Male Transsexuals." In *Proceedings of the Second Interdisciplinary Symposium on Gender Dysphoria Syndrome,* ed. Donald Laub and Patrick Gandy, 152–62. Stanford: Stanford University Press.

"On the Warpath." 1883. *Milwaukee Sentinel,* Nov. 5, 3.

Padgug, Robert. 1990. "Sexual Matters: On Conceptualizing Sexuality in History." In *Forms of Desire: Sexual Orientation and Social Constructionist Controversy,* ed. Edward W. Stein, 43–67. New York: Garland.

Pagliassotti, Druann. 1993. "On the Discursive Construction of Sex and Gender." *Communication Research* 20(3): 472–93.

Pauly, Ira. 1969. "Adult Manifestations of Female Transsexualism." In *Transsexualism and Sex Reassignment,* ed. Richard Green and John Money, 59–87. Baltimore: Johns Hopkins University Press.

———. 1974a. "Female Transsexualism: Part I." *Archives of Sexual Behavior* 3(6): 487–507.

———. 1974b. "Female Transsexualism: Part II." *Archives of Sexual Behavior* 3(6): 509–26.

———. 1998. "Gender Identity and Sexual Orientation." In *Current Concepts in Transgender Identity,* ed. Dallas Denny, 237–48. New York: Garland.

———. n.d. "Sexual Preference of Transsexuals." Unpublished ms., Reno.

Perham, John. 1887. "Manangism in Borneo." *Journal of the Straits Branch of the Royal Asiatic Society* 19: 87–103.

Perry, Mary Elizabeth. 1987. "The Manly Woman: A Historical Case Study." *American Behavioral Scientist* 31(1): 86–100.

Person, Ethel, and Lionel Ovesey. 1974. "The Transsexual Syndrome in Males: I. Primary Transsexualism." *American Journal of Psychotherapy* 28: 4–19.

Phillimore, Peter. 1991. "Unmarried Women of the Dhaula Dhar: Celibacy and Social Control in Northwest India." *Journal of Anthropological Research* 47: 331–50.

Ponse, Barbara. 1976. "Secrecy in the Lesbian World." *Urban Life* 5(3): 313–38.

Poole, Fitz John Porter. 1981. "Transforming 'Natural' Woman: Female Ritual

Leaders and Gender Ideology among Bimin-Kuskusmin." In *Sexual Meanings: The Cultural Construction of Gender and Sexuality,* ed. Sherry B. Ortner and Harriet Whitehead, 116–65. New York: Cambridge University Press.

———. 1996. "The Procreative and Ritual Construction of Female, Male, and Other." In *Gender Reversals and Gender Cultures: Anthropological and Historical Perspectives,* ed. Sabrina Ramet, 197–218. London: Routledge.

Povinelli, Elizabeth A. 1991. "Organizing Women: Rhetoric, Economy, and Politics in Process among Australian Aborigines." In *Gender at the Crossroads of Knowledge: Feminist Anthropology in the Postmodern Era,* ed. Micaela di Leonardo, 235–56. Berkeley: University of California Press.

"Presto! Ralph Kerwineio Now Miss Anderson." 1914. *Milwaukee Sentinel,* May 5, 1–2.

Prieur, Annick. 1998. *Mema's House, Mexico City: On Transvestites, Queens, and Machos.* Chicago: University of Chicago Press.

Prince, Virginia. 1992. "Rose by Any Other Name." *TV/TS Tapestry Journal,* no. 60, 20–21.

Queen, Carol, and Lawrence Schimel. 1997. "Introduction." In *PoMoSexuals: Challenging Assumptions about Gender and Sexuality,* ed. Carol Queen and Lawrence Schimel, 19–25. San Francisco: Cleis Press.

Ramet, Sabrina. 1996. "Gender Reversals and Gender Cultures: An Introduction." In *Gender Reversals and Gender Cultures: Anthropological and Historical Perspectives,* ed. Sabrina Ramet, 1–21. London: Routledge.

Raymond, Janice G. 1994 [1979]. *The Transsexual Empire: The Making of the She-Male.* New York: Teacher's College Press.

Rees, Mark. 1996. *Dear Sir or Madam: The Autobiography of a Female-to-Male Transsexual.* London: Cassell.

Reich, June L. 1992. "Genderfuck: The Law of the Dildo." *Discourse* 15(1): 112–27.

"Returned Home." 1883. *Milwaukee Sentinel,* Nov. 6, 2.

Richmond, Marisa J. 1996. "Transgender History of Nashville and Middle Tennessee." Presented at meeting of the Tennessee Vals, Aug. 10, Nashville.

Robertson, Jennifer. 1989. "Gender-Bending in Paradise: Doing 'Female' and 'Male' in Japan." *Genders* 5 (Summer): 50–69.

———. 1992. "The Politics of Androgyny in Japan: Sexuality and Subversion in the Theater and Beyond." *American Ethnologist* 19(3): 419–42.

———. 1998. *Takarazuka: Sexual Politics and Popular Culture in Modern Japan.* Berkeley: University of California Press.

"Romance and Reality." 1883. *Milwaukee Sentinel,* Oct. 31, 5.

Rosario, Vernon A. 1994. "Trans [Homo] Sexuality? Double Inversion, Psychiatric Confusion and Hetero-Hegemony." Presented at the Sixth North American Lesbian, Gay, and Bisexual Studies Conference, Nov. 17–20, Iowa City.

Roscoe, Will. 1987. "Bibliography of Berdache and Alternative Gender Roles among North American Indians." *Journal of Homosexuality* 14(3–4): 81–171.

———. 1988. "The Zuni Man-Woman." *Out/Look* 1 (Summer): 56–67.

———. 1991. *The Zuni Man-Woman.* Albuquerque: University of New Mexico Press.

———. 1995. "Strange Craft, Strange History, Strange Folks: Cultural Amnesia and the Case for Lesbian and Gay Studies." *American Anthropologist* 97(3): 448–53.

Roth, H. L., ed. 1892. "The Natives of Borneo. Edited from the Papers of the Late Brooke Low, Esq." *Journal of the Anthropological Institute of Great Britain and Ireland* 21: 110–37.

Rubin, Gayle. 1989. "Thinking Sex: Notes for a Radical Theory of the Politics of Sexuality." In *Pleasure and Danger: Exploring Female Sexuality*, ed. Carole S. Vance, 267–319. London: Pandora.

———. 1992. "Of Catamites and Kings: Reflections on Butch, Gender, and Boundaries." In *The Persistent Desire: A Femme-Butch Reader*, ed. Joan Nestle, 466–82. Boston: Alyson Publications.

Rubin, Henry. 1996. "Report on the First FTM Conference of the Americas: A Vision of Community." *Journal of Gay, Lesbian, and Bisexual Identity* 1 (2): 171–77.

———. 1999. *The Subject Matters: FTM Transsexual Embodiment and Subjectivity.* Chicago: University of Chicago Press.

San Francisco Lesbian History Project. 1989. "'She Even Chewed Tobacco': A Pictorial Narrative of Passing Women in America." In *Hidden from History: Reclaiming the Gay and Lesbian Past*, ed. Martin Duberman, Martha Vicinus, and George Chauncey, 183–94. New York: New American Library.

Schaeffer, Claude E. 1965. "The Kutenai Female Berdache: Courier, Guide, Prophetess, and Warrior." *Ethnohistory* 12: 193–236.

Scheper-Hughes, Nancy, and Margaret Lock. 1987. "The Mindful Body: A Prolegomenon to Future Work in Medical Anthropology." *Medical Anthropology Quarterly* 1 (1): 6–41.

———. 1991. "The Message in the Bottle: Illness and the Micropolitics of Resistance." *Journal of Psychohistory* 18: 409–32.

Scott, D. Travers. 1997. "Le Freak, C'est Chic! Le Fag, Quelle Drag! Celebrating the Collapse of Homosexual Identity." In *PoMoSexuals: Challenging Assumptions about Gender and Sexuality*, ed. Carol Queen and Lawrence Schimel, 62–68. San Francisco: Cleis Press.

Scott, Joan W. 1990. "Deconstructing Equality-versus-Difference; or, The Uses of Poststructuralist Theory for Feminism." In *Conflicts in Feminism*, ed. Marianne Hirsch and Evelyn Fox Keller, 134–48. New York: Routledge.

———. 1991. "Gender: A Useful Category of Historical Analysis." In *Women's Studies International: Nairobi and Beyond*, ed. Aruna Rao, 13–37. New York: Feminist Press.

"A Secret Song." 1989. *Time Magazine*, Feb. 13, 41.

Serematakis, C. N. 1991. *The Last Word: Women, Death, and Divination in Inner Mani.* Chicago: University of Chicago Press.

"Sex Concealment Revives Memory." 1914. *Milwaukee Sentinel*, May 6, 3.

"Sex Concealment Revives Memory of Waupun 'Man.'" 1914. *Milwaukee Sentinel*, May 5, 20.

Shapiro, Judith. 1991. "Transsexualism: Reflections on the Persistence of Gender and the Mutability of Sex." In *Body Guards: The Cultural Politics of Gender Ambiguity*, ed. Julia Epstein and Kristina Straub, 248–79. New York: Routledge.

Sherzer, Joel. 1987. "A Discourse-Centered Approach to Language and Culture." *American Anthropologist* 89 (2): 295–309.

Silverman, Kaja. 1986. "Fragments of a Fashionable Discourse." In *Studies in En-*

tertainment: Critical Approaches to Mass Culture, ed. Tania Modleski, 139–52. Bloomington: Indiana University Press.

Smith, Dorothy E. 1987. *The Everyday World as Problematic: A Feminist Sociology.* Boston: Northeastern University Press.

Smith-Rosenberg, Carroll. 1989. "The Body Politic." In *Coming to Terms: Feminism, Theory, Politics,* ed. Elizabeth Weed, 101–21. New York: Routledge.

Spender, Dale. 1985. "On Feminism and Propaganda." In *For Alma Mater: Theory and Practice in Feminist Scholarship,* ed. Paula A. Treichler, Cheris Kramarae, and Beth Stafford, 307–15. Urbana: University of Illinois Press.

Spier, Leslie. 1930. *Klamath Ethnography.* California University Publications in American Archaeology and Ethnology 30. Berkeley: University of California Press.

"Standards of Care." 1990. Harry Benjamin International Gender Dysphoria Association, Sonoma, Calif.

Stanley, Liz, and Sue Wise. 1991. "Feminist Research, Feminist Consciousness, and Experiences of Sexism." In *Beyond Methodology: Feminist Scholarship as Lived Research,* ed. Mary Margaret Fonow and Judith A. Cook, 265–83. Bloomington: Indiana University Press.

Steele, Valerie. 1996. *Fetish: Fashion, Sex and Power.* New York: Oxford University Press.

Steiner, Betty, 1985. "Transsexuals, Transvestites, and Their Partners." In *Gender Dysphoria: Development, Research, Management,* ed. Betty Steiner, 351–64. New York: Plenum Press.

———, ed. 1985. *Gender Dysphoria: Development, Research, Management.* New York: Plenum Press.

Steiner, Betty, Ray Blanchard, and Kenneth J. Zucker. 1985. "Introduction." In *Gender Dysphoria: Development, Research, Management.* New York: Plenum Press.

Stoller, Robert. 1965. "Passing and the Continuum of Gender Identity." In *Sexual Inversion: The Multiple Roots of Homosexuality,* ed. Judd Marmor, 190–219. New York: Basic Books.

———. 1968. *Sex and Gender, Volume I.* London: Hogarth Press.

———. 1972. "Etiological Factors in Female Transsexualism: A First Approximation." *Archives of Sexual Behavior* 2(1): 47–64.

———. 1973. *Splitting: A Case of Female Masculinity.* New York: New York Times Book.

———. 1975. *Sex and Gender.* Vol. 2: *The Transsexual Experiment.* New York: Jason Aronson.

———. 1982. "Transvestism in Women." *Archives of Sexual Behavior* 11(2): 99–115.

———. 1985. *Presentations of Gender.* New Haven: Yale University Press.

Stone, Sandy. 1991. "The Empire Strikes Back: A Posttranssexual Manifesto." In *Body Guards: The Cultural Politics of Gender Ambiguity,* ed. Julia Epstein and Kristina Straub, 280–304. New York: Routledge.

"Strange Stories—Whereabouts of 'Dubois' and His Young 'Wife.'" 1883. *Milwaukee Sentinel,* Nov. 3, 3.

Strassberg. Donald, Howard Roback, Jean Cunningham, Embry McKee, and Paul Larson. 1979. "Psychopathology in Self-Identified Female-to-Male Transsexuals, Homosexuals, and Heterosexuals." *Archives of Sexual Behavior* 8(6): 491–96.

"Suicide of a Woman." 1870. *San Francisco Daily Morning Call,* Jan. 1, 10.

Sullivan, Louis. 1989. "Sullivan's Travels." *The Advocate,* July, 68–71.

———. 1990a. *From Female to Male: The Life of Jack Bee Garland.* Boston: Alyson Publications.

———. 1990b. *Information for the Female to Male Cross Dresser and Transsexual.* Seattle: Ingersoll Press.

Taylor, John, and Mary Taylor. 1983. "Dear Child." *Friendly Woman,* Spring, 13.

Thompson, C. J. S. 1974. *The Mysteries of Sex: Women Who Posed as Men and Men Who Impersonated Women.* New York: Causeway Books.

Thompson, Raymond. 1995. *What Took You So Long? A Girl's Journey to Manhood.* London: Penguin Books.

Transgender Tapestry. 1999. Waltham, Mass.

Tremain, Rose. 1992. *Sacred Country.* New York: Washington Square Press.

Tuzin, Donald. 1991. "Sex, Culture and the Anthropologist." *Social Science and Medicine* 33(8): 867–74.

Tyler, Carole-Anne. 1989. "The Supreme Sacrifice? TV, 'TV,' and the Renée Richards Story." *Differences: A Journal of Feminist Cultural Studies* 1(3): 160–86.

Ulrichs, Karl Heinrich. 1975 [1898]. *Forschungen über das Rätsel de mannmännlichen Liebe.* New York: Arno Press.

Ulstein, Stefan. 1993. "'Jo' Views the West through a Woman's Eyes." *Seattle Post Intelligencer,* Sept. 10, 11.

Van Cleve, Janice. n.d. "How to Run a Successful Support Group." Unpublished ms., Seattle.

Vance, Carole S. 1980. "Gender Systems, Ideology, and Sex Research: An Anthropological Analysis." *Feminist Studies* 6(1): 129–43.

———. 1989. "Pleasure and Danger: Toward a Politics of Sexuality." In *Pleasure and Danger: Exploring Female Sexuality,* ed. Carole S. Vance, 1–27. London: Pandora.

———. 1991. "Anthropology Rediscovers Sexuality: A Theoretical Comment." *Social Science and Medicine* 33(8): 875–84.

Velazquez, Loreta Janeta. *The Woman in Battle: A Narrative of the Exploits, Adventures and Travels of Madame Loreta Janeta Velazquez, Otherwise Known as Lieutenant Harry T. Buford, Confederate States Army.* Ed. C. J. Worthington. Richmond: Dustin, Gilman, 1876.

Verschoor, A. M. and J. Poortinga. 1988. "Psychosocial Differences between Dutch Male and Female Transsexuals." *Archives of Sexual Behavior* 17(2): 173–78.

Vicinus, Martha. 1992. "'They Wonder to Which Sex I Belong': The Historical Roots of the Modern Lesbian Identity." *Feminist Studies* 18(3): 467–97.

Walworth, Janis R. 1997. "Sex Reassignment Surgery in Male-to-Female Transsexuals: Client Satisfaction in Relation to Selection Criteria." In *Gender Blending,* ed. Bonnie Bullough, Vern L. Bullough, and James Elias, 352–69. Amherst: Prometheus Books.

Weeks, Jeffrey. 1977. *Coming Out: Homosexual Politics in Britain from the Nineteenth Century to the Present.* London: Quartet Books.

———. 1980–81. "Inverts, Perverts, and Mary-Annes: Male Prostitution and the Regulation of Homosexuality in England in the Nineteenth and Early Twentieth Centuries." *Journal of Homosexuality* 6(1–2): 113–34.

————. 1986. *Sexuality*. London: Routledge.

————. 1989. "Questions of Identity." In *The Cultural Construction of Sexuality,* ed. Pat Caplan, 31–51. New York: Routledge.

Weigert, Andrew J., J. Smith Teitge, and Dennis W. Teitge. 1986. *Society and Identity: Toward a Sociological Psychology.* New York: Cambridge University Press.

West, Candace, and Don H. Zimmerman. 1987. "Doing Gender." *Gender and Society* 1(2): 125–51.

Weston, Kath. 1993. "Lesbian/Gay Studies in the House of Anthropology." *Annual Review of Anthropology* 22: 339–67.

Wheeler-Voegelin, Erminie W. 1942. *Culture Element Distributions: XX, Northeast California.* California University Publications, Anthropological Records 7, no. 2. Berkeley: University of California Press.

Wheelwright, Julie. 1990. *Amazons and Military Maids*. London: Pandora.

"When the Bough Breaks." 1992. *People Weekly,* Feb. 24, 61.

Whitehead, Harriet. 1981. "The Bow and the Burden Strap: A New Look at Institutionalized Homosexuality in Native North America." In *Sexual Meanings: The Cultural Construction of Gender and Sexuality,* ed. Sherry B. Ortner and Harriet Whitehead, 80–115. New York: Cambridge University Press.

Whittle, Stephen. 1993. "The History of a Psychiatric Diagnostic Category." *Chrysalis Quarterly* 1(5): 25–32, 49.

————. 1996. "Gender Fucking or Fucking Gender? Current Cultural Contributions to Theories of Gender Blending." In *Blending Genders: Social Aspects of Cross-Dressing and Sex-Changing,* ed. Richard Ekins and Dave King, 196–214. London: Routledge.

Wieringa, Saskia, and Evelyn Blackwood. 1999. "Introduction." In *Cultures, Identities, Sexualities,* ed. Evelyn Blackwood and Saskia Wieringa. New York: Columbia University Press.

Wilchins, Riki Anne. 1997. *Read My Lips: Sexual Subversion and the End of Gender.* Ithaca: Firebrand.

Williams, Walter L. 1992. *The Spirit and the Flesh: Sexual Diversity in American Indian Culture.* Boston: Beacon Press.

Wilson, Elizabeth. 1990. "Deviant Dress." *Feminist Review,* no. 35 (Summer): 67–74.

"Woman Who Cross-Dressed Found Dead with Two Others." 1994. *Seattle Times,* Jan. 1, A12.

Woodhouse, Annie. 1989. *Fantastic Women: Sex, Gender and Transvestism.* New Brunswick: Rutgers University Press.

Woodward, Grace Steele. 1963. *The Cherokees*. Norman: University of Oklahoma Press.

"Writing Life's Last Chapter." 1914. *Milwaukee Journal,* May 4, 1–2.

Young, Katharine. 1989. "Disembodiment: The Phenomenology of the Body in Medical Examinations." *Semiotica* 73(1–2): 43–66.

"Young Woman Differs from Man." 1914. *Milwaukee Journal,* May 24, 7.

Index

Jason Cromwell is an anthropologist who conducts research on sex, sexuality, gender, and identity. He received his Ph.D. in anthropology from the University of Washington in 1996 and is an independent scholar. He is a long-time member of the transcommunity and has served on the boards of directors of the Ingersoll Gender Center, International Foundation of Gender Education, and American Education Gender Information Service. He is also a co-founder of the FTM Conference and Education Project/Spectrum.

Typeset in 10/12.5 New Baskerville
Composed by Celia Shapland
at the University of Illinois Press
Manufactured by Versa Press, Inc.

University of Illinois Press
1325 South Oak Street
Champaign, IL 61820-6903
www.press.uillinois.edu